The Brooklyn Dodgers
in the 1940s

For my ever-patient and loving wife, Betty

The Brooklyn Dodgers in the 1940s

How Robinson, MacPhail, Reiser and Rickey Changed Baseball

RUDY MARZANO

Foreword by Dave Anderson

McFarland & Company, Inc., Publishers
Jefferson, North Carolina, and London

LIBRARY OF CONGRESS CATALOGUING-IN-PUBLICATION DATA

Marzano, Rudy, 1927–
    The Brooklyn Dodgers in the 1940s : how Robinson,
Macphail, Reiser, and Rickey changed baseball / Rudy
Marzano ; foreword by Dave Anderson.
        p.   cm.
    Includes bibliographical references and index.

    ISBN 0-7864-1987-3 (softcover : 50# alkaline paper) ∞

    1. Brooklyn Dodgers (Baseball team)—History—20th
century.   2. Brooklyn Dodgers (Baseball team)—Influence.
I. Title.
GV875.B7M34   2005
796.357'64'0974723—dc22   2005000876

British Library cataloguing data are available

On the cover: background: ©2004 Photospin. Foreground: Ebbets
Field (National Baseball Hall of Fame Library, Cooperstown, N.Y.).

Manufactured in the United States of America

McFarland & Company, Inc., Publishers
  Box 611, Jefferson, North Carolina 28640
    www.mcfarlandpub.com

Table of Contents

Acknowledgments

Without the help of a number of Brooklyn Dodgers this book, whatever its merits, would have lacked the insight and scope necessary to describe the most turbulent and interesting decade in the 44-year history of Ebbets Field.

My thanks to Bobby Bragan, Pete Coscarart, Carl Erskine, Herman Franks, Gene Hermanski, John (Spider) Jorgensen, Clem Labine, Eddie Miksis and Howie Schultz. Also to St. Louis Cardinals pitcher Max Lanier and St. Louis Browns outfielder Roy Sievers.

I am indebted to Dr. Arthur Häfner, head of the Seton Hall University Library, for the cooperation of his entire staff, to those great folks at the Cleveland headquarters of there American Society for Baseball Research, and to staff members of the Rutgers University Library in New Brunswick and the Brooklyn Public Library at Grand Army Plaza. On a local level I appreciate the help of Roland Bennett and his fine people at the Public Library of Maplewood, New Jersey, where I have lived most of my life.

I appreciate the help of my children who, after convincing me to put aside my typewriter, taught me the wonders of the computer, thereby hauling me into the 21st century.

To friends such as baseball writer Ron Mayer, *Newark Star-Ledger* cartoonist Tom Walker and his brother John, and *New York Times* sports columnist Dave Anderson, my thanks for the advice and encouragement that helped me over some rough spots.

Above all to Betty, my wife of 50 years, thanks for putting up with a Brooklyn Dodger fanatic who to this day has never forgiven those who moved the team to Los Angeles.

Foreword

by Dave Anderson

Ebbets Field's only remaining contemporaries are Fenway Park and Wrigley Field, but those two baseball museums in Boston and Chicago, as well as the World Series museum known as Yankee Stadium, have never been quite the same as Ebbets Field.

Quite simply, they don't make 'em like Ebbets Field anymore. Because they can't.

In retrospect, as this richly researched and so-easy-to-read history shows, much of today's baseball structure was developed in the Ebbets Field laboratory. Nobody thinks twice today about black players, whether African-American or Latin American, in the major leagues. Nobody thinks twice now about padded walls to protect outfielders from themselves. Nobody thinks twice now about batting helmets.

In time maybe all of these developments would have occurred in another ballpark somewhere, if not in several ballparks, but the fact is that each happened at Ebbets Field.

Jackie Robinson, the first African-American in modern major league history, joined the Brooklyn Dodgers at Ebbets Field for the 1947 season opener. The following spring, Dodger president Branch Rickey had the outfield walls of Ebbets Field padded in order to protect center fielder Pete Reiser from another concussion if he crashed into them in pursuit of a fly ball. And when Larry MacPhail was the Dodgers' combustible general manager, he created the basis for today's batting helmets: plastic inserts that fitted into zippered pockets in specially designed baseball caps.

MacPhail also oversaw the first telecast of a major-league game as it was beamed out of Ebbets Field in 1939, back when newspapers and radio were baseball's only links to its fans.

Baseball today would be the same, but if those four elements had not happened at Ebbets Field each surely would have taken longer to occur.

Ebbets Field is where almost everything in this book happened. It closed after the 1957 season when the Dodgers moved to Los Angeles. In 1960 it was razed to make way for the sprawling Ebbets Field Apartments that are there now with an entrance on Bedford Avenue. Nearby is the area's tribute to Jackie Robinson, the aptly-named Jackie Robinson Middle School.

It's too bad Ebbets Field wasn't allowed to just fall apart, its girders and 32,000 seats scattered like the ruins of ancient Greece. Those ruins would deserve to be a baseball shrine. As it is, when people drive or walk by the Ebbets Field Apartments many do stop and stare, as if the ballpark were still there. And for all those people who went to Ebbets Field through the years, almost everything that happened there is still happening there—at least in their memories.

Those people talk about Ebbets Field as if they were still walking over from the Prospect Park subway station, or over from the Grand Army Plaza past the Botanical Gardens, or as if they were about to buy a *Brooklyn Eagle* newspaper (with a free scorecard) before going into the Italian marble rotunda to get a box seat or grandstand seat, or go around behind center field to sit in the bleachers. Sorry, no luxury suites.

Wherever the seat's location—behind home plate, along the foul lines or in the upper deck in center field—you were on top of the game. In the silence before a pitch you could often hear the infielders talking or vulgar voices growling in the dugouts.

Between pitches you might hear Hilda Chester clanging her cowbell from the front row of the upper center field bleachers, or see Jack Pierce launching balloons as he shouted "Cookeee" from his seat near third base, or hear the Dodger Sym-Phony band tootling through the grandstand along the aisle behind home plate. The view from there, looking toward the outfield, was different from the round, bland stadiums of recent years.

In deep center field was the "exit gate." After the game you could stroll across the outfield grass and leave through the metal gate that opened onto the Bedford Avenue sidewalk. The scoreboard in right field, with its red "Schaefer" beer sign on top and its black-and-white "Hit Sign, Win Suit" offer at the bottom, hid much of the screen atop the concave right field wall.

Across the slanting screen behind home plate, Red Barber and later Vin Scully perched behind a microphone in a gray metal coop. When Old Gold cigarettes sponsored the radio broadcasts a Dodger home run was an "Old Goldie" and the Ol' Redhead would bounce a carton down the screen. The batboy would retrieve it and hand it to the home run hitter as he approached the dugout wearing his creamy white uniform with "Dodgers" in blue script across his chest.

Hanging from the roof was a long gray metal press box where the newspaper beat writers clacked away at typewriters, and Western Union operators dot-dashed the stories on telegraph keys.

The clubhouses were adjacent to each other under the stand along the right field line. Small, high windows overlooked Sullivan Place from the Dodgers' clubhouse where Pee Wee Reese, in his years as team captain, was ensconced in a rocking chair. Near him sat Jackie Robinson, Gil Hodges and Duke Snider. Also in that clubhouse during Pee Wee's career were Roy Campanella, Carl Furillo, Whitlow Wyatt, Kirby Higbe, Billy Cox, Don Newcombe, Carl Erskine, Johnny Podres, Preacher Roe, Joe Black, Clem Labine and the many others who contributed to Dodger championships during that era.

Going to and fro from the dugouts, both the Dodgers and the visiting team walked along the dirt runway behind a high wrought-iron fence. Above them, fans gathered on a ramp to hoot or root.

This was Ebbets Field in the seasons this book brings to mind so well. This was a ballpark, not a stadium. This was a baseball stage where baseball games were meant to be played, where baseball history was meant to be written and where a baseball era was meant to be remembered.

They don't make 'em like Ebbets Field anymore. Because they can't.

Dave Anderson, a Pulitzer Prize–winning sports columnist for The New York Times, *is the author of 22 books and more than 350 magazine articles.*

Introduction

Before the rise of the Brooklyn Dodgers in the 1940s, baseball was a game of white men, cloth caps and concrete walls. Four men changed all that: Branch Rickey, Larry MacPhail, Jackie Robinson and Pete Reiser. Looking back, we can see that their accomplishments made the Dodgers the most important team during the most important decade in American baseball history.

Consider: How many years would black ballplayers have been denied opportunity if Rickey hadn't had the courage to bring Jackie Robinson up from Montreal? How many careers, and even lives, have been saved by MacPhail developing the batting helmet and by Rickey ordering padded walls and a warning track at Ebbets Field in his efforts to save Reiser's career?

In a less dramatic move, overlooked at the time, in 1947 Rickey hired Alan Roth, the first team statistician in baseball history. During his years at Ebbets Field, Roth's statistical innovations changed the way managers and front office executives make decisions both on and off the field. As an example, it would be unthinkable for today's managers to ignore stats on who hits well or poorly against right-handed or left-handed pitchers or how certain pitchers fare against individual hitters. Similarly, Roth's on-base percentage, which didn't become official until 1984, is viewed by many today as far more indicative of a hitter's value to his team than his batting average.

So Ebbets Field, gone these many years from the Borough of Brooklyn, was the spawning ground for all these historic advances between the years 1941 and 1948. Baseball, as you can see on any day of any season, was transformed by those men of Ebbets Field. In combination, they made the game much safer, more interesting, and, by breaking the color line, opened it up to all men of all nations.

MacPhail's impact went even further, eventually extending the game to just about every home in the country, the long-range result of his signing with NBC for the first telecast of a major league game. It took place at Ebbets Field on the threshold of the '40s—August 26, 1939—in a doubleheader split by the Dodgers and the Cincinnati Reds. In these pages is an account of that historic broadcast, and the innovations of MacPhail and Rickey as they changed forever the game's offense and defense. These are the years when Pete Reiser destroyed himself against the concrete walls, and when Jackie Robinson suffered the racial slurs and insults of that 1947 season and then two years later won the National League batting title.

The desperate years of World War II brought on the only amputees who ever played in an official major league game, the youngest battery mates who ever put on a major league uniform and the wartime rejuvenation of one of the nastiest men who ever played in the big leagues.

In mid-decade, as the Mexican raiders lured major leaguers south of the border, there was the first playoff in baseball history, the formation of the short-lived but important American Baseball Guild, and Danny Gardella, an obscure wartime outfielder, who was bought off by baseball's owners when he challenged the reserve clause.

There are sad times in this book, as when young Ray Chapman was killed by an errant fastball in the Polo Grounds, when young Willard Hershberger committed suicide in his Boston hotel room and when Lou Gehrig and Babe Ruth died. And happy times, as when the people of Brooklyn danced in the streets in the fall of 1941 and made a demigod out of Pistol Pete Reiser, a 22-year-old who led them to the pennant. And exciting times, as when Joe DiMaggio hit in his record 56 straight games.

There are the good men of baseball here, men like MacPhail and Rickey, and Baseball Commissioner Albert Chandler, who would not join those who would prevent Jackie Robinson from being the first black man to play in the major leagues.

And there are the other kind of men, like Leo Durocher, who once blackjacked a medically discharged veteran under the stands of Ebbets Field, and Walter O'Malley, who broke the heart of his native city when he took the Dodgers to the West Coast.

The 1940s, they're a long way back, but in many ways they're still with us. When you see a game on television, when you see padded walls and warning tracks in outfields across America, when you see batters wearing helmets and when you see black ballplayers on virtually every team in every league in the country, you are seeing the 1940s in 21st century dress, and you will come to understand the impact the Brooklyn Dodgers had on our great American game.

As they used to say on radio's *Lone Ranger,* come with me in this book to the "days of yesteryear" and meet again the Dodgers of my youth: Pete Reiser, Dixie Walker, Pee Wee Reese, Mickey Owen, Hugh Casey, Whitlow Wyatt, Cookie Lavagetto, Dolf Camilli, Spider Jorgensen, Carl Furillo, Gil Hodges, Duke Snider, Billy Cox, Pete Coscarart, Eddie Miksis, Gene Hermanski, Jackie Robinson, Roy Campanella, Don Newcombe, Billy Herman, Carl Erskine, Clem Labine, Don Zimmer and all the rest who brightened the lives of millions of people from the 1940s until those dark days of 1957.

Rudy Marzano
Point Pleasant, N.J.
January 2005

1

The $100 Superstar of 1939

It was the most sensational debut in the history of baseball—a three-run homer off Cardinals rookie Ken Raffensberger followed by two more home runs, five singles and a walk. Before he was stopped by Lefty Gomez his line read: 11 times up, 11 times on base, eight hits, three walks, total bases 20, runs batted in eight, runs scored six.[1]

It was spring training, Clearwater, Florida, 1939. The Dodgers had brought shortstop Pete Reiser up from Elmira for a look and soon all baseball was looking and asking: who is this kid and where did he come from?

The kid was Hal Reiser, Pistol Pete to his childhood friends, 20 years old, and a switch hitter with power and speed. And he wasn't totally unknown. Five years earlier Branch Rickey had put him under contract at age 15, after which he forgot about going back to school.

Rickey knew the boy would be a star. Rickey always knew when it came to baseball talent. He was president of the St. Louis Cardinals at the time and his baseball antenna, infallible as always, had zeroed in on this teenager as he was tearing up the St. Louis Municipal League, hitting and fielding like a pro.

The boy had it all, Rickey saw, and could play any position. Though he was only 15, Branch didn't want anyone else to get at him, so he instructed his Midwest scout, Charley Barrett, to sign him and then hide him as he matured.

The Cardinals at the time were supreme in St. Louis, the Gashouse Gang, with Frankie Frisch, Joe Medwick, Pepper Martin, Leo Durocher and the Dean brothers ruling the National League. Barrett therefore had a certain cachet as he cajoled parents into signing with him. He was from the *Cardinals,* not those perennial losers, the St. Louis Browns. But he knew he'd have to do some explaining to the Reisers, to convince them that he had a good reason for cutting Pete from a tryout session.

"I want to talk to about your son," he said to George Reiser as he walked up the front steps onto the Reiser porch.

"I want to talk to you, too," George replied. "Why'd you cut him?"

"We didn't want anyone else to see him," Barrett said. "That's why we didn't ask him to come back. We know who he is."[2] The flattery worked and Barrett got his contract, but he would have gotten it anyway once he and Reiser remembered playing in the old Trolley League back before the First World War.

George was a pitcher then, when the Trolley League was a big deal in the St. Louis area and stretches of lower Illinois. But as his family grew he gave up the idea of playing professionally and settled for pitching weekends in a local industrial league, a decision he later regretted, as all his children came to realize.[3]

Such leagues were flourishing in areas of the East and Midwest during those years. Companies would hire local athletes and pay them well to keep them from going elsewhere. But their leagues started to die in the late 1940s as television beamed major league games into taverns and then homes. Finally, when U.S. manufactured products like steel went overseas, the leagues went the way of their sponsors.

Like many a father George Reiser dreamed of reliving his life through his sons, of having one of them reach the heights he never tried for or couldn't reach. But unlike most others he had an edge: two of his sons had remarkable baseball talents, and he was in a city where he could see to it that they developed them.

St. Louis was a baseball town, ideally suited for George

Pete Reiser was known back in the late 1940s as "the man they padded the walls for." Branch Rickey, realizing something had to be done to protect Pete from himself, padded the walls of Ebbets Field. It was too late to salvage Pete's career, but Rickey's idea has been copied by all, saving careers and even lives, and changing the way the outfield is played.

Reiser's fatherly dreams. The fans were loyal to the game, the kind of loyalty they gave the St. Louis Browns through year after year of futility; St. Louis was a city of 815,000 that supported two teams for more than 50 years until television inroads drove one of them to Baltimore in 1954.

The town was heavily industrialized, although in Pete's youth it still had a whiff of the frontier in that St. Louis was still the world's largest raw fur market. It also had shoe factories and three large breweries, a combination that brought out the humor and tolerance of Brownie fans in the slogan: "First in booze, first in shoes and last in the American League."[4]

George had an older son, Mike, who at 17 was one of the best ballplayers in the area, better, in Pete's own words, than Pete. "I was always good" Pete once said, "but Mike was the real ballplayer in the family and could do anything. But he died just after he signed with the Yankees."

With Mike, George Reiser's dream seemed about to come true when a Yankee scout knocked at his door. A practical man—he had to be while raising nine children—he signed for Mike, not waiting for Charley Barrett.

Five days later Mike was dead, in the winter of 1931 of scarlet fever, a scourge at the time. "I caught it from him," Pete said, "and we both ended up with sore throats. About two in the morning he told me he had something in his throat and then blood came rushing out. My mother yelled for someone to get a priest so I ran out of the house, heading for the church. It was snowing and I ran for 12 blocks. I got to the door of the rectory and pounded on it. When it opened I said 'my brother is dying' and I collapsed."[5]

Some parents never get over a devastating blow like that but George, heartbroken as he was, had eight other children to worry about. And there was still Pete, the other baseball prodigy. He helped him develop and then, as he always hoped, Charley Barrett showed up with that contract in hand.

After George signed for his son, Barrett hired Pete for scouting trips, listing him as his chauffeur at $50 a month. When they got to a town where Pete would work out with the local team the manager usually asked Barrett to "leave the kid here." Charley always refused, saying that Pete was only 15. "Don't worry," he was told, "we'll change his name and play him. Nobody'll know."[6] At that age most of Pete's contemporaries were in school, but it was 1934, deep into the Depression and attendance was down. Many a youngster had to work to help the family in an age when welfare was unheard of. To the Reisers the $50 a month was particularly important, for George was a warehouse foreman[7] raising that family of eight. The extra money made a striking difference.

The chauffeuring pretense went on for almost two years until in 1937 Pete was assigned to the Cardinals team in New Iberia, Louisiana, and later that year to Newport in Eastern Arkansas. The following spring, on March 23, 1938, Baseball Commissioner Kenesaw Mountain Landis, in a possible vendetta against Rickey, decided the Cardinals were stockpiling young ballplayers illegally.

There was a rule that each major league organization was allowed a working relationship with one team in each minor league. St. Louis, Landis ruled, had cheated by forming secret illegal bonds with additional teams. He then freed some 100 ballplayers, among whom only Reiser and James (Skeeter) Webb made it to the majors. The account in the *Times* termed the ruling a sweeping denunciation of the Cardinals' system of "working agreements" with minor league clubs, and the opening gun of a campaign aimed principally at Rickey.[8]

It would be naïve to believe that at least some of the other clubs weren't doing the same, but Landis went after the Cardinals in particular, perhaps because of their extensive farm system, but much more likely because Landis was jealous of Rickey.

Veteran sportscaster Stan Lomax thought it a vendetta. "Landis had a real hatred for Rickey," he told writer Harvey Frommer. "He knew Rickey was too smart for him. Rickey should have been the commissioner."[9]

Landis was aware of Rickey's accomplishments and, given his vanity and sense of self-righteousness, was uncomfortable in his presence. The commissioner was born in Millville, Ohio, son of a Union Army surgeon who was gravely wounded at the battle of Kennesaw Mountain in Tennessee. Nevertheless, he was instrumental in keeping blacks out of baseball and resented Rickey's moves to integrate the Dodgers. It wasn't just coincidence that Jackie Robinson arrived only after Landis died.

Bill Veeck says in *Veeck as in Wreck* that he had planned to buy the Phillies in 1943 and hire some black ballplayers to fill the void caused by the draft. He went to Commissioner Landis for approval, he wrote, and Landis "wasn't exactly overjoyed" at the idea. Veeck then points to Ford Frick, National League president, as the heavy who prevented the sale by having Phillies owner Gerry Nugent, then in bankruptcy, turn the team over to the league, which then sold it to lumber dealer William Cox. Frick, of course, was working for Landis.

"Word reached me soon enough," Veeck said, "that Frick was bragging about how he stopped me from contaminating the league." He added that he had been willing to pay about twice what Cox paid for the team.[10]

Memoirs are tricky things. Events often cloud over as the years go by. Veeck was a totally honest man, honorable in all his dealings, but there are doubts today about his recollection. The Society for American

Baseball Research looked into the matter recently and discovered that Veeck never gave any corroborating proof, and that Phillies owner Gerry Nugent denied that any such offer was made.

Of even greater significance, the black press, including the local *Philadelphia Tribune,* never printed a word of any Phillies sale or Veeck signing black ballplayers during this period, a story they would have leaped on if there had been a shred of truth to it.[11] But it made no difference. The baseball world knew of the commissioner's mindset and of his influence over Frick. The story was believed because it was common knowledge that Landis was vehemently against blacks coming into the major leagues.

Rickey seethed at Landis' freeing his minor leaguers; he was not accustomed to losing when it came to his dealings with ballplayers. In selling Dizzy Dean, for example, he took the biggest chance of his career and won. The Cubs knew Diz was having arm trouble but wanted him anyway. They thought at 27 his arm would heal, but Rickey knew instinctively that Dean was through, and he was.

Other deals that Rickey made were right out of the horse trader's manual, with the other guy invariably the victim. Dodger Secretary Harold Parrott recalled that when he was Dodger beat man for the *Brooklyn Eagle,* Rickey, as Cardinal president, pulled off a deal where Brooklyn traded Frenchy Bordagaray, Dutch Leonard and a minor leaguer for supposed slugger Tom Winsett.

Tom was awesome in batting practice, hitting ball after ball into Bedford Avenue. He became known around the league as a two o'clock hitter, an earlier version of Tommy Brown of the 1940s, the Dodger pre-game power hitter who hit 15 homers in six years before being shipped to the Phillies.

As Winsett floundered during the season Parrott approached Rickey when the Cardinals were in town and asked him why Winsett couldn't hit during a game as he did in batting practice.

"Watch that beautiful swing my boy," Rickey answered. "Mr. Winsett sweeps the bat in the same plane every time. Woe unto the pitcher who throws the ball where the Winsett bat is functioning, but throwing it almost anywhere else in the general direction of home plate is safe." In three years with the Dodgers Winsett hit a total of eight home runs. It was a master Rickey sales job.[12]

This time, however, Rickey was the victim and, angry as he was, he dared not challenge Landis, the "savior" of baseball after the Black Sox scandal. And it was not that Rickey lacked guts. Back in 1923 when he was manager of the Cardinals, he had a fistfight at the Polo Grounds with none other than Rogers Hornsby, who was bigger, 15 years younger, and in playing shape.

The *Times* reported that the fight had taken place in the dugout toward the end of the season,[13] but Rickey's biographer, Murray Polner, has it in the privacy of the clubhouse, the culmination of disagreements over Rickey's managing style and Hornsby's tendency toward lateness and sometimes absences at game times.[14]

Ed Fitzgerald, in his history of the Dodgers, wrote that their differences were such that "Rickey, the Sunday School teacher and YMCA man, took on Hornsby in a fierce fistfight" in the visitors' clubhouse that ended only when Cardinal coach Burt Shotton stepped in and stopped it, although the entire team knew the violence hadn't settled anything.[15]

After the fight Rickey and owner Sam Breadon made trips to New York to trade Hornsby, a further *Times* account reported. But Rickey should have realized Breadon had no intention of letting Hornsby go when he turned down an offer of $275,000 from the Dodgers, an unheard amount at that time.[16]

Even so, Rickey never really felt threatened, not until Hornsby took over the team in 1925. Breadon, however, was aware of Rickey's talents and kept him on as vice president, a move that Hornsby opposed.

Sam later got a taste of what it was like to deal with Hornsby directly. Rogers often swore at the owner, demanded a three-year, $150,000 contract and finally wore out his welcome at a time when his batting average was down to .316 from .403 of the previous season. Breadon, fed up with the constant profanity and griping, finally traded him to the Giants.[17]

This strange and unpleasant man lasted just one year with the flinty John McGraw. He was traded to the Boston Bees "for the good of the Giants," with no cash involved and no explanation offered.[18] It was known, however, that Giants owner Charles Stoneham had tired of Hornsby's continued insults and profanity and reacted much faster than Breadon did.[19]

For Rickey, taking on Hornsby was part of being manager, but Landis was another matter. He was baseball's absolute ruler, credited with having saved the game after the Black Sox were found to have thrown the 1919 Series to the Cincinnati Reds, even though a jury of fans later found them innocent.

In truth the credit more likely belongs to a combination of Babe Ruth and a livelier ball. Babe hit those home runs—29 in 1919, 54 in 1920, 59 in 1921—and new fans by the thousands filled the parks wherever he played. The dead ball era, when a man could hit 96 home runs in 13 seasons and be called Home Run Baker, was ending.

Just how dead the ball was is shown in the stats of four Hall of Famers who had long careers, were big for their day (all around six feet tall), and were excellent hitters: Ty Cobb, .367, 24 seasons, 124 homers;

Tris Speaker, .344, 22 seasons, 117 homers; Sam Crawford, .309, 19 seasons, 97 homers, and Nap Lajoie, .339, 21 seasons, 82 homers.

The dead, or softer, ball had been part of the game since it was first played in the mid–19th century. Some 70 years later the manufacturers started using a cork center, better wool and they wound the ball tighter,[20] making it harder and thus easier to hit for distance. Within two years the dead ball era was itself dead, swept away by baseballs flying into the stands and over the fences. Wee Willie Keller's "hit 'em where they ain't" became hit 'em where they can't catch 'em.

It was an unlikely pair that brought on the long ball craze. Ed Barrow, a non-ballplayer, had replaced shortstop Jack Barry as manager of the Red Sox in 1918 and soon noticed that one of his pitchers, Babe Ruth, could hit with power he'd never seen before.

Barrow had courage here and the judgment that later got him the job as president of the New York Yankees, for he was messing around with one of the premier pitchers of the day, and the figures prove it. In 1915–18 and 8 with a 2.44 ERA; 1916–23 and 12 with a league-leading 1.75 ERA; 1917–24 and 13 with a 2.01 ERA. And he gave you innings: 216, 323, and 326 for those years.

I once had the privilege of asking Joe DiMaggio who he thought was the greatest baseball player who ever lived. "Babe Ruth, without question," he answered immediately. "A lot of people don't know he was one of the best pitchers of his time, probably good enough to make the Hall of Fame if he kept at it. And he was possibly the best right fielder of his time, with that pitcher's arm. Cobb comes close but I think Ruth is number one."

Earlier that day a friend called and asked if I'd like to meet Joe. The occasion was the opening of a restaurant in the northern section of Newark, an area where Joe spent many evenings during his playing career. It was owned by the grandson of one of Joe's Newark friends, with Joe there as a favor.

When we arrived DiMaggio was sitting at the head of a rectangular table with three elderly Italian gentlemen on each side. I sat opposite him and waited for someone to say something. The elderly gentlemen seemed awed, even frightened, sitting at a table with *Joe D.*

DiMaggio was tall, handsome, and impeccably dressed. It was 1968 so he was still a young 54. He looked affable so, being an ex-reporter, I decided to speak up.

"Joe, how's Dom?" I asked, boldly using his first name to make things as informal as possible. The old gentlemen looked at me like I was crazy, *talking to Joe D and calling him Joe.*

"Oh he's fine," DiMaggio replied. "He owns half of Boston."

"How about Vince?"

"Vince is fine too. He owns most of Pittsburgh. I'm the only bum in the family. I'm the only one without a job."

Everyone laughed, the ice was broken, and there was conversation around the table. DiMaggio stayed for another two hours, walking around and talking to everyone. He was among friends, affable to all, knowing there was no press around to ask about Marilyn or anything else he didn't like talking about. In that atmosphere no one was crass enough to ask for his autograph and he seemed to know they wouldn't.

Ruth's pitching record, looked up later, proved Joe's point: 94 and 46 for a .671 percentage, and a 2.28 ERA. Barrow must have had some misgivings in remaking him, for that is one of the best performance sheets in the game's history.

But when he first started hitting those home runs it was too early to know that this 23-year-old, who came to baseball out of a Baltimore orphanage, or reform school as some called it, had forever changed the game's offense. So it was Landis who was lionized as the man who banned those 1919 fixers for life and thereby restored the game's integrity. Or so it seemed to the public. His shock of white hair, craggy features and regal speech and bearing had the press mesmerized. Whatever he said was written in the stone of the Georgia mountain he was named for.

It was this seeming omnipotence that made it impossible for Rickey to fight Landis's ruling and thus keep Reiser and the others. Brooklyn soon signed Pete for a $100 bonus, a laughable amount today but not so in 1938 at a time when World War II hadn't yet lifted us out of the Great Depression.[21]

When asked in 1941 how he felt after Brooklyn scout Ted McGrew offered him the money, he said: "A hundred dollars. I agreed then and there. I felt like a bum who had suddenly become a millionaire."[22] (For those too young to remember: in 1938 a person could walk into most taverns, order a beer for a nickel, and partake of a free lunch.)

So Pete took the money and spent his first season as a Dodger farmhand with New Iberia of the Evangeline League. The next year, with Superior in the Northern League, he taught himself to hit from the left side, closer to first base. As he learned, groundballs that were previously outs by a step were becoming base hits[23] and soon it was assumed by all that he was a natural switch-hitter, something he never denied.

Before he was promoted to Elmira in 1939 the Dodgers brought him to spring training. Leo knew about Pete through MacPhail, who was close to Rickey at the time. Larry and Branch had feuded in the past to the point where Rickey fired MacPhail as president of the Cardinals' Columbus club. But that was forgotten, as were many of MacPhail's feuds.

Pete's arrival infuriated Rickey since it was in violation of a promise

MacPhail supposedly made that he would hide Reiser in the low minors for the two years it would take before the Cardinals could sign him again. The *Brooklyn Eagle*'s Harold Parrott wrote that Larry, in turn, was furious with Durocher for exposing Pete to scouts from other teams.[24]

No one asked Parrott why MacPhail, if he wanted to hide Pete, allowed him to come to camp in the first place. Some said he didn't know Pete was there, but that is absurd. Larry knew everything about his team, even when he was drinking.

MacPhail was a hard drinker but he wasn't a drunk. Far from it, for he had one of the great minds of modern baseball and proved to be the most innovative executive the game has ever known. Within just seven years he introduced night baseball and television to the major leagues, developed the first batting helmet for general use and turned the Brooklyn franchise around. When he got out of control, which happened more often than with most men, the problem was usually his temper, not his drinking. On the occasions that his drinking got out of hand associates steered clear, knowing that Larry could turn mean. In what became known as the "Battle of the Biltmore" he once attacked a former employee for writing a magazine article he didn't like, and then, in a drunken rage, attacked others indiscriminately.[25]

He introduced night baseball before he took over at Ebbets Field when he was general manager at Cincinnati. And ever the promoter, he did it in spectacular fashion. On May 24, 1935, the lights he had installed were ready and so was President Franklin Delano Roosevelt, a MacPhail friend. Larry had a telegraph installed in the White House and at the proper moment FDR, from 500 miles away, touched the key and Crosley Field was bathed in light. The 20,000-plus crowd then saw Paul Derringer six-hit the Phillies for a 2 to 1 win.[26]

His genius, not only for innovation but as a baseball man, transformed the Dodgers from one of the worst organizations in the game— heavily in debt and with a crumbling ballpark—into a dynasty that virtually ruled the National League until the team was taken away by a city unwilling to form a major league club on its own. Stealing the Brooklyn Dodgers was easier than doing the hard groundwork.

Larry was the ideal man for the Dodgers as the 1940s approached, for the franchise needed not only a physical overhauling, but a psychological one as well.

For some 20 years the team had been the orphan of New York, laughed at as the Daffiness Boys, called "The Bums" in the press, and were constantly finishing in the second division. While the Yankees swaggered under Miller Huggins and the Giants snarled under John McGraw, the Dodgers were out there in Brooklyn, a long subway ride away and separated from Manhattan by a world-famous bridge.

"Brooklyn's resentment at being treated like a poor relative was real," broadcaster Red Barber wrote in *Rhubarb in the Catbird Seat*. "It had the bridge, but Manhattan had the skyscrapers, the theaters, Wall Street. Brooklyn was suffering from a borough-wide inferiority complex."[27]

The press condescended to Brooklyn's baseball team by coining funny names and reporting the false "three-men-on-third" type of story the metropolitan writers reveled in. The worst offender was Red Smith, the revered leader of the corps, the one other writers took their cues from. Smith simply disliked Brooklyn and the Dodgers and his writing often showed it.

Back in the mid–1930s, for example, when Harold Parrott was sports editor of the *Brooklyn Eagle*, he tried to hire Smith when Smith was working in Philadelphia. Smith's reply: "I decided that Brooklyn was farther from New York than Philadelphia was."[28] Can anything be more patronizing than that? Or more stupid? And he never changed. Through the years as the Dodgers rose in prestige throughout the country, as centerfield changed from Reiser to Snider and Walker gave way to Furillo, Red Smith seldom relented.

Take the 1947 World Series, for example, at a time when the Dodgers were the lords of the National League. The scene was Ebbets Field and the Brooks had just routed the Yankees' Bobo Newsom in the second game.

"As soon as the attack began," Smith wrote, "the species of fauna described as typical of Brooklyn came out of the woodwork. With half the capacity of Yankee Stadium the joint shuddered with noise."[29]

Fauna coming out of the woodwork? Brooklyn fans as cockroaches? Red Smith never wrote anything like that about the Polo Grounds or Yankee Stadium. And he never called the stadium a joint.

Roger Kahn wrote in *The Era* that Smith was not alone in his condescension, that many of the Manhattan writers adopted the same patronizing tone about the borough, the team and Ebbets Field. He quotes Duke Snider as saying that a number of Dodgers picked up on it and resented it. Kahn also wrote that Smith, a native of Green Bay, Wisconsin, regarded Brooklyn as a provincial outpost. From Green Bay no less.[30]

MacPhail could never change that pressbox attitude, but he brought the rest of the country around. His brashness and confidence, his temper and his genius, started to rub off on the entire team and they began walking around and talking like the winners they would soon become. Manhattan still looked on with disdain but there were now Brooklyn fans in Peoria and Dubuque and points west.

The Brooklyn Trust Company, as owner of 51 percent of the team, backed him as he bought stars, and men like Dixie Walker who, to the

Red Barber was the voice of the Brooklyn Dodgers for 15 years, a man so respected that he set the tone for many who came after him. Red was always calm, not matter what was happening. During the '47 Series he broke an old taboo by reminding his listeners that Yankee Bill Bevens was deep into a no hitter, thereby banishing that superstition forever. (National Baseball Hall of Fame Library, Cooperstown, N.Y.)

surprise of many, became a star. But MacPhail's wasn't the checkbook baseball of a George Steinbrenner, buying stars the Yankees often didn't need. Larry had to spend to appease Brooklyn fans who were tiring of second-division baseball.

While he was building the team he brought both radio and television to the baseball world of New York. As to radio, the three New York teams had agreed in 1934 not to broadcast games on the theory that people would listen at home rather than buy tickets. But for the 1939 season Larry brought in his Cincinnati broadcaster, Walter (Red) Barber, to announce Dodger games over WOR. The Giants and Yankees were furious but wrong, as attendance at Ebbets Field increased, proof of MacPhail's contention that radio would stimulate interest and make new fans. The Giants and Yankees were forced to follow along reluctantly.[31]

Barber was one of the major reasons for the success of radio in

Brooklyn. He brought a thorough knowledge of the game and the team to the microphone and was always neutral, never a "homer" like Mel Allen or Russ Hodges. And that voice with its slightly Southern accent never deceived the listener. Unlike Allen, with Barber a fly ball at the wall was just that, not a home run caught at the last moment.

His acceptance of Jackie Robinson showed the fairness of the man. He was Southern to the core, born in Mississippi to Southern-bred parents. When he found that Montreal manager Clay Hopper was fair in his treatment of Robinson, he asked himself: "When you get around to life, isn't that what it's all supposed to be? Be a *fair* man?"

"If I did anything constructive in the Robinson situation," he wrote, "it was simply in accepting him the way I did—as a man, as a ballplayer. I didn't resent him, and I didn't crusade for him. I broadcast the ball."[32]

Red's integrity was finally his undoing. Back in 1947 he got away with his precedent-shattering reminders that Bill Bevens was pitching that no-hitter against Brooklyn because in time it came to be seen he was right, that superstitions such as not mentioning a no-hitter have no place in the broadcast booth. But later when broadcasting for the Yankees, that same type of honest reporting got him fired by CBS when he described something at the stadium that was seen as unfavorable to the team, and therefore the network.

Red had gone to work for the Yanks in 1954 because he'd had enough of Walter O'Malley's deviousness. He had a good 12-year run working with Mel Allen and others when he was dismissed at the end of the 1966 season, two years after CBS had taken over and made Mike Burke president. The team had struggled all that year, with Mantle obviously near the end on those crippled knees. The previous season Mickey hit .255 with but 19 home runs.★

With two weeks to go in that '66 season, the Yankees—to the shock of all New York—were in last place, about to finish an unbelievable 26½ games behind Baltimore. Red showed up for a day game and looked over the stands. He could hardly believe what he was seeing: the huge stadium—*The Stadium*—was deserted, with visiting White Sox manager Eddie Stanky saying he could count the people in the ballpark.

Red always considered himself a reporter, not just a broadcaster, and when he saw those thousands upon thousands of empty seats he knew the game was secondary, that the smallest crowd by far in the history of Yankee Stadium was the story. He asked a number of times for a camera to pan the empty stands and was refused each time.

★*Mantle later regretted playing his last three seasons, during which his lifetime batting average dipped below .300 to .298. Had he retired in '66 he would have been .307 lifetime: 2,108 hits in 6,894 at-bats.*

Realizing he could not get a TV picture of the scene, he decided to say what he had to say "as a reporter," to tell his listeners what was going on. He leaned into the mike, knowing he could not be cut off, and said: "I don't know what the paid attendance is today, but whatever it is, it is the smallest crowd in the history of Yankee Stadium, and this smallest crowd, not the ballgame, is the story."[33]

He was soon told by Burke that his contract would not be renewed.[34] Maybe he would have been fired anyway, given the extreme situation in the Bronx. CBS had never bargained for last place when it bought what had seemed to be the perennially mighty Yankees. The crowd business was just too much. It was never given as the reason for Red's dismissal, but everybody knew. CBS was furious, convinced his honesty was misplaced not only in his opening remarks but by him compounding the situation later in the game by announcing a paid attendance of 413.

This, then, was the man MacPhail brought in from Cincinnati to become the voice of the Dodgers. As such he was the announcer during that historic first telecast of a major league game—on August 26, 1939, at Ebbets Field, with Cincinnati the opposition. It was transmitted to the NBC studios in Manhattan, to the television exhibit at the New York World's Fair and could be picked up by the handful of people who had sets within 50 miles of the game. There were even televised interviews of players Bucky Walters, Dolf Camilli, Dixie Walker and Whitlow Wyatt and managers Leo Durocher and Bill McKechnie—another MacPhail innovation that changed baseball forever.[35]

Red had done all the groundwork for NBC in getting MacPhail's permission and setting up the telecast. NBC knew it and expressed appreciation. He wanted a memento of the historic event and the company complied, sending him a silver cigarette box with his name and the date engraved on it. Enclosed was a bill for $35. Red, integrity intact, paid it.[36]

By this time MacPhail's relationship with Durocher alternated between affection and fury, with Leo later estimating that "he fired me sixty times if he fired me once."[37] The most memorable took place after the Dodgers were on their way home by rail from Boston after Wyatt's shutout had clinched the pennant on September 25, 1941. MacPhail went to the 125th Street station to board the train and ride in triumph with the team into Grand Central Station.

Durocher, however, heard that some of his players were going to get off at 125th Street to avoid the crowd at Grand Central. Leo felt the fans, after a 21-year wait, deserved to greet the entire team so, not knowing Larry was waiting to board, told the conductor not to stop, stranding MacPhail. Larry, tipsy and furious, confronted Leo later in the Hotel New Yorker and, not waiting for an explanation, fired him.

The next morning Larry winked at Durocher, saying: "I got a little drunk last night, didn't I."[38] Even if he had meant it, not even MacPhail would have had the nerve to fire his manager on the eve of a World Series.

He did have the nerve, however, to ignore whatever promise he made to Rickey about hiding Reiser. But even though he and Durocher knew a rookie of great promise had arrived in camp, Pete had to wait his turn. He was an infielder and had to sit while Leo gave Tony Lazzeri, his old Yankee teammate, a shot at second base. There was no place for Pete, since the other infielders were Durocher himself, Camilli, Cookie Lavagetto and Pete Coscarart. Leo's decision is understandable, for even at 36 Tony deserved a look, having hit .292 with 174 homers over a 13-year career that was ending.

Pete finally got his start on March 22 and the hitting streak began. During the next three games he homered off Ken Raffensberger, walked, then hit singles off Bob Bowman, Mort Cooper and Paul Gehrman, homered off Big Jim Weaver, bunt-singled and homered against Ray (Peaches) Davis and then pulled a muscle scoring after singling against Fred Hutchinson. He was now eight for eight and two walks.

Three days later Lefty Gomez ended the streak. Gomez walked him in the second, but in the sixth with Goody Rosen on first, Lefty got him on a force play. By this time writers were surrounding Pete after every game, still calling him Hal, not knowing that he had been Pistol Pete to his friends while growing up.

As opening day approached Durocher and MacPhail got into one of their many shouting matches, this time over Reiser's status. Larry ordered him farmed out to Elmira and Durocher said no, loudly.[39] After all, Pete had a sensational spring, hitting .417 (15 for 36) and expected to stay with the big club.

Durocher wasn't alone in his regard for Pete. MacPhail at that time turned down an offer of $100,000 and five players for him.[40] Pete knew something was doing after Yankee Manager Joe McCarthy told him he would play third for the Yankees that year.

McCarthy operated that way for years. Backed by Jacob Ruppert's beer millions, he was used to getting whatever players he wanted and was therefore derided in the press and around the major leagues as a "push button manager." Maybe so, but he always knew what buttons to push, knew the skills of the players available.

And during those spring training weeks he wanted Reiser, and for good reason. Lou Gehrig was having the worst spring of his career, hitting .132 on five singles in 39 at-bats, plus five errors in 10 games played.

He had reported in March after a winter of workouts, determined to improve on his 1938 figures: .295 average with 29 home runs and 114

RBIs—a wonderful year for most players but not the numbers of one of the great sluggers in baseball history.

So McCarthy was concerned. He thought Lou may have just needed a rest, but there were doubts. The baseball instincts that made Joe a Hall of Fame manager told him that Lou, at 36, might be finished. He substituted Tommy Henrich for him in a spring training game so he could rest for a day. But in case Gehrig was through he wanted a hitter to replace him and in Reiser he saw that hitter.

Word soon got around about the Yankee offer and that MacPhail had turned it down. McCarthy had done his best, but MacPhail didn't budge and Barrow wouldn't go higher. And it soon became clear that Gehrig needed far more than a day's rest, that his career might well be over.

On opening day Lou was no better and by this time everyone around the league knew it. That the pitchers felt he was through became obvious as the Yankees faced Lefty Grove, trying for win number 272 on his way to 300. DiMaggio was up with Jake Powell on third and Gehrig on deck.

Baseball, like all competitive sports, is tough and unsentimental. Lefty had gotten Lou to ground into a double play after DiMaggio had singled in the third inning. This time he walked Joe to pitch to Lou. The strategy worked as Gehrig hit a soft line drive into another double play. The unthinkable had just happened. After Babe Ruth retired no one walked anyone to get at Gehrig. There were some pitchers who wouldn't even walk the Babe to face Lou. But on this day some 30,000 fans at Yankee Stadium saw one of the greatest hitters in the game humiliated by one of the greatest pitchers.

So the ballplayers weren't taken unawares when on May 2 the man known as the Iron Horse sat out a regular season game and thereby made headlines all over the country. As the Yankee first baseman he had played in 2,130 consecutive games, a record no one thought would ever be broken. Lou still felt he just needed a rest as Babe Dahlgren replaced him that day.

"I'm not sick, my eye is sharp, yet I was not swinging right," he said. "I reduced the weight of my bat from 36 to 33 ounces thinking a change might work. Maybe a rest will do me good."

But as he took to the bench Gehrig broke down and wept, and there were moist eyes throughout the Stadium as one of the most emotional moments in all of baseball swept through the Yankee team. This was their leader, this quiet, confident man the writers called the Iron Horse. Men such as he did not cry, nor did his teammates. They were physical and tough, but the thought that Gehrig might never play again was too much even for them. Lou didn't realize it, but the general feeling was that his skills had eroded so quickly that something was desperately wrong, that he had played his last game.[41]

They were right and soon amyotropic lateral sclerosis became known as Lou Gehrig's disease, a degenerative affliction that affects the spinal cord and would kill Lou within two years.

With Gehrig down McCarthy had to settle for Ellsworth "Babe" Dahlgren, up to that time a .259 hitter with 10 home runs, numbers that would change little over a 12-year career. Joe had "pushed the button" for Reiser but there had been no response.

After the Yankees were turned down Durocher and Reiser were stunned at the Elmira order. But MacPhail thought Pete was not ready and he may have been right. He softened the blow somewhat by sending Pete to Class AAA Montreal Royals camp for the rest of spring training but he never relented. Pete would play in the Eastern League.

Even though it was in the low minors, Elmira was a good place to live and was a good baseball town, with a tradition going back to 1888. It was a town of 45,000, mostly white blue collar, with Mark Twain's grave its principal tourist attraction. The Eastern League's eight teams were close enough together so that overnight bus trips, the bane of minor league play, were not the rule.

And any worries Leo had that Pete might be ruined by some know-nothing manager proved groundless. Elmira had Clyde Sukeforth briefly and when Suke was promoted to Montreal, Bill Killefer replaced him. Bill knew the game and how to handle men. He was 52 and had spent 13 years in the majors as a catcher, five of them as the battery mate of 373-game-winner Grover Cleveland Alexander.[42] A man who could keep Alexander, one of the game's all-time drinkers, under even partial control for that length of time could be trusted with any rookie, no matter the potential.*

Pete did well there at first, but Elmira proved a forerunner of things to come: it was there that the injury jinx and hospital stays started.[43] He played shortstop for 38 games and hit .301, but was bothered by a sore arm and had to quit in August.

He was sent to Johns Hopkins for an operation when the sore arm turned out to be a broken right elbow. While his arm was in a cast for two months he learned to throw left-handed, starting with a tennis ball and then working up to long throws of a baseball in a nearby park.[44] It was then true that he was ambidextrous and a switch-hitter.

*One of the saddest and most touching ads ever printed appeared on page 6 of The Sporting News, January 30, 1941: "I'd like to have a job. What have you to offer. Available any type position I can handle. Sober, reliable, and I will give my best efforts wherever I succeed in locating. Grover Cleveland Alexander, Times Square Hotel, New York." Voted into the Hall of Fame just three years earlier, he was telling the world he was off the booze and needed work. He was never offered a baseball job. The Times reported that at one time he was an "added attraction" in a sideshow on 42nd Street in Manhattan (obituary, November 5, 1950, p. 92).

Pete expected to stay with Brooklyn that 1940 spring, or at least be assigned to Montreal since he'd hit .301 at Elmira the previous year. But he forgot that because of injuries he had played in only 38 games. MacPhail remembered. It was back to Elmira.

To Larry's satisfaction Pete had a spectacular summer with Elmira that 1940 season. He was healthy and hitting .378 when he was brought up to Brooklyn toward the end of July. But he was brought up at a price. It is one of the few, if not only, times that a minor league team's fans rebelled the way Elmira's did when Pete (and then pitcher Ed Head) was taken from them. As Al Mallette, retired sports editor of the *Elmira Star-Gazette* tells it:

"We lost Reiser and Head in mid-season. Pete was hitting .378 and Ed had 12 wins. We were in second place then but when they left the team started losing and we were down to sixth when the fans started staying away.

"They were so angry with MacPhail and the Dodgers they stayed away for the rest of the year. By October MacPhail had had enough. He wanted no more of Elmira. Signed the franchise over to the city, no money, no anything."[45]

Head didn't do much that year but Pete had a very respectable major league beginning: 58 games as an outfielder and substitute at third base, a .293 average, 3 home runs, and 20 RBIs. MacPhail was right. That extra time at Elmira made a difference in that Pete wasn't one of those who were brought up too soon, or who never played in the minors. Think of Dick Wakefield, Ron Swoboda, Tommy Brown, and Clint Hartung, names recognizable even today as might-have-beens.

Those 58 games proved that Pete's minor league years were over. In his first full season he won the batting championship at 22 1/2 years old, the youngest to do so in the history of the National League. He is in illustrious company there, for the only two younger batting champions were American Leaguers Al Kaline and Ty Cobb. Kaline, at 21, hit .340 in 1955, and Cobb, just one day older than Kaline, hit .350 in 1907.

2

1940: MacPhail Starts a Dodger Dynasty

Reiser arrived at Ebbets Field on the 23rd of July, 1940, with Cincinnati in town for a double-header. Whoever compiled the attendance figures must have been working on commission, for there is no other way to explain the 40,538 who supposedly jammed Ebbets Field that day. Even after the centerfield stands were expanded in 1946 the old park could never hold that many.

Whatever the number, it was a balmy, festive day, the major league debut of 21-year-old Pete Reiser. After the Dodgers left the dugout many wondered why the new kid was playing in right field. For most of his minor league career he had been a third baseman and shortstop, not an outfielder.

Durocher, however, had a set infield: Dolf Camilli at first, a solid fielder with great power; Pete Coscarart at second, who would make the All-Star Team that year; Pee Wee Reese at short with a space awaiting him up at Cooperstown and Cookie Lavagetto at third, steady and coming off a .300 year. There was no room for a rookie, no matter the potential.

With that infield added to the solid pitching of Whitlow Wyatt, Freddie Fitzsimmons, Curt Davis and Hugh Casey, plus Walker and Medwick in the outfield, Durocher was going to stick it in Bill Terry's eye. Terry, the manager of the hated Giants. Brooklyn had already burned Big Bill out of a pennant in 1934, the year of his "Is Brooklyn still in the league" taunt.

Terry later defended his remark by saying he had heard nothing of any Dodger player deals and wondered what they doing in that area. Very unlikely from a man both embarrassed and chastened after being

The 1939 infield that helped make Brooklyn a first division ballclub. Manager Leo Durocher is on the left next to Dolf Camilli, Pete Coscarart and Harry Lavagetto. After a seventh-place finish in 1938, Brooklyn was third in '39, second in '40 and pennant winners in '41, the year they became one of the dominant teams in the National League.

beaten out of a pennant by a sixth-place team he demeaned unnecessarily.

The truth is that Terry was being interviewed by baseball writers in New York before spring training began. Memphis Bill was obviously full of himself at the time. He had succeeded John McGraw—legendary applies here—in 1933 and had led the Giants to the pennant and a World Series win over the Senators in his first year as manager. He had also hit .401 in 1930 although, in truth, if that season had been a movie it would have been titled "Year of the Hitter."

So, buoyed by success, he was giving the writers his opinion of the Giants and other teams as pennant contenders when the *Times'* beat man Roscoe McGowen asked him how the Dodgers would do. Always ready to rub it in where second-division Brooklyn was concerned, he replied with mockingly raised eyebrows: "Brooklyn? Is Brooklyn still in the league?"[1] The gods didn't like it, and sure enough at season's end the Dodgers beat the Giants in the final two games, enabling the Gashouse Gang to win its only championship.

The Giants had a six-game lead that early September but slumped in mid-month and continued to slide until Friday, September 26, when Dizzy Dean won his 29th game of the season, a 4–0 shutout over the Reds. It brought the Cardinals into a tie for the lead with the Giants, who had beaten Brooklyn that day.

The next day Paul Dean beat the Reds 6 to 1 while at the Polo Grounds, Van Lingle Mungo, with Brooklyn fans marching in the aisles carrying signs taunting Terry, beat the Giants 5 to 1, putting them one game behind. It ended the next day when Brooklyn, down by four runs in the first inning, came from behind to rout Carl Hubbell 8 to 5, giving the Cards the pennant. The aisles were filled with even more taunting Dodgers fans and their signs, including: "Yes, Bill, the Dodgers Are Still in the League."

Now it was 1940 and the Giants were the local second-division team. Brooklyn, the Flatbush Faithful were sure, would not just be in the league but would represent the league. It was not to be, not yet. But fan hopes were up for the first time in years, as MacPhail, with Brooklyn Trust Company backing, was upgrading the park, buying players and improving the lighting system that had brought night ball to Brooklyn two years before.[2] He bought his first star ballplayer on March 6, 1938, when he purchased Camilli from the Phillies for $45,000 and Eddie Morgan, who couldn't hit and was soon gone. Dolf was 31, a compact 5 foot 11 and a hitter, coming off a .339, 27-homer season.

When MacPhail told Brooklyn Trust's board of directors that he had paid $50,000 [sic] for his new first baseman, one director thought he hadn't heard right. "You mean the $50,000 is for a whole team, don't you?"[3] He didn't realize that Larry was just getting started.

This man knew what he was doing; he was spending money to build a winner. His next major moves were masterful: in 1939 he bought Hugh Casey from Memphis and Whit Wyatt from Milwaukee. Wyatt was seen as washed up at 31 but over the next two seasons would win 15 and then lead the league with 22 wins. Casey, at 26, would be one of the game's premier relievers over the next decade.*

MacPhail's moves continued and, surprisingly, no one at the bank

---

*Casey committed suicide July 3, 1951, as he was talking on the telephone with his wife, she trying desperately to talk him out of killing himself with a rifle he told her he was holding. He was declaring to her his innocence of a charge that he fathered a child out of wedlock. She then heard the blast that killed him instantly. (New York Times, 7/4/51, p. 18.)

objected. On July 24 he got Walker from Detroit for the waiver price and then bought Pee Wee Reese from Louisville for what was said to be $75,000. The purchase price was actually $35,000 in cash plus four no-name players valued, by MacPhail's estimate, at $10,000 each. The deal specified that Pee Wee report to Brooklyn during spring training of '39, thus allowing Louisville to use him in the 1938 playoffs.[4]

The Walker deal is a mystery. He was only 28 and had averaged better than .297 over the previous four seasons. Though he was seen by many as damaged goods because of injuries, MacPhail heeded his instincts and was rewarded when Dixie became a late-blooming star. Some aspects of the Reese deal were even stranger.

According to Durocher, MacPhail got the shortstop because Joe Cronin was afraid that if Red Sox owner Tom Yawkey bought the 20-year-old he would take Cronin's job after showing "how the position should be played."

Harold "Pee Wee" Reese held the Brooklyn infield together for 15 seasons and is now in the Hall of Fame. Brooklyn bought Pee Wee after Boston Red Sox shortstop Joe Cronin scouted him down in Louisville and reported back to owner Tom Yawkey that the "pasty-faced kid would never make it." Cronin, no fool, was trying to protect his job.

"Cronin went down to see him (play)," Durocher says in *Nice Guys Finish Last*, "and reported back that Reese was a pasty-faced kid who would never make it."[5] At the time, Cronin had been in the league since 1926, a manager since 1933, and a solid hitter (he would end a 20-year career at .301 and be elected to the Hall of Fame in 1956). There's much talk about the Curse of the Bambino, of course, but little about how a Hall of Fame shortstop who never got rattled might have helped that often jittery Red Sox infield through the 1940s and '50s.

As things stood, Cronin had reason to be afraid. He was 34 and the 20-year-old Reese would have blown him right out of his shortstop job, probably onto first base, where the next year Jimmy Foxx would start drinking his way off the team. Joe hung on for a couple of years but by 1942 he was down to 79 at-bats as Johnny Pesky replaced him at short-stop.

So Pee Wee came to Brooklyn where he held *that* infield together for 15 seasons. He became the team captain, respected not only for his skills on the field but for his sense of discipline, and diplomacy when called for, in the clubhouse.

The nickname Pee Wee was the result of a marble tournament he won as a boy in Kentucky,[6] but it no longer fit, as at 5 foot 9 and 160 pounds he became one of the most durable infielders of his day. His at-bats ranged between 500 and 600 a season and he compiled a lifetime .269 average. This would have been higher had he not taken so many first pitches in becoming known as the best two-strike hitter in the game.

MacPhail figured Reese would anchor the infield but he wasn't satisfied with the outfield. He had Walker, but Leo kept shuffling him in and out of the lineup with a group of journeymen. Larry knew he needed a star, a hitter with power.

And he got him when the Cardinals agreed to send Joe Medwick and Curt Davis to Brooklyn for $125,000, outfielder Ernie Koy, pitchers Carl Doyle and Sam Nahem, and infielder Bert Haas. And no one at the bank even blinked. They were used to MacPhail by now and, besides, they were fans.[7]

This looked to be one of the best deals in Dodger history. The quality and durability of Medwick were extraordinary. He was a lifetime .338 hitter with power when he arrived in Brooklyn, having won the triple crown and MVP awards in 1937, when he hit .374 with 31 home runs and 111 runs batted in. As for hit totals: for the five years before 1940 he had 224, 223, 237, 190, and 201.

Why did the Cards trade a player of that quality? Word was going around about dissension on the team because Medwick was said to have become selfish to the point where he was partly responsible for the their failure to overtake the Reds in '39.[8] And the Cards had that great farm system. There was always somebody coming along, in this case Stanley Frank Musial at Rochester, brought up the following season to take Joe's left field spot.

Davis proved to be a sleeper. He had been a workhorse for years with mostly mediocre results. But now he was 37 and had a miserable start because of a sore arm. So even though he was 22 and 16 the year before, the Cards dealt him. He was only 8 and 7 for Brooklyn that year but then 13 and 7 on the pennant winners in '41 and 15 and 6 when the Cards won the flag at the very end of '42 by winning 106 games to the Dodgers' 104.

So now Larry had the nucleus of the great team the Dodgers would become. The finishing touches would be added at the end of the year when he purchased right-handed fastballer Kirby Higbe and catcher Mickey Owen. He got Higbe for $100,000 (possibly more) and Pitcher Vito Tamulis because the Phillies needed the cash. Owen, one of baseball's really fine defensive catchers, went for $65,000 and Gus Mancuso because the Cards had Walker Cooper coming along. As a result of these deals the Dodgers would be poised to win a pennant the next year, fight the Cardinals down to the final day in other seasons and, finally, dominate the league for years.

But Durocher wasn't looking at tomorrow. He never did. He wanted that 1940 pennant and might have won it if he hadn't lost Reese, Medwick, Camilli, and Lavagetto for long stretches during the season: Reese, the glove that held the infield together, Medwick, his best hitter, Camilli, his power hitter, Lavagetto, his solid third baseman.

Reese went down twice, first on June 1 at Wrigley Field when he was hit behind the left ear by a fastball thrown by Cubs righthander Jake Mooty, and on August 15 when he broke his heel sliding into second at Ebbets Field, finishing him for the year.[9]

In Chicago the background prevented him from seeing the ball that hit him. In those days center field stands were not roped off and darkened as they are today for the benefit of the hitter. Years later he recalled for Peter Golenbock that he lost the ball in "a lot of white shirts out there. Mooty released the ball and I never saw it."[10] Reese was out a total of seven weeks and therefore played only 84 games all season.

Medwick was struck on the left side of his head by a fastball thrown by Cardinal righthander Bob Bowman on June 18, just six days after he arrived at Ebbets Field.[11] It was one of the more serious beanings since Cleveland shortstop Ray Chapman was killed by a Carl Mays fastball at the Polo Grounds in 1920, major league baseball's only fatality.

There might have been bad blood there. The Cards had just traded Joe away and the Dodgers were sure the beaning was deliberate, with some saying they heard Bowman yell from his dugout the previous day that he would "get" some of the Brooklyn players. As a result, Brooklyn District Attorney William O'Dwyer conducted an investigation, inconclusive, of course. But publicity never hurts, and O'Dwyer was even then driving toward his mayorship.[12]

Bowman denied it all. Medwick, he told the *Herald-Tribune*, had been a friend of his on the Cardinals, and was hit because he had been expecting a curveball and therefore never made a move to get out of the way. There were Dodgers who denied this, saying Bowman's encounter with Durocher and Medwick that morning precipitated the beaning.

In an elevator at the Hotel New Yorker, Bowman heard Leo say he wouldn't be playing that day because of bruises he suffered the day before. "Of course you aren't going to play," Bowman said to him. "You know I'm going to pitch."

"You won't be in there when I get to bat," Durocher replied, apparently deciding at that instant to play, a logical conclusion given Leo's extreme combativeness. "I don't throw at punk hitters," Bowman answered.[13]

In any event, Medwick was knocked cold by Bowman's first pitch and lay prone at the plate. He was carried off the field on a stretcher and spent almost a week in the hospital with a concussion but, luckily, no fracture. He healed perfectly, but when he got back to the team he was no longer the great hitter he had been when the Dodgers bought him just two weeks before.

The *Brooklyn Eagle's* Tommy Holmes watched Joe play for several seasons after the beaning and felt that Joe was plate-shy for a long time afterward, never again digging in and swinging hard as he had for years.[14] But he hit .301 in 1940 and .318 in 1941, followed by .300 in 1942, very respectable averages, but not for Joe Medwick. The beaning turned an extraordinary hitter into a good .300 hitter. As we shall see, it also led to the batting helmet, one of the great innovations of modern baseball, without which no game would be played today.

Camilli went down next, hospitalized July 7 after a collision with Bees first baseman Buddy Hassett, who also went out with injuries. Dolf was out for almost two weeks, with Jimmy Wasdell filling in. The day before he came back, the Dodgers, on July 19, became embroiled with the Cubs in a way that showed how combative they had become, how much they were now a reflection of their brash and aggressive manager.

In an afternoon game at Wrigley Field, Hugh Casey not only dusted off Claude Passeau twice but then hit him in the back. This is unheard of, since a pitcher can easily retaliate, especially a guy like Passeau, who was 6 foot 2 and tough. Passeau threw his bat at Casey and they went at each other, starting a bench-clearing but injury-free melee. Strangely, Passeau was banished but Casey wasn't.[15]

That game obviously showed the tension the team was under, what with all the injuries and Durocher's constant umpire-baiting. Things seemed bad enough, but they got worse. After August 15, when Reese was lost for the year, Lavagetto suffered an attack of appendicitis on the 29th and was gone, the fourth major player to go down for an extended period. These injuries struck at the heart of the Dodgers: right field, shortstop, first base, and third base.

When Medwick was beaned the team was in first place that morning. But Cincinnati started pulling ahead and Durocher saw the pennant slipping away, injury by injury. Then came the first of the "wait till next year" cries in the press, a cry that was never heard at Ebbets Field, not even after Bobby Thomson in 1951. It was pure press box mythology, but at this time it would have been apt, for this '40 team became so strong that there was a next year.

With all those injuries, a major question for the team was how this new kid Reiser would fit in with this big-time talent. Had he learned to hit the curve ball and could he come anywhere near the .378 average that brought him up from Elmira? Pete was a good hitter from the start but at first, like thousands of rookies before him, he found that those minor league averages, like fine wine, do not travel well.

With Reiser, however, there was one constant everyone knew about by then: his wondrous speed, his 3.2 seconds from home to first after he taught himself to hit left-handed down in the low minors. The Dodgers, of course, knew about his speed from the beginning, from the day he reported to their New Iberia farm team in 1937 after Landis freed him from the Cardinal chain.

Durocher often bragged about his fast rookie, even back in '39 when he was supposed to be "hiding" him. Pete tells of his arrival that first spring in Clearwater when Leo pitted him against a kid named Cesar, said to be the fastest man in the Dodger organization. Durocher sucked MacPhail into a $100 bet that Pete could beat Cesar by 10 yards in a foot race—and MacPhail lost.[16]

Roger Kahn tells of Reiser's speed in his book *The Era*: "In full baseball uniform, wearing spikes, Reiser sprinted 100 yards in 9.8 seconds. Although he didn't compete at track, Reiser was probably the fastest man on earth. He had it all, everything, and he was tough."[17] To say he was the fastest on earth is debatable, but Kahn knew his Dodgers. Unlike Red Smith, say, he was not just an occasional visitor to Ebbets Field. He and his father, Gordon, lived near the park and were there often.

The fans knew of Pete's speed but they wanted to see if he could hit, especially against frontline, pennant-bound pitching. As the first-place Reds came in for a three-game series, the Faithful hungered for a Dodger sweep, two victories that would cut the Cincinnati lead to three games.

It was not to be. Not only did they lose all three games, but Pete's debut was an embarrassment. Bad enough he went 0 for 3, but in his second at-bat he accounted for all three outs, as follows: Reiser up, men on first and second, nobody out. Ordered to sacrifice, he missed the pitch and Babe Phelps was caught off second. Then he grounded into a double play. Two pitches, three outs.[18]

Some Dodgers used the day as payback time, revenge for what they considered recent dirty play by Cincinnati second baseman Lonnie Frey. It started in the eighth inning as Frey came in "hard and high" at Coscarart as he was trying to complete a double play. The ball went over Camilli's head and Coscarart came up swinging. This, you can tell from the *Times'* account, wasn't your typical baseball fight with both sides milling around and no punches thrown.

This was a brawl and the crowd loved it. Coscarart punched Frey several times and as Frey went down both teams swarmed around second base. Wyatt, who had suffered a serious knee injury the previous season in a collision with Frey, was seen (and photographed) slapping the downed second baseman with his glove. Both Frey and Coscarart were banished and Cincinnati starter Gene Thompson suffered a spiked ankle and had to leave the game. Coscarart also had a spike wound and Frey a swollen, discolored eye.

"He came in very high," Coscarart said later. "It's the third time he's done it."[19] Although the fight was broken up fairly quickly, it never really ended, since the Dodgers and Reds kept snapping at each other for the rest of the season.

That series just about finished the Dodgers. If they could have won even one of the three it might have been different. They had hopes for the third game but came up against Bucky Walters, who won his 15th on the way to a 22–10 season. So Cincinnati left Brooklyn with an eight-game lead, insurmountable, even at July's end, as long as that Red pitching staff—Walters, Paul Derringer, Jim Turner and Joe Beggs—stayed healthy. And they did.

New Jerseyans were aware that in that first game Reiser went hitless against none other than Joe Beggs—none other because if you lived anywhere near an International League city in the late '30s you'd remember Joe Beggs as the ace of the best minor league club in baseball history—the 1937 Newark Bears (Charley Keller, Joe Gordon, George McQuinn, Spud Chandler, etc.).

That club could have beaten a number of the major league teams of its time, certainly my 1937 Dodgers. I was 10 then, a few years away from solo trips to Ruppert Stadium and Ebbets Field, but I read about those Bears and Dodgers every day in the *Newark Evening News*, memorizing their stats and collecting their pictures—a 10-year-old in love with two baseball teams.

There was a *Newark News* item about Tommy Henrich joining the Bears. He was with Newark for only seven games when he was called up by the Yankees, but before that, though, his story is interesting in revealing how cavalierly young minor leaguers were treated back during the Depression when for many it was baseball or nothing.

As told by Ron Mayer in his seminal book on the 1937 Newark Bears,* Henrich was being shifted around the Cleveland organization,

For an excellent account of that wonderful Ruppert Stadium year see The Newark Bears, A Baseball Legend *by Ronald A. Mayer, Rutgers University Press, New Brunswick, NJ, 1994.*

deprived of a chance at the majors, even though he hit over .300 wherever he played. He finally appealed to Commissioner Landis who, recognizing the injustice involved, declared him a free agent, thus clearing
the way for the Yankees to sign him for a bonus of $2,500. He was called
up in mid–1937 as Joe McCarthy was having injury problems with his
outfielders.[20]

Meanwhile, Beggs was having a 21 and 4 year but the parent Yankees, pitching rich as they were, later really had no room for him. He just
couldn't break into a staff that had Lefty Gomez, Red Ruffing, Monte
Pearson, and Spud Chandler as starters and Johnny Murphy in the
bullpen. They traded him to the Reds in 1940 and he was a key to their
pennant with a 12–5 record and a terrific ERA of 2.00.

Cincinnati with its eight-game lead was cruising to the pennant, a
proud and happy group as July ended. Then on August 3 a tragedy,
unexplainable and almost unbelievable, struck the team: one of its catchers committed suicide. Willard Hershberger, only 29 years old, ended
his life in Boston's Copley Hotel in the most brutal fashion: he opened
his throat with a straight razor while kneeling at the bathtub.[21] The
Newark native had been one of the catchers on the 1937 Bears. In fact,
the year before he had been voted the International League Catcher of
the Year.

He is the only player in the history of the game to take his own life
during the baseball season, and there is no concrete explanation why. He
left no note, nor did he show any obvious hints during the previous day
that he would kill himself. There were signs later noted, however, that
darkness had been closing in.

The Hershberger suicide, covered extensively in *The National Pastime,* a publication of the Society for American Baseball Research, ended
a life of depression and melancholy, with paranoia developing toward the
end. A few days before his suicide outfielder Morrie Arnovich was sitting with him in the dugout when Hershberger told him "there's a lot of
fellows on this club who are down on me."

Cincinnati Manager Bill McKechnie said afterward that Hershberger
was worried about his failure to hit consistently. This would seem consistent with paranoia since he was a lifetime .316 hitter over three seasons. McKechnie added that he and Hershberger talked through most
of the night before the suicide, with Hershberger saying that he would
probably kill himself, as his father did. McKechnie said he left the room
convinced he had talked him out of it.

There were also reports that Hershberger was upset at being Ernie
Lombardi's backup, but he must have heard that Cincinnati came close
to trading Lombardi to the Cubs during the '37 off-season to make room
for him. The trade never came off but everybody on the team knew the

Reds had faith enough in Bill to make him their first-string catcher at the appropriate time.

That fatal day, McKechnie waited until the end of their doubleheader before telling his players the news. When they gathered in the clubhouse he simply said: "All right, now be quiet. Willard Hershberger has just destroyed himself." He then told the team that the suicide was not related to baseball problems and that he had given his word that he would never reveal what was talked about the night before. And he never did.[22]

Although the reasons for Hershberger's suicide will never be known, the consensus among all involved was that in addition to his fits of depression as a factor, there was a legacy of suicide in the family. Not only had his father taken his own life, but two first cousins died the same way.[23]

What poor Hershberger never realized through his depressions and anxieties was that his teammates were genuinely fond of him and deeply concerned about what they saw and sensed was happening. And that's not just hearsay. The team vowed to win the Series in his honor and then backed that up with a touch of real class: after they won it they voted his mother a full Series share, $5,803, a small fortune in the fall of 1940.[24]

As the pennant race moved on, the Reds were pulling ahead until at the close of the season they were 12½ games in front of the Dodgers, helped along the way by those key Dodger injuries. Most important among the fill-ins was Reiser, as he came in from the outfield to play third base for the rest of the year when Lavagetto went down. He played in 58 games with a record of 66 for 225 at the plate for a .293 average, 11 doubles, 4 triples, 3 home runs and 20 RBIs.

And, not to forget, he protected Abe Stark's sign during his time in right field, just as all the other right fielders did down through the years until the team left for Los Angeles. Abe was one of Brooklyn's leading citizens, a one-time borough president and longtime owner of one of the biggest clothing stores in town, Abe Stark's, naturally. Abe knew publicity and he hired space for a sign at the base of the Ebbets Field scoreboard and advertised that any batted ball that hit the sign would win the hitter a suit.

"Hit Sign, Win Suit," it said. Clever, clever idea. Often when a ball went near that sign Red Barber or Connie Desmond would tell listeners that, again, Abe Stark had been saved. Everyone knew it was almost impossible to hit it since it was at ground level and balls did not get through skilled outfielders like Dixie Walker and Carl Furillo.

Of course Abe didn't care about a suit or two. He was an amiable multi-millionaire and was involved in almost every charitable activity in the borough. The sign made his name, though. There was even a famous cartoon showing Stark, glove in hand, standing in the outfield guarding against hits that might cost him a suit.

But it never happened. Harold Parrott, who covered the Dodgers for 15 years before being hired as the team's road secretary in 1944, wrote that "not once in all my years at Ebetts Field [1927 to 1957] did I see Abe Stark give up a suit."[25]

It was now mid–September, with the Dodgers some 12 games out when, on the 16th in a meaningless game with the first-place Reds, Durocher's usual umpire-baiting got out of hand. He jawed with George Magerkurth on a disputed play for so long that by game's end Ebbets Field was in turmoil. As Magerkurth was leaving the field he was attacked by one Frankie Gernano, a 21-year-old, stocky 200-pounder.

It all started when the usually sure-handed Coscarart erred in the 10th inning, dropping the ball as he was throwing to first for the double play. Umpire Bill Stewart called the runner out, ruling that Pete was in the act of throwing. He was overruled by Magerkurth, who called the runner safe.

As the game ended with a 4–3 Cincinnati win, the crowd surged onto the field and Gernano made his move. Maje, 6 foot 3 and 240 pounds, was taken by surprise and went down with Gernano on top of him. Some blows were exchanged before Stewart dragged him off Magerkurth so that the police could handcuff him.[26]

On previous occasions Maje had had the usual run-ins with Durocher that all umpires had to suffer through, Leo being what he was. But after this violence it was always vendetta time between the big umpire and the entire Dodger family: players, executives and fans. As a result, there were some very tense moments between the Brooks and Maje right up until he retired after the 1947 World Series.

Even though they finished so far out, the Dodgers were not discouraged at season's end. Everyone knew they were a strong team. Six of them had made the All-Star team: Coscarart, Durocher (filling in for Reese at short), Medwick, Lavagetto, Wyatt and Higbe. They felt, they *knew*, their time was coming, for MacPhail, that underrated baseball genius, was making moves that would very soon pay off. He continued his drive toward a winner by rescuing Wyatt and Walker from the scrap heap, buying Medwick, Higbe and Mickey Owen, and bringing Reiser up from Elmira.

The Higbe deal caused a furor among Philadelphia's stockholders and fans, since he was the latest Phillie star to be sold by club president Gerry Nugent to pay off a mortgage and other expenses. This was and has been done in other eras but Connie Mack and Charley Finley were owners and thus answerable only to themselves.

The $100,000 plus Vito Tamulis that Brooklyn paid for Higbe was a good sum of money then but not enough to hold off talk of a fan boycott and stockholder revolt in Philadelphia. Things quieted down after what the *Brooklyn Eagle* called a "stormy" stockholder meeting during which Nugent promised to get some fresh capital.[27]

As the result of all of MacPhail's moves, the Dodgers were but one year away from becoming one of the dominant teams in the National League for years to come. It was the MacPhail-Durocher era now, with that press-driven bogus daffiness business long behind them.

3

1941: The Year of the Batting Helmet

Just before the start of spring training for the 1941 season Larry MacPhail called Pete into his office to ask a question and then issued a command. The question delighted Pete; the command doomed him to a brief career.

"Do you want to play for the Dodgers this year?" MacPhail asked.

"Damn right I do," was the reply.

"Well, then you learn to play center field," MacPhail ordered, finally coming out with what he had intended for Pete all along, as indicated in his order that Bill Killefer switch him to the outfield at Elmira. Even today, looking back and knowing of the tragedies ahead, the decision at that time made sense, since Brooklyn had that set infield of Lavagetto, Reese, Coscarart, and Camilli.

MacPhail, aware of Reiser's speed, had Durocher play him in right field when he came up the previous year. Things had gone well until Lavagetto went out for the season, forcing Durocher to bring Pete into the infield, where he looked to have the makings of a great third baseman.

He loved third base, but he loved playing baseball more, so when he returned to center field he was happy. Hell, he thought to himself with the brash confidence of a 22-year-old, anybody can play center field. All you had to do was run the ball down.[1]

But the walls out there were waiting, at Sportsman's Park where all chances of an illustrious career ended the next year, and at Ebbets Field, the smallest park in the league and therefore the most dangerous for the Reiser combination of speed and daring.

Howie Schultz, Dodger first baseman during and after the war, feels

39

that other outfielders might have had Reiser's problems with the walls but that they weren't fast enough to put themselves in that kind of danger. "He was so fast he tried for everything," Schultz said during a telephone interview. "He was never gun-shy like some others I knew. Pete just kept his eye on the ball and kept going."[2]

Eddie Miksis, also reached by phone, agreed. "The walls were never there for Pete," he said. "He just wanted to get to the ball and run full tilt all the time."[3]

Joe McCarthy thought Yankee Stadium's center field was the toughest in baseball, that only the best could play it. He told writer Maury Allen that he put Joe DiMaggio out there when he thought Joe was ready. "He needed that room to roam in Yankee Stadium. That's the toughest center field in baseball and only the real great ones can play out there. That's a lot of ground for a man to cover."[4]

McCarthy's point is true to this day, the Stadium's size makes it tough to cover, but he failed to point out that there is no danger in playing center field there. He should have, because among the three New York ballparks of that day, only Ebbets Field made most outfielders cautious, aware at all times of the nearness of the walls. Consider the center field distances at all three parks at that time: Yankee Stadium: 461 feet from home plate to the center field bleachers, left center 457, right center 407; the Polo Grounds: 490 to the dead center clubhouse steps, left center 447, right center, 449; Ebbets Field: 400 to center, 365 to left center, and 352 to right center.[5]

Yankee Stadium and the Polo Grounds were made for fast center fielders, a DiMaggio, a Willy Mays. With their speed they could get to most fly balls, and both had plenty of room to run, as Mays did when he caught Vic Wertz' long drive in the 1954 World Series. As for dangerous, no outfielder was ever hurt by a triple flying over his head. And there has never been a center fielder at either park carried off on a stretcher after hitting the wall out in center field. At both parks they were simply too far away.

But not the ones at Ebbets Field. Consider again those outfield measurements: 400 to center, 365 to left center, 352 to right center. The ballpark, built in 1913 during the dead ball era, was much larger then but years of alterations had made it a bandbox, a fan's dream but a pitcher's and a center fielder's nightmare.

In March, however, Ebbets Field was weeks away as the team headed for Havana for spring training, sun and Cuban cigars, among other things. Once they got there Reiser picked up where he had left off in his 1939 spring debut. But with the center field question settled, he had to defend his decision to bat only left-handed.

At first MacPhail was dead against it, but Pete was hitting so well from the left side that Paul Waner, in his brief stay with Brooklyn that spring, advised him to stop hitting right-handed altogether, that his stroke left-handed was perfect. Waner, who knew something about hitting, added: "I know you've got more power right-handed, but you uppercut right-handed; left-handed you don't. With your speed, you stay left-handed, kid."[6]

Pete took his advice, even though MacPhail was still opposed. Larry gave way, however, after Pete had another sensational spring. Hitting against all opposition, he was 48 for 126, a .381 average; against major-league pitching, 31 for 80, a .387 average.

The season started in the worst possible way, a three-game sweep by the Giants, the Dodgers leaving a total of 30 men on base, a stark difference from the 1940 start when they won nine straight. The next day the pennant drive started up in Boston as Reiser hit a long three-run homer in the second to open the scoring in an 11–6 Brooklyn win. In a scheduling nightmare, it was back to New York where the next day Pete went 4 for 5 to help beat the Giants 10–9 before more than 56,000 at the Polo Grounds.

Three days later Pete suffered his first major league injury when he was struck on the side of his head by a pitched ball in the third inning of a Dodgers win over the Phillies. Luckily, however, he was wearing the new protective cap MacPhail had developed. There was one out and a man on first when a fastball by sidearmer Ike Pearson sailed in and hit Reiser so hard that, as it struck one of the plastic inserts in his cap, it could be heard all over Ebbets Field. Pete reeled and slumped to the ground and was carried off the field and taken to Brooklyn's Caledonian Hospital.

At first the injury was thought to be serious because of the sound and force of the impact, but X-rays showed no fracture of either the cheek or skull. The attending doctor said the injury would have been far more serious had Pete not used the inserts MacPhail ordered issued at the start of spring training.

Luckily for Pete, and countless others to follow, the Dodgers were the first team in baseball to be equipped with the "protectors" MacPhail had been considering since 1939.[7] The idea of some kind of helmet had been around for some time but never adopted because many ballplayers ridiculed the concept as unmanly.

But the idea was coming on. The first major leaguer in modern baseball to wear what the New York Times described as an "aluminum helmet" was Lamar "Skeeter" Newsome, shortstop for the Philadelphia Athletics, who designed his own aluminum undercap after he suffered head injuries twice from pitched balls. The New York Times ran a picture of Newsome wearing his device on page 33 of their April 27, 1939, edition.

MacPhail took action with his idea after Reese and Medwick were both struck down in June of 1940, with Medwick's beaning far more serious. "Medwick was really badly hurt," MacPhail said later, "worse than we knew at the time. We rushed him back into action too quickly, partly because Ducky insisted on playing."[8]

The Medwick beaning was it for MacPhail. His super hitter was seriously hurt and he decided to stop just thinking about protectors and have them developed. Jockeys at that time were wearing protective caps, so Larry went to Alfred Gwynne Vanderbilt, the noted race horse owner, and got one and sent it down to Baltimore where Drs. Walter Dandy and George Bennett of Johns Hopkins studied its design before developing one for baseball.

The protector covered the vital parts of the head and, as MacPhail described it, "weighed practically nothing," being made of plastic strips that were inserted into specifically designed caps with zipper compartments. Some players wore an insert only on the side facing the pitcher but MacPhail wanted both sides protected. His point was proved when Reese, in spinning to avoid a pitch by Paul Center of Cleveland in an early March exhibition game, was hit on the "other" side of his head but not injured.[9]

Looking back, the surprising thing is that it took so long for such sensible protection to catch on. Between 1910 and 1920 four minor leaguers were killed by fastballs.[10] Then on August 16, 1920, at the Polo Grounds, major league baseball's only fatality resulted when Ray Chapman, star Cleveland shortstop, was felled by a fastball thrown by the Yankees' Carl Mays. Chapman's skull was so severely fractured that a midnight operation failed to save him and he died the next day, one of the most popular players in the country dead at 29.[11]

There were rumors of petitions to have Mays banned from baseball but nothing came of them, possibly because, as the *Times* pointed out, Ray was leaning over and crowding the plate when he was hit. That the petitions were mentioned at all was because of Mays' unpopularity through years of controversy over his coming close or "dusting" hitters.[12]

It has been written often that Chapman's death has kept Mays out of the Hall of Fame. He was certainly a great pitcher with a 208–126 record and a 2.92 ERA and might well be worthy, especially when compared to Lefty Gomez for one, with his 189–102 record and 3.34 ERA while pitching for Yankee teams that included Ruth, Gehrig, Dickey, and DiMaggio.

Although Chapman's was the only death, a number of careers were ruined in the pre-helmet days, the most famous being Mickey Cochrane's early retirement, the result of being hit in the right temple by an Irving "Bump" Hadley fastball at Yankee Stadium on May 25, 1937. Cochrane was then the playing manager of the Tigers and had a .320 lifetime batting average over 13 years, numbers that got him into the Hall of Fame in 1947.

When he was struck, Mickey had worked the count to three and two, important in that pitchers, to avoid walking the batter, never pitch high and tight in that situation. The next pitch was, however, high and inside and, according to the *Times*, Cochrane fell into the path of the ball as he tried to duck.[13]

He suffered a triple skull fracture, an injury so severe that he was not permitted to sit up until more than a month later, and then only for short periods. When he was released from the hospital on July 8 he was allowed to resume managing but, because of the lasting effects of the injury, never played again.

For an example involving a man still in the game, Don Zimmer comes to mind. While playing for St. Paul he was at bat without a helmet when he was struck on the side of his head on July 7, 1953.[14] It turned out to be one of the worst non-fatal beanings on record, as Zim was hospitalized for 28 days, 13 of them in a coma, and had to be operated on twice to remove blood clots near his brain. He was released from the hospital on August 3, advised by his doctors to take the rest of the season off before reporting to the Dodgers the following spring.[15]

St. Paul trainer Bill Buhler told reporters that Zimmer had been struck near the back of the head above the level of the ear, matching reports that Zimmer had lost the ball in the lights and ducked into the pitch. *St. Paul Pioneer Press* sportswriter Joe Hennessy wrote that observers at the game believe that Zimmer would not have been so seriously injured had he worn the protective helmet the Saints provided all team members. Hennessy had been urging the team to wear the protection since Bob Ramazzotti, another future Brooklyn Dodger, had suffered a fractured skull in 1948.[16]

During the off season Don had to undergo a third operation, reportedly to insert a silver plate in his skull to protect the damaged area. In his book *Zim*, Zimmer reveals that he does not have such a plate, as the baseball world has long believed.

"I had been hit on the side of the head that was my speech center," he said. "They had to drill three holes in the left side of my skull to relieve the pressure, but when my condition didn't improve, a couple of days later they drilled another hole in the right side of my skull. People think I've got a metal plate in my head but the fact is they filled those holes up with what they call tantalum buttons that act kind of like corks in a bottle. Those players [who] sometimes thought I managed like I had a hole in my head were wrong. I actually have four holes in my head."[17]

Plate or whatever, this gutsy little guy (his baseball height is listed at 5 feet 9) used to worry the fans every time he came up during his four years at Ebbets Field. There was that "plate in his head" with him facing fastballs with the distinct possibility that he could be killed if struck again. At least he was wearing a helmet during those years, but still....

That worry carried over into the entire baseball world. Everybody knew about "the plate" and didn't want Zimmer hurt again. In 1976, for example, when he was managing the Red Sox, a brawl started in Cleveland when Bernie Carbo slammed into Cleveland third baseman Buddy Bell, who came up swinging. Both benches cleared and Zimmer wound up at the bottom of a heap of players. Dave Garcia, a Cleveland coach who later managed there and at Anaheim, ran up screaming, "Don't hurt Zim, don't hurt Zim. He's got a plate in his head." And nobody did. Even at the bottom of the heap Zimmer escaped with only a small spike mark on his cheek.[18]

Years before, those first MacPhail inserts probably would have saved Chapman's life and Cochrane's career had a Larry MacPhail been around during their playing days. Those inserts have evolved into today's full head and cheek protectors, and anyone doubting the value of helmets need only look at the film clip of Mike Piazza being hit square in the forehead by that Roger Clemens fastball during an interleague game on July 8, 2000. Had he not been wearing a helmet there is little doubt that Piazza would have been killed outright or maimed for life. Pitchers like Clemens, who don't have to face retaliation, are one potent argument against the designated hitter.

Clemens was interviewed by Morley Safer on *Sixty Minutes* about his pitching inside, today's euphemism for intimidating batters. He kept saying that he had to pitch inside to set up the batter for an outside pitch. Safer used a clip showing Piazza being hit and another in which Clemens hit Scott Brosius in the middle of the back. Clemens, with a straight face, denied that either had been deliberate.[19]

Piazza differed, declining to take a post-game phone call from Clemens. And Met Manager Bobby Valentine was incensed. "We've handed his lunch to him every time we've played him," he said after the game. "So the first hitter he throws at his head, the third hitter he throws at his head and the fourth hitter he hits him in the head. My player who had pretty good success against that pitcher got hit in the head."[20] Bobby's meaning was clear. Before the beaning Piazza had been 7 for 12 against Clemens, including three homers.

Of the dwindling number of retired Dodgers old enough to have played both with and without any protective headgear, three agreed that the presence of any kind of protection made them feel safer and somewhat more confident at the plate.

Pete Coscarart, Eddie Miksis, and Bobby Bragan felt there was no doubt that even the early inserts, primitive as they were compared to today's full helmets, gave them a sense that there was at least some protection where there had been none before. Bragan felt that even the pitcher got a psychological lift knowing an errant (and from some pitchers deliberately errant) pitch would probably not seriously injure. "Of course fellows like Sal Maglie, Don Drysdale, and Early Wynn wouldn't give a damn if you had a helmet or not," he said. "They were headhunters."[21]

Miksis pointed out that the full helmets developed later made even the basepaths safer. He said the first team to use the full helmet was Branch Rickey's Pirates in the early 1950s. "They had this bonus kid, a left-handed pitcher and he gets on base and I'm playing second. A grounder goes to short and he comes running into second base *standing up*. I hit him right where the P was on his helmet and it split right in half. The first thing he said was 'thank God for Mr. Rickey's helmet.' That helmet saved his life. If he didn't have it on he'd a been dead."[22]

By May 1 it was springtime and the fans were turning out. The Associated Press reported attendance of more than 1.5 million in only the fourth week of the season. And, what must have warmed MacPhail's heart, the Dodgers, with one of the game's smallest parks, drew one-fifth of that total. The fans no doubt sensed that Larry's trading and spending were starting to pay off.

Or was it that baseball was allowing us to look inward, away from Europe where the war was in its second year? But there was no real forgetting, for that very week one of the game's great sluggers, Hank Greenberg, was inducted into the army.[23]

On the day Greenberg went in, MacPhail made the trade that solidified the Dodgers' infield for the long pennant drive ahead. Coscarart could not get his stroke back and had to be replaced at second base, so Larry turned to the Cubs and gave them infielder Johnny Hudson, outfielder Charley Gilbert, and $65,000 for Billy Herman.

With Herman's arrival somebody had to go and the following week Alex Kampouris was sent down to Montreal. As I read the *Herald-Tribune* clip detailing this trade, my mind went back more than 60 years to a day in the summer of 1940 when I was standing near the players' entrance at Newark's Ruppert Stadium. I was having a good day for autographs: Tommy Holmes (later a star with the Boston Braves), Tommy Padden, Georgie Scharein, Leo Nonenkamp, Big Ed Levy, and Montreal catcher Joe Cratcher. Then out came Kampouris, who snarled: "Get away from me kid." He had struck out four times that day.

As he got into a cab I yelled: "Yeah, home run king. You're the strikeout king, too." He reached out the cab window and I ducked as he threw a punch at me, screaming: "You little son of a bitch." It wasn't until years later that I realized the kind of pressure Kampouris and other Newark Bears were under.

I had just turned 13 and thought those guys had it made, playing ball on the Triple A level. I later found many of them were on their way down, the Paddens, the Schareins and the rest. Kampouris had also been demoted, sent down by the Giants after six years in the National League. How was a 13-year-old kid supposed to realize that sort of thing?

So here it is in 1941 and again Kampouris is being sent down, this time a victim of the numbers game. As he again left the majors and headed for Montreal, he was hitting .314 and had hit several homers. To keep him on the team the Dodgers had intended to send Coscarart down since he was still not hitting well.

But Bill Terry refused to waive Pete out of the league so Kampouris had to go. Terry's reasoning is understandable: Coscarart had hit a solid .277 the year before, and even though slipping at the plate, was one of the best fielding second basemen to ever play the game. He was selected for that year's All-Star team while hitting only .241, a tribute to his wonderful glove. And in those days the eight managers in each league picked the teams, so the game was not a popularity contest as some are today.

When the cause of all this maneuvering arrived in Brooklyn he was hitting only .194. Herman, one of the great hitting second basemen, had had one of his worst springs. But, as happens often when a man is traded, he went on a spree: four for four in his first game as a Dodger and 18 for 31 until he was stopped by Chicago's Big Bill Lee at Wrigley Field on May 20.

Two days after Billy's arrival in Brooklyn, Reiser had his first encounter with the outfield walls in the second game of a two-game sweep of the Cardinals at Ebbets Field. Pete struck the metal gate in center field in the second inning, making a gloved-hand catch of a drive by Enos (Country) Slaughter. It was the first of his do-or-die catches that put him out of action for a week or more.

The injury was a gash below his left hip and, though dazed, he soon walked off the field. The press was told the injury was not serious and that Pete would be ready for the Phils the next day. He was out for eight days, missing five games as the team was rained out twice.[24]

No one took much notice at the time because, unlike his later injuries, the cut healed and left no aftereffects. But the daring was shown, the intensity obvious. If Durocher had been paying attention he would have seen the first warning flag go up. But Durocher was never concerned with warning flags. With him it was win today, worry about tomorrow, or, as he once told *The Sporting News*: "What's tomorrow? Maybe a flood will wash out the ballpark. Maybe there won't be any tomorrow. I'm only interested in today."[25]

That philosophy paid off for him in the two-game sweep of the Cardinals, games that were just about as exciting as baseball can be, with the first game decided in the ninth inning and the second in the twelfth. They proved to be a prelude to five pennant fights, some right down to the last day, with the one in 1946 resulting in the first playoff in baseball history.

Brooklyn was down 3–2 in the bottom of the ninth in game one. Billy Southworth had started Lon Warneke and replaced him with Clyde Shoun and then Ira Hutchinson in the eighth. Billy yanked him when he walked the first batter in the ninth. In came Max Lanier, who walked Camilli and threw too late to third on a Walker bunt. Bases loaded, none out, and Lanier out. After reliever Bill McGee walked in the tying run Reese lined a single to left for the game winner.

The second game, after Reiser left injured, proved to be a combination hitter's game and pitcher's battle. Brooklyn scored four runs in the first two innings but the Cards tied it with one in the third and three in the fourth. There was no further scoring until the last of the twelfth, when Medwick led off and got to second on a throwing error. Lavagetto followed with a grounder into left field, allowing Medwick to score the winning run.

That first Dodgers–Cardinals series of the season was the start of a superb rivalry that World War II could only interrupt, not stop. From the moment Medwick scored that 12th inning run, 1941 was one long Brooklyn–St. Louis battle that wasn't decided until the final week.

It was now mid–May and on a hazy Thursday afternoon at Yankee Stadium what many consider to be the greatest individual achievement in the history of sports began. It was May 15 and in a game in which the Yankees got pounded 13–1 by the White Sox, Joe DiMaggio hit a single off lefthander Eddie Smith, the start of a 56-game hitting streak that lasted until July 17.[26]

The streak ended in Cleveland as pitchers Jim Bagby and Al Smith and third basemen Kenny Keltner stopped Joe in four at-bats. Keltner made two great plays on hard-hit grounders, one a back-handed stab and long throw, to stop DiMag as he topped by 12 the previous streak of 44 by Wee Will Keeler in 1897. Joe's batting average during the 56 games was .408—91 hits in 223 times at bat.

Joe started a 16-game streak the next day that lasted until August 3, when he went hitless against Johnny Niggeling of the St. Louis Browns. During this streak he hit .395 on 30 for 76, so if it weren't for Keltner and the pitching of Smith and Bagby, DiMaggio might have hit in 72 straight games with a .401 average over that stretch.[27] It's hard to imagine anyone ever equaling such sustained hitting over that length of time.

When Pete returned to the lineup he hit .400 (10 for 25) in the next seven games, but despite Pete's hitting they lost a couple to the Cardinals and were 2½ out when they came home for a series with Philadelphia. They won the opener and faced Ike Pearson the next day, May 25, in a game the *Times'* Louis Effrat described as Reiser's "big test."

In an inning that could have been concocted by a Hollywood screenwriter, Reiser came up to face Pearson for the first time since he was hospitalized after being struck by that Pearson fastball on April 23, a month earlier. All who were aware of this, as Effrat certainly was, were wondering: would Pete be gunshy, especially against the Pearson sidearm fastball, the one that hit him a month earlier?

The bases were loaded and the count went to 3-and-1 when on the next pitch Pete hit a grand slam home run to center field, leading his team to an 8–4 rout of Pearson and the Phillies, the first win of a four-game sweep.[28]

There is a totally bogus account of this home run from a respected source, quoted occasionally. It has it that Reiser paced his hospital room floor the night after he was hit, went to the ballpark the next afternoon, and pinch-hit the grand slam off the same Ike Pearson. The truth: Pearson beaned Reiser on April 23 and didn't face him again until May 25, when Pete hit the grand slam. The *Times'* box scores of April 24 and May 26 tell the real story, two games a month apart.

That same week the baseball world turned to New York where, at his home in the Bronx, Lou Gehrig died at the age of 37, victim of the spinal affliction that had struck him two years earlier.

The national outpouring of grief at Gehrig's death was not lost on Samuel Goldwyn. As shrewd a producer as Hollywood ever saw, he knew that the death of a relatively young and world-famous athlete was box office, so not long after Lou's death plans were underway for the movie that became *The Pride of the Yankees.*

The Sporting News, in its role as the bible of baseball, got itself involved by urging its readers to mail in their preferences as to who should play Gehrig, whether he be an actor or a ballplayer. The paper assured its readers that the choices would be forwarded to Samuel Goldwyn himself.

Among the actors, the final choice, Gary Cooper, was number one, followed in order by: Spencer Tracy, Eddie Albert, John Wayne, William Gargan and number six, George O'Brien. Unranked choices were Ronald Reagan, Brian Donlevy, Guinn "Big Boy" Williams, Cary Grant, George Tobias, Pat O'Brien, Dennis Morgan, William Holden, Joel McCrea, Randolph Scott, Lon Chaney Jr., Michael Whalen, Lionel Barrymore, Johnny Mack Brown and Richard Dix.

Knowing *The Sporting News,* the poll had to be legitimate, but to movie buffs it seems obvious that some voters were joking around. Cary

Grant as Lou Gehrig? Lionel Barrymore? George Tobias? Brian Donlevy? Lon Chaney Jr.? All good men, but not to play Lou Gehrig.

The Sporting News should have drawn the line at Lionel Barrymore. This was the time of the Lew Ayres *Dr. Kildare* movie series when Barrymore, as Dr. Gillespie, was so crippled by rheumatoid arthritis that he had to play the role in a wheelchair.

Ballplayers nominated, in no rank order, were Hank Greenberg, Wally Pipp, Waite Hoyt, Frank McCormack, Babe Ruth (Babe Ruth??), Babe Dahlgren, Lefty O'Doul, Jimmie Foxx, Elbie Fletcher, Al Hollingsworth, Charlie Grimm, Bill Nicholson and Johnny Humphries.[29] It's obvious the Babe Ruth voters were jokers, too.

The movie was certainly very effective as the story of the early death of a very good man, but many viewers agreed with the assessment of the *Times'* film critic Bosley Crowther that it should have had more baseball and that Gary Cooper would never be mistaken for Lou Gehrig or any other ballplayer.

As Lou was being eulogized and then buried in Kensico Cemetery in Valhalla, New York, baseball teams across America did what the Dodgers and Cardinals did in Sportsman's Park: both squads lined along the foul lines for a minute of silence as the centerfield flag was lowered in tribute to the Iron Horse.

It was early June now, the best baseball weather of the year, but as the flowers bloomed the war kept creeping nearer, with Hank Greenberg in basic training and other ballplayers reporting for duty. The first big leaguer to be drafted, Hugh Mulcahy of the last-place Phillies, had gone in months before, on March 8. Hugh was a good pitcher on a bad team and he lost so often that he was nicknamed "Losing Pitcher," as the box scores would list: Losing Pitcher, Mulcahy. He served almost five years, the longest hitch of anyone in baseball. Like a number of other good pitchers, notably Johnny Beazley of the Cardinals, Hughie didn't have it when he returned, weakened by a tropical disease he caught while serving in the South Pacific.[30]

There were many who felt the country was already at war, what with the draft and 50 overage destroyers being turned over to Britain, an act that Churchill called a justification for Germany to declare war on the United States. Ahead was an undeclared shooting war in the North Atlantic as German U-boats attacked the destroyer *Greer* and then sank the destroyer *Reuben James* with a loss of 96 officers and men.

Against this background, a type of special status for baseball, different from the anti-trust provision but equally important at the time, was about to be tested. Pitcher Johnny Rigney, a White Sox righthander, requested a deferment that was to be decided at the highest level, President Roosevelt himself.

The president would have to rule on the validity of a section of the National Selective Service Act that granted deferments to baseball players for financial reasons, permitting them to complete their current seasons. Rigney, 26, was ordered to report for induction June 20, but his local draft board granted a 60-day deferment so that he could complete about half the season.

The Illinois Selective Service director opposed the deferment as favoritism for "high-salaried people." Under the law the director was allowed to appeal any decision of the local and county boards, but his appeal, or the appeal of the draftee, had to go directly to the president for a decision.[31]

When compared to the madness of today's baseball salaries, the players of that day hardly seem "high-salaried." But the average major league salary back in 1941 was $7,000[32] at a time when industrial workers were happy with $1 an hour. With many Americans making $40 a week, $7,000 went a long way.

A Packard Clipper, one of the best cars of the day, went for $905 to $1,395. Or down the scale, a new Studebaker could be had for $547. Beer was 5 cents, the best Goodyear tire was $10.95 and a six-room, two-bath house in Kew Gardens on Long Island could be had for $6,890 complete with playroom and garage. The higher social levels could buy a mansion in Westchester's Pelham Manor for $21,000.[33]

So the extra 60 days' pay that Rigney wanted to earn through the deferment was substantial for that time, but within a day he withdrew his request, saying that the interpretation of the draft code was "in controversy," meaning that the public outcry against his deferment request made him change his mind.

Rigney duly reported for induction on June 20 and was rejected. Doctors found a chronic eardrum perforation that made him unfit for service. After Pearl Harbor, though, it was a different story. Many perforated eardrums were downgraded as reasons for deferment,[34] Frank Sinatra excepted. Johnny went in for three years and, like Beazley, had nothing when he returned.

On that June 19, the day before the Rigney soap opera ended temporarily, the Dodgers were in Chicago when Dick Wakefield arrived at Wrigley Field and put on a Brooklyn uniform to show Durocher what he could do. Roscoe McGowen reported in his *Times* story that the young Michigan All-American hit a few into the right-field bleachers in batting practice and that Durocher was favorably impressed.

This was just a stopover for Wakefield, however. He was shopping himself around and Brooklyn was the sixth club he performed for. All those journalists and others who railed against Pete Rose for doing the same thing in the 1980s apparently never heard of Wakefield. Dick soon became the first of the "bonus babies" when he signed with Detroit for $40,000, leaving the baseball world groggy.[35]

MacPhail was smart to lay off this one. Wakefield, at 6 feet 4, had everything but real talent. He hit wartime pitching in '43 and '44 for a combined .327 but wasn't much when real baseball began again. He hung on for the better part of six seasons, as several managers waited for that picture swing to produce power that just wasn't there against post-war pitching.

After the Wakefield show the Dodgers headed for Cincinnati and into a typical Midwest heat wave. They won the series opener on Friday, beating Bucky Walters 6–2. Then during a doubleheader the next day the temperature at Crosley Field hit 95, with humidity to match, as the Brooks faced Paul Derringer. They won the first game in 16 innings on an unearned run. Reiser singled, reached third when first baseman Frank McCormick threw wildly to first on the next batter, and then scored on a Walker squeeze bunt.

Wyatt was unhittable until the heat, and especially the humidity, got to him. He broke a scoreless tie in the 11th inning with a home run off Derringer. But after running it out he became ill from the heat and had to quit. Casey took over and was the winner in the 16th when Walker bunted Reiser home. Derringer went all 16 innings in that heat, the 2–1 loser. Games like that were the reason he was 12 and 14 that year. A terrific pitcher, he won 223 games with mostly second-division Cincinnati teams and probably would have been in the Hall of Fame years ago had he played for a New York team.

The second game was far less dramatic but no less important. It enabled Brooklyn to leave town just one game behind the Cardinals as they beat Johnny Vander Meer 3–2. No heroics here, but the crowd saw one of the weirdest double plays ever recorded. Reiser singles, Lavagetto singles, and both advance on a wild pitch. Medwick hits a sharp grounder to Lonnie Frey who gets Reiser at the plate. Catcher Dick West rolls the ball to the mound thinking there are three out. As Lavagetto breaks for home, Frey recovers and for the second time in about six seconds nails a man at the plate. It was a weekend to remember.

It was Forbes Field the next day where Brooklyn took the opener. In the eighth inning, with the score 4–4, Herman Franks hit a pinch-hit, three-run homer for the winning runs. The Dodgers swept the other two games, one a relatively peaceful 8–0 shutout by Curt Davis, and the other a raucous 5–4 with Higbe the winner.

That final game was one in a series of confrontations between Durocher and umpire George Magerkurth that dated back to the September 1940 game in which Leo had the fans so worked up that one of them attacked Maje as he was leaving the field.

The big umpire had never forgiven Durocher, and was not about to put up with him now, a year later. In the very first inning Durocher came out to protest a called strike on Reiser, but before he could say a word Maje thumbed him out. Then Frankie Frisch, the Pirates' manager, was ejected by Maje in the sixth as he, too, protested a called strike. Finally even Pirate coach Mike Kelly, in charge in Frisch's absence, was thrown out by Umpire Tom Dunn for protesting an out at third base in the seventh.

This was first time Durocher had been banished that year, but it was apparent there was heightened tension between Magerkurth's crew and both teams whenever Durocher started to go into his act. Within a month that tension would erupt into violence again, with Durocher completely losing his head during a tight pennant race.

The next week Brooklyn arrived in Boston for a series with the Braves that started with a distinctly tavern-league touch. The umpires sent a telegram telling Braves manager Casey Stengel they were fogbound on the night boat from New York (oh beautiful bygone days). Casey called Durocher over and said: "We'll start the game anyway. I'll have Johnny Cooney umpire and you get one of your fellows."

Leo Durocher, the Dodgers' brawling, gambling manager, gives a signal from his Ebbets Field dugout. Leo was among the most contentious managers in the game's history, constantly arguing with umpires, and sometimes fans, one of whom he blackjacked under the stands. Pete Reiser felt the team should have got combat pay while playing for him.

Lord knows if it was legal or not but the game began with Cooney calling balls and strikes from behind the mound, tavern-league style, and Freddie Fitzsimmons working the bases. Boston took a one-run lead in the bottom of the inning as Sibby Sisti got to second on a Walker two-base error, took third on an infield out, and scored when Buddy Hassett singled to left. The umpires, led by Babe Pinelli, arrived for the second inning and major-league baseball resumed. Boston won, 3–2, and there was no subsequent word from Landis, so the Brooks lost a half game in the standings.

An injury to a front-line

player hit the Dodgers again when, on the last day of June, Owen was felled by a Johnny Podgajny pitch that sailed in and struck him beside the left eye. As the flow of blood from the resultant cut was stopped, Mickey was taken to Caledonian Hospital.

Tommy Holmes, in the *Eagle* the next day, wrote that probably no team in modern big-league history ever experienced anything like the series of beanings Dodger players had suffered during the 1940 season and the first half of 1941. He cited Pee Wee Reese, Joe Medwick and Hugh Casey in 1940, and Pete Reiser and now Mickey Owen just midway through 1941. The plastic headgear MacPhail ordered for the team had helped, Holmes wrote, but "apparently what the Dodgers need is a suit of armor." This was pointing up the fact that no kind of headgear would have protected Owen, since he was hit just beside the eye, an area that cannot be covered by anything.[36]

The opposing pitcher in every case claimed innocence, saying the ball somehow "sailed" into the hitter. Maybe so, but the Dodger combativeness that practically radiated from their manager has to be taken into account. Durocher was a man who over the span of years met a heckling fan under the stands and broke his jaw with a blackjack, floored a much larger sportswriter by getting in the first punch and was generally hated around the league. Reiser once said: "There were times I thought we should've got combat pay playing for Leo."[37]

The feeling among most ballplayers was summed up by Pete Coscarart: "When I played for him I loved him and when I played against him I hated him. Most of us felt that way."[38]

Durocher had little respect for anyone, not even the game's greatest player, Babe Ruth. When MacPhail hired Babe as a coach in 1938 Durocher was resentful, thinking Ruth was being groomed to manage the Dodgers. One day Leo executed a perfect hit-and-run play that the writers thought Ruth had signaled for from his first base coaching spot.

"For Christ's sake," Leo is quoted as saying. "How could he call the play? He doesn't even know the fucking signals." Ruth got mad and after some shouting Leo shoved him into a locker. Luckily for the manager, others intervened before Ruth, 6 feet 2 and 215 pounds, could retaliate.[39]

Ruth was only with the club till the end of that season but while there he put on a hitting show every day, as both fans and ballplayers watched in awe. Coscarart was there in his first year as a Dodger and recalls, "He'd hit about 15 minutes every day [in batting practice] and everybody just stopped everything to watch him, the players, the fans, and all. As a designated hitter he might have lasted another 10 years. My brother [Joe] was playing third for Boston [Bees] when Ruth was playing there. Babe hit three home runs the last day of his career."[40]

Leo's aggressiveness, even toward an idol like Ruth, extended, of course, to the pitching mound, where he encouraged Wyatt, for example, to discourage hitters from digging in. Dan Daniel, writing in *The Sporting News*, spelled out Leo's philosophy: dusting the hitter is part of the game.

"What's wrong with loosening up the hitter. Is the pitcher supposed to [give] the batter confidence and let him dig in? I don't believe in throwing at a batter's head, but I do think knocking the batter down once in a while in an innocent sort of way is part of the game,"[41] Durocher told the writer.

Leo never explained how a knockdown pitch could be "innocent" and he didn't have to, since Ford Frick, who had warned Durocher about brushbacks a month earlier, apparently chose to ignore the remarks.

Brooklyn's best pitcher during the early 1940s lived by that Durocher philosophy. John Whitlow Wyatt was 34 years old during the 1941 season and had banged around the minor and major leagues from 1929 until he landed in Brooklyn in 1939. At 32, thanks to something Larry MacPhail sensed about him, he was about to become one of baseball's dominant pitchers after all those years of struggle.

And he wasn't about to give up the chance and go back to all those so-so years, going from one American League team to another during the 1930s. During his Brooklyn years he became one of the league's top pitchers, a brushback righthander who, at 6 feet 1 and 185 pounds, was afraid of no one.

Wyatt hit Marty Marion once because he was laughing, Reiser recalled. "Marty was in the box smoothing the box, taking his time. Wyatt fires it in and down Marion goes. I guess he was expecting it because he got up laughing. Next pitch, right in the ribs. 'Don't laugh at me when I'm on the mound,' Wyatt says."

Not even Joe DiMaggio was immune. After beating the Yanks 3–2 in the second game of the World Series, Wyatt faced them in game 5, apparently tired of DiMag digging in on him. There were some tense moments in the fifth inning as Wyatt pitched inside and after the second or third brushback DiMag seemed to lose his temper and took a step toward the mound, shouting something. Of course no one could hear what he was saying, but years later Reiser described what went on:

"He [Wyatt] knocked Joe down. I was talking to DiMaggio not too long ago about that."

"You know the meanest guy I ever saw in my life?" Joe asked.

"Yeah," I said, "Whitlow Wyatt."

"Oh, you remember that," Joe said.

Reiser explained the problem between the two: "Joe liked to dig in and Wyatt didn't like that. First pitch, Joe goes down. He didn't say anything. He gets up, digs in again. Second pitch, down he goes again."

By this time they were shouting at each other, Reiser recalled, with Wyatt continuing to threaten DiMaggio if he hept digging in.[42] But according to the *Times* it became more volatile than Reiser remembered. After the last brushback Joe flied to Pete and as he rounded second on his way to the dugout more words were exchanged with Wyatt. Both benches started emptying, with the ever-aggressive Owen headed for The Jolter. Joe, expecting a fight, struck a defensive posture as the umpires converged on the mound and took control.

After the game Joe told the press that he was angered by two pitches at his head. "When I was crossing the field I reminded Wyatt the Series wasn't over yet. He came with a remark that made me go for him, and he came for me. I was just waiting for him to throw the first punch but I don't recall that he did."[43]

One thing from all that is certain: if Durocher had been a pitcher he would have been Whitlow Wyatt, with one difference: Wyatt, regardless of DiMaggio's opinion, was tough but not mean. Durocher was at times tough and often mean.

As a result of the beaning Owen was out for a week and recovered just in time for the All-Star game, held that year in Detroit. Six Dodgers were named to the team and all six played: Reiser, Lavagetto, Medwick, Herman, Owen and Wyatt. Whit went two scoreless innings and Herman got two hits as the American League, winners almost every year in that era, won 7–5 on a three-run homer by Ted Williams in the last of the ninth off Claude Passeau.

For once, the All-Star game had to share the spotlight, for on the minds of baseball fans throughout the country was Joe DiMaggio's one-man show, now going into its seventh week. Ten days before the All-Star exhibition Joe had broken George Sisler's 41-game hitting streak, and then Keeler's as he continued hitting right up to the three-day break. In Cleveland he went 3 for 4 in his 56th straight game on July 16.

The next day, after he was stopped by Bagby and Smith, aided by those great plays by Keltner, Joe was philosophical in talking to sportswriter Dan Daniel: "Well, that's that," he said. "I've been under a strain even after the record was broken. But that's gone now. I'll be out there now still trying to win games. That's all that has counted, anyway."[44]

Brooklyn opened the second half of the season being shut down by three Cincinnati pitchers, Vander Meer, Joe Beggs and Whitey Moore. Games with the Reds had quieted down from the previous two seasons. For one thing, the Frey-Coscarart battles were over since Coscarart had been benched with the arrival of Billy Herman.

The following day Cincinnati won again, another tough loss for Wyatt, who gave up three runs on six hits in eight innings, the kind of pitching that wins much of the time. He was having a tremendous year but games like that one limited his record to 22 and 10, excellent of course, but with his 2.34 ERA it should have been even better.

During the next week MacPhail picked up Johnny Allen, another pitcher from the scrap heap, and he paid immediate dividends. After the disastrous series against Pittsburgh and St. Louis, Durocher started Allen against the Cubs and he won the first of his three victories as a spot starter. Allen was 36 and came to the Brooks via the waiver list from the sixth-place St. Louis Browns.

Johnny was only 3 and 0 for the Dodgers but he gave Leo more than 100 innings during the next two hot summer months. He had been a superb pitcher for the Yankees in the early 1930s, compiling a 50 and 19 record between 1932 and 1935 when McCarthy traded him to Cleveland in the off-season for Monte Pearson and Steve Sundra.

McCarthy was criticized by the New York press for trading a 50 and 19 pitcher, but Joe must have known something. Sundra was never much, but Pearson went 56 and 22 over the next four years until he started losing his touch in 1940. Again, if Joe was a "push-button manager" he always seemed to know what buttons to push.

On August 9 the Brooks played in one of the wildest double-headers of the season as they faced Stengel's Boston Braves at Ebbets Field. Casey's relief pitcher, Dick Errickson, started it all by hitting three Dodger All-Stars within two innings.

It began when Medwick was hit in the elbow and had to leave the game. Moments later Camilli was hit in the back of the head and in the next inning Reiser got it in the side of his head. Neither was hurt, thanks to MacPhail's protective inserts, but that made no difference to the fans. Bottles started flying out of the stands and one fan was arrested and later fined $10 in Night Court.

The *Times'* Roscoe McGowen, from his seat in the pressbox, felt that Medwick had been dusted, probably because he had hit one into the left-field stands foul by about a foot. "But in justice to the pitcher, who appeared quite flustered thereafter," McGowen wrote, "his hitting of Camilli and Reiser seemed accidental." Durocher apparently agreed since there was no retaliation. The Dodgers swept the two games 11–4 and 4–0.

The next day one of those pivotal events that help decide pennant races took place at Sportsman's Park, where St. Louis was playing the Pirates. Enos Slaughter was racing back into right center when he swerved to avoid Terry Moore, who was making a diving catch. Slaughter bounced off the wall and fell heavily, breaking his collar bone. The *Post-Dispatch* reported the injury as a broken left clavicle and that Slaughter would be out for the rest of the season.[45] He came back in mid–September to pinch hit a few times but was unable to play full time.

Slaughter was missed because he was one of those who played

beyond their skills. This is always said of Eddie Stanky, but Slaughter was on a much higher level than Eddie. Few players have made the Hall of Fame on intangibles, but Slaughter is one of them. His batting average was an even .300 over 19 years. And his 169 homers isn't that bad when you consider that he was only 5 foot 9 and 180.

But it was his competitive fire and baseball instincts that got him into the Hall. Slaughter was among the most driven men ever to play the game. Baseball was war to the man. Bill Dickey once said that competitive fire is what separates the best from the mediocre, what makes a ballplayer great. "I'll give you two examples," he added, "Pete Rose and Enos Slaughter."[46]

And Slaughter had an instinctive feel for the game in all situations. Only one example is necessary, his "Mad Dash" in the seventh game of the 1946 World Series. There's more on this at the end of Chapter 7, but the essence of "The Dash" is that Slaughter's scoring from first on what was essentially a single to left-center surprised just about everyone in Sportsman's Park, giving rise different versions of the play down through the years.

A man like that cannot be replaced in the middle of a pennant race, especially against a team as good as the 1941 Dodgers. Johnny Hopp took over Slaughter's right field spot when he wasn't backing up Mize at first. Hopp was among the leading hitters that year but he wasn't Enos Slaughter. Utility outfielders Coaker Triplett and Estel Crabtree and backup catcher Don Padgett proved adequate but also were a cut well below an Enos Slaughter.

At the time of the injury, Enos was batting .311, with 129 hits, 69 runs scored, and 71 RBIs, second to Mize in that category. He had played in every inning that year and didn't want to leave the game until Manager Billy Southworth went out to get him.

"When I reached him in right field I asked him if he could raise his right arm," Southworth said. "He said sure, but when he tried his face went white, and I knew there was something radically wrong."[47]

The day after Slaughter's injury, the Dodgers came home and lost a doubleheader to the Giants but then swept the Pirates four straight. The first Pittsburgh game was a fans' delight and they showed it. In the third inning, Reiser hit a triple off the center field wall, driving in two runs. The Pirates tied it in the ninth but it was Reiser's day; he won it with a home run in the bottom of the inning.

As his drive cleared the right field screen, dozens of cheering fans rushed onto the field and escorted him around the bases. From third base on, the crowd was so dense that Umpire Jocko Conlon had to clear the basepath so that Reiser could score.[48]

As Brooklyn was beating Pittsburgh, the Cardinals suffered another serious blow to their pennant chances when Terry Moore, one of the game's greatest center fielders, was struck on the right side of his head as a pitch by Boston Braves' lefthander Art Johnson sailed in on him. Terry was carried off the field on a stretcher and taken to a Boston hospital, where doctors found he had suffered a concussion.

Many of the Cardinals had been injured during the season, but Moore going down, especially after they had just lost Slaughter for the season, was devastating. When he was struck he was hitting .299 and the Cardinals were only one game out, ready for a stretch drive for the pennant. None of the attending doctors speculated as to whether headgear would have prevented the injury, but the Cardinals' trainer, Dr. Harrison J. Weaver, said the protector would not have helped, since the point of contact was below the edge of the cap.

Moore, as team captain, set an example by not wearing the cap because he didn't like the feel of it. After he was hit, however, the other Cardinals who had not been wearing them changed their minds and from then on the protective caps became part of their batting gear.[49]

At first Moore's injury didn't seem too severe, and it was thought he would miss perhaps a week or so, but he remained in the Boston hospital eight days and after he was flown back to St. Louis he was hospitalized again, suffering from dizzy spells. In all, Moore missed 28 games and none of the replacements could spark the team the way Moore (and Slaughter) did.

For the time Terry was out both Brooklyn and St. Louis played decent ball, not inspired by any means, but well enough. The trouble for the Cards was that they needed to play inspired baseball to pass Brooklyn down the September stretch. Instead they played 17–10 ball while Brooklyn was going 18–10, a half-game better.

Looking back so many years later, it is apparent that the Cardinals lost the pennant during the previous month. The team simply could not overcome the loss of Slaughter and Moore. Not even their great pitching could make up for the loss of two of the best outfielders in the game. For example, the first week Terry was gone Brooklyn played just .500 ball, four wins, four losses, but the Cardinals could not pick up any ground. Their offense was just too crippled.

On August 30, however, the Dodgers gave the Cards a lift. They were leading by 1½ games as they arrived at the Polo Grounds to face Bill Lohrman and Bill McGee, two so-so pitchers but good enough that day to knock them out of first place. Out in Cincinnati Lon Warneke was no-hitting the Reds 2–0.

Warneke was a hell of a pitcher, another one of those really good ones just short of Hall of Fame caliber. Or was he? It's hard to tell, with the Veterans Committee often sneaking in cronies that the baseball writers rightfully ignore. In any event, Lon won 193 and lost 121 with a 3.18 ERA over 15 years. At 6 foot 2 and 185 pounds he was built much like Wyatt and, like Wyatt, tough but not mean. As a result of his no-hitter and the Dodger double loss, the Cardinals and Dodgers were virtually tied at the end of the day, with St. Louis just two percentage points ahead of Brooklyn at .640.

In the batting race Pete was hitting at .327 as Nick Etten led the league at .332, followed by Johnny Hopp at .329. Over in the American League Williams was hitting .405, just a point off his final average that year. Cecil Travis followed at .361. *Cecil Travis.* One of the unsung heroes of the game, a man mostly forgotten today except by many convinced he should be in the Hall of Fame.

Travis was one of the best-hitting shortstops of all time and ranked with Arky Vaughn and Luke Appling as the best of his era. Before he went into the army in 1942 he hit better than .300 eight out of nine seasons for the Senators and entered the service with a lifetime batting average of .327—1,370 hits in 4,191 at-bats. In 1941 he was second to Ted Williams' .406 with a .359 average as he led the league with 218 hits.

But then came the war and, while many other ballplayers were playing service ball, Cecil wound up in Belgium and fought in the Battle of the Bulge. As Shirley Povich wrote in *The Sporting News*: "The war dealt pretty harshly with Travis. He came out of the Battle of the Bulge with frozen feet and never did regain the bounce so essential to an infielder." The base doctors were able to save his feet but when he "joined the Nats late in 1945 he could scarcely move around on the frostbitten feet he suffered."[50]

So figure this: Travis went to war and suffered a career-ending injury, while Hal Newhouser won 70 of his 207 wins during the war and was eventually elected to the Hall by the Veterans Committee.* After the war Newhouser was a good major league pitcher, but the Hall isn't about good, it's about excellence over a long period of time, or should be. In any event, there ought be a place somewhere at Cooperstown for someone like Travis and others who lost so much in the war.

As Travis was trailing Williams in what proved a hopeless fight for the American League batting title, Reiser started his drive for the batting championship as he and Dolf Camilli led the Dodgers to their first pennant in two decades. He began by going 6 for 12 against the Giants in that double loss and then the following day in a double-header at Boston he went 5 for 9. With that start he hit .409 in his last 28 games to win the batting title at .343, followed by Johnny Cooney at .319 and Joe Medwick at .318.

In all justice to Newhouser, he tried several times to enlist but was turned down each time because of a heart condition.

After Pete's 5 for 9 in Boston, St. Louis was still leading the Brooks by two percentage points, a virtual tie. A week later, however, the Dodgers had opened up a three-game lead on September 7 when they swept the Giants in a three-game series at Ebbets Field.

In the Saturday afternoon series opener, Davis held the Giants to nine hits and one run as the Brooks won, 4–1, the big hit being Camilli's 30th homer. Meanwhile, in St. Louis, the Cards were shut out 2–0 by Vander Meer.

Johnny had been having a rough time since his back-to-back no-hitters in 1938. The next two years he had arm trouble and spent some time in the minors. In '39 he was 5 and 9, and in '40 just 3 and 1. Shutting out the Cards at that crucial time was the high spot in a brilliant comeback year: 16 and 13 with a 2.82 ERA and a league-leading 202 strikeouts.

The sweep of the Giants went into the next day, a Sunday doubleheader. The first game was a runaway, Higbe winning 13–1. The second was one of those last-inning comebacks that fans love. The Giants were up 3–1 in the ninth when Medwick tied the game with a two-run single. As the tying run scored, the crowd of 34,000-plus roared and threw so much confetti and paper on the field that the game had to be stopped. The *Eagle*'s Tommy Holmes wrote that the cheering went on for a couple of minutes and that a snowstorm of torn paper and confetti almost obscured the Giants' outfield. When things calmed down, it took some time before the field was cleared enough to resume play.

Brooklyn won it in the 10th when Owen singled, was sacrificed to second and scored the winning run on Pistol Pete's hit to deep left that was scored a single as Mickey crossed the plate. The crowd poured out onto the diamond, hundreds of them forming a line behind the Sym-Phony as it marched around the field playing victory tunes.[51]

The cheers were premature. Two days later Big Bill Nicholson drove in the winning runs in both ends of a double-header at Wrigley Field while the Cardinals were taking two from Philadelphia. The race had now tightened down to a one-game Brooklyn lead as the team arrived in St. Louis for probably the most crucial three-game series in its history up until then.

Sportsman's Park was always a factor in those years, especially toward the end of the season. Visiting teams knew they would be playing on the worst field in baseball, with a rock-hard infield and an outfield that toward season's end began to look mangy, spotted with clumps of grass that caused strange bounces. One reason was the Midwestern weather, relentless heat and little rain. But, more important, the field never got a rest, since both the Cardinals and the Browns used the one stadium, each playing at home while the other was on the road. So there was little repair time, with the result that as the season wore on, conditions got even worse.

In this the home team had somewhat of an advantage if only from familiarity. They were in their home park and knew its quirks. But even an outfielder as skilled as Enos Slaughter had problems. "That ball would come to you ever' which way," he told the writer Frederick Turner. "Sometimes you'd get hit in the throat, sometimes in the leg, sometimes in the stomach. You'd try to get in front of it and stop it, but, boy it was tough."[52]

Roy Sievers, the American League's first Rookie of the Year, remembered the infield as so hard that sliding became hazardous. "The infield was like a rock," he recalled, "so hard that when we'd slide into second, for instance, most times we'd come up with a big strawberry on whatever hip hit the ground.

"I was with the Browns then and everytime we'd come home from a road trip we'd see the park the same as we left it. I was an outfielder then and I can tell you the outfield was no better than the infield. With so little maintenance it sure was a tough park to play in."[53]

Fortunately for all it was mid–September as the series opened, the weather moderating as fall was approaching. The first game was typical of the St. Louis–Brooklyn rivalry. It went 11 innings until Dixie Walker's single with the bases loaded drove in Medwick and Lavagetto for a 6–4 victory.

The teams were so argumentative throughout the game, getting on Umpire Al Barlick constantly over ball and strike calls, that League President Ford Frick decided to meet with the managers and umpires the next day. He was upset by the umpire badgering and became more so during a lengthy rhubarb in the Dodger eighth after Reiser slammed a triple to right center. On the next pitch Medwick claimed that Ernie White balked, but Barlick didn't agree. Joe stepped out of the box with the pitch and Barlick called a strike on him. It was then Durocher time.

He got his players riled up, as usual, starting with a long harangue at the umpires, followed by kicking dirt on the plate. Other Dodgers followed suit, kicking dirt and arguing. The umpires acted with restraint, particularly when Fitzsimmons, upset over a call, threw his hat high in the air, a breach of baseball discipline that is almost never tolerated. They didn't run Fitz, but many other umpires would have.

The next morning Frick called the two managers and four umpires together and laid down the law. "This is not an argument," he said. "We're telling you that we're going to run [today's] ball game. We're going to treat you as though you were eighth-place ball clubs and if a man's actions call for dismissal he'll be dismissed. If it hurts either club, that's just too bad."[54]

The next day's game was a 4–3 squeaker, a quiet squeaker, with Lanier getting the win after relieving Pollet in the sixth inning. The Cardinals came into that sixth inning tied at 2–2 and won it on triples by Gus Mancuso and Crabtree off Dodger loser Curt Davis. The Brooklyn lead was down to one game again as Wyatt and Mort Cooper were rested up for what turned out to be one of the best-pitched games in National League history, Wyatt over Cooper, 1–0.

Cooper was certainly one of the best pitchers of his day but the trouble was that his day, his best years, were during the war. By 1941 he was 28 and big, 6 foot 2 and 210 pounds, and with his brother Walker formed one of the two best known brother batteries in baseball history (Rick and Wes Ferrell being the other). But there was always the taint of "wartime star" to his career. Between 1943 and 1945 he was 52 and 19, thus 42 percent of his 123 wins were against retreads, kids, and those judged unfit for military service.

But on this mid–September peacetime day Cooper pitched a masterpiece, a no-hitter through seven, and three hits over nine. His problem was Wyatt, who pitched even better. In the best game of his career, Whit also gave up three hits but no runs and was the winner when Cooper gave up back-to-back doubles to Walker and Herman in the eighth inning for the game's only run. Those two had a number of memorable battles in the next few years, but none could match this one for drama, given the pressure and the stakes involved.

Wyatt, with nine strikeouts to Cooper's six, finished with a flourish by striking out Mize and Crabtree in the eighth and, for the final out, got Slaughter on strikes as Enos was making his first appearance since his shoulder injury on August 10. That night Brooklyn left St. Louis for the last time that season and headed for Cincinnati with a two-game lead.

The Cards, game as ever, came snapping back the next day against the Giants, with Warneke leading the way again. Lon beat the great Hubbell, who pitched his best game of the year, a three-hitter that he lost 1–0. The lone run was unearned as Triplett scored on an error by second baseman Mickey Witek. Of the 154 games Hubbell lost (against 233 wins), that must have been one of the toughest.

Meanwhile the Dodgers played one in Cincinnati that lasted four hours, commonplace today but a rarity then. Johnny Allen, whom the Dodgers got on waivers from the sixth-place St. Louis Browns because both leagues believed he was finished, pitched the game of his life. In the longest game of the year Allen went 15 innings, giving up six hits and no runs before he was relieved by Hugh Casey.

What happened next has driven starting pitchers nuts over the years. It was getting dark and the umpires, after conferring, decided to allow one more inning. Reiser, first man up in the 16th, hit a home run into the right center field stands for the first run, as Brooklyn went on to score four more to win it. Then Casey took the mound, got three outs and was the winner. For his 15 innings, Allen probably got a pat on the shoulder from Durocher, useless when it came time to talk salary. But, of prime importance to the team, the Allen-Casey effort kept the Dodgers two games up.

A sad sidelight of the game was, again, Paul Derringer, who pitched shutout ball for 16 innings until he was relieved by Joe Beggs in the 17th. It was the second time in less than a month that Derringer lost such a heartbreaker to Brooklyn in Cincinnati. On July 22 he had gone those 16 innings and lost 2–1 in that 95-degree heat. Derringer was another great pitcher with Hall credentials: a 223-game winner with often second division and sometimes last-place clubs.

Within the next few days the Cardinals cut the lead to one game by sweeping a double-header from the Braves. Both of their starters went all the way, with the rookie Pollett winning the first 6 to 1, and Lanier the second as the Cards scored a run in the ninth to win 3 to 2.

Since the Cards eventually lost the pennant, the double win turned out to be less important than the arrival of the rookie Stanley Frank Musial, 20 years old and up from Rochester, where he had been hitting well over .400. Things to come: in the nightcap batting third in his first major league game Stan went 2 for 4, with a two-run double in the third inning.

On the same day in Pittsburgh, the Dodgers won a beauty to keep their lead at one game, partially offsetting the Cardinals' sweep of the Braves. Trailing 3–1 in the ninth, Brooklyn scored five runs to preserve that slim one-game lead with 11 to play.

The next day Brooklyn lost a weird one because of what Roscoe McGowen termed "an astounding piece of pitching by Hugh Casey." The Brooks were up by one in the eighth when Magerkurth called a balk on Casey that brought in Vince DiMaggio with the tying run. Hugh, after getting two strikes on Pirate catcher Al Lopez, "threw three consecutive balls behind and above Lopez's head."

Out comes Durocher and, after a loud argument, Leo is again thumbed out by Magerkurth, more fuel to what later erupted into the most contentious player/umpire confrontation in memory. Casey then walked Lopez and gave up the winning run on a triple by shortstop Alf Anderson, causing a clubhouse explosion by a seething Durocher. "Alf Anderson," he shouted. "For Christ's sake, Alf Anderson. Who the fuck is Alf Anderson?"[55]

For some crazy reason Frisch was favoring this .215 hitter over Arky Vaughn. There was constant friction between the outspoken Vaughn and hot-tempered Frisch that finally resulted in a trade with Brooklyn on April 12: Vaughn for Coscarart, Phelps, Wasdell and Luke Hamlin.

It turned out Frisch had traded a future Hall of Famer to make room for a 27-year-old rookie who as a part-timer hit .239 through 1942, played two games after he came out of service in 1946, and was gone, never to play another major league game.

Arky was a Dodger for four years, during which he hit .291 but again had troubles getting along with his manager. After a particularly acrimonious dispute with Leo he quit the team for two years but came back for the '46 and '47 seasons. He was released in 1948 and was virtually forgotten until the Veterans Committee voted him into the Hall of Fame 33 years after he drowned in a boating accident in 1952 at age 40.

Durocher, in his seething over Anderson, broke all the lights in the runway leading to the clubhouse and threw a chair through the transom of the umpires' dressing room. Meanwhile a number of Dodgers were ganging up on Magerkurth as he was leaving the field. In a hearing to investigate what the *Herald-Tribune* called a brawl, Owen testified that things were heating up in the very first inning when Magerkurth greeted him with: "Hello horseshit." Mickey replied: "Hello horseshit yourself." (The *Tribune* used the euphemism "horsefeathers.")

"You know what I mean," the big umpire replied. "You tried to make me look bad in that series with the Giants."[56] Like all umpires, Magerkurth hated being "showed up." Too many showups meant back to the minors.

Things really got nasty as the Dodgers—Medwick, Coscarart, Franks, Wyatt, and Camilli—confronted Magerkurth under the stands. There were later rumors that Durocher was there and got into a fight with the big umpire. That is untrue, since Durocher wasn't called to testify later and was not fined by the commissioner, as all the others were.

In fact, there was no physical violence, just swearing and shouting, with nasty insults back and forth. No one dared challenge Maje physically in those days. He was 6 foot 3, 250 pounds, and had been a prizefighter, and a pro football player with the Moline Indians. There's a story that in the 1920s when he was umpiring in the International League, five Baltimore Orioles attacked him after a game. He knocked all of them out, throwing one through the clubhouse door.[57]

None of the Dodgers, though all big and very physical men, dared touch him, but they were fined anyway, $25 for the use of "vile and profane" language. Durocher was fined $150 for his abuse of Magerkurth in the game against the Pirates. The biggest loser, however, was Magerkurth, who was not assigned to the World Series because of opposition by Durocher and the Dodgers' front office.[58]

The turmoil seemed to be over, but it wasn't. The real violence took place on the evening of September 19 outside Philadelphia's Warwick

Hotel when Durocher decked Associated Press sportswriter Ted Meier with three quick punches after some words were exchanged.

Observers said Durocher had lost 12 pounds during the tumultuous road trip and appeared under great stress when Meier asked for an interview. Durocher replied curtly and Meier came back with: "You're not talking to Magerkurth now." Both men walked down a nearby alley and appeared to have settled their differences when Durocher suckered the reporter, a much larger man, with a quick right and two more as he tried to get up twice. Dodger Road Secretary John McDonald finally broke it up and all three went into the Warwick's lobby where Meier and Durocher shook hands.[59]

To those not in the newspaper business Meier's actions might seem strange: a big man gets surprised by three sucker punches and shakes hands almost immediately. But, as any newspaperman can tell you, Meier wanted to hold his job. Covering the Dodgers put him at the top of his profession and he didn't want a transfer. And that still goes.

In the 1960s it was common knowledge in sports departments in Northern New Jersey that Ralph Houk often physically abused reporters who wrote things he didn't like. The worst instance involved a young man on *The Bergen Record* who was beaten up to the point where Houk was throttling him on the floor before he was pulled off.

When it was over the beat writer refused to report the incident to the police or anyone else. He was covering the Yankees and didn't want to be assigned elsewhere. Houk, supposedly a Ranger hero during the war, had size on his side as well as position. He was 193 and just under six feet, a catcher who was one of the luckiest men ever to play the game. In eight years as a Yankee backup he caught in just 91 games, collecting salary and World Series checks all that time. Because of Yogi Berra's skills and durability he was never put to the test and therefore enjoyed a long career as player and manager. Durocher and Houk were two of a kind, mean bastards who took advantage of people they knew would not fight back.

Durocher, ever the hustler, made some good money by using his attacks on umpires in comic sketches on the Milton Berle and Jack Benny radio shows and at Duffy's Tavern. At $1,500 a shot he would make fun of Beans Reardon, Jocko Conlon, Babe Pinelli and Magerkurth—particularly Magerkurth.

Example: Central Casting would send some big hulk onto the stage to ask Durocher in menacing tones, "Did I hear you call me a blind bat, Durocher?" Leo would reply "What, can't you hear either, Magerkurth?" Audiences would roar, but from today's perspective I guess you had to be there.[60]

September 21 was a terrible day for the Cardinals. Lon Warneke did his job as usual, eight hits and two runs into the ninth inning. But he left with two on and Howie Krist, a top reliever at 10 and 0 that year, intentionally walked Clyde McCullough before Bob Scheffing, hitting at .242, pinch-hit a grand slam home run.

With that loss the curtain was starting to close on Billy Southworth and his men, and there was worse to come as the Dodgers, playing in Philadelphia, won both ends of a doubleheader 3–2 and 6–1, Wyatt and Higbe the victors. Pete had another great day, 3 for 8 and 4 runs scored. Thanks to those three clutch players the Brooklyn lead was now two full games, with the Cards having eight to play and the Brooks seven.

But the Cardinals still had some fight in them. The next day, with the rookie Musial getting 6 hits in 10 trips, they took two from the Cubs by 6–5 and 7–0. Meanwhile Brooklyn, amid the ferment and unrest caused by their manager, did well to split a doubleheader at Philadelphia. The Durocher assault on Meier was exactly the sort of thing that prompted Reiser to suggest combat pay should go with playing for him. Here he was in the tightest pennant race in baseball history and unable to control his fists.

(It's hard for us today to imagine the pressure the two contenders were under. Winning wasn't just for the prestige as it is with our million-dollar ballplayers in this free-agent age. It was for the money back in 1941. Those players knew that even the loser's share of the World Series proceeds was more than some of them earned all season long, enough not only for the wife's fur coat, but in many communities a house as well.)

Durocher sent the 38-year-old Davis against the Phils the next day and he pitched a 5–0 shutout with RBIs by Camilli, Reese, Lavagetto and Reiser. Curt had never before pitched under such pennant pressure as he did that year. He had knocked around in the minors for years before the Phillies brought him up in 1934, a 31-year-old rookie, and then briefly starred for St. Louis until they traded him off with arm trouble in 1940.

The lead was now 1½ games and the next day the *Times'* John Drebinger wrote that hopes were dimming for the Cards. They had split a doubleheader with Pittsburgh at a time when they both had to win, since there were only four games left for each team. Now time wasn't the only factor: Brooklyn was playing the seventh-place Braves while St. Louis was in Pittsburgh for a doubleheader against the much stronger Pirates. They split that day, but in the second game the young Musial hit the first of his 475 career home runs, in the fifth inning off Rip Sewell.

The following day, September 24, the Brooks went up to Boston where the combination of Higbe and Casey held the Braves to five hits and two runs for a 4–2 victory. The winning runs came in the seventh when Walker belted a triple to left with the bases loaded, overcoming a 2–0 Braves advantage. It was Dixie's 31st birthday.

Walker proved, in that year alone, to be worth a hundred times the waiver price the Dodgers paid for him. He hit .311 with nine homers and 71 RBIs, and he was death to pitchers in the clutch. Dixie was brought up by the Yankees in 1931, but they never had room for him in that outfield of Ruth, Combs and Chapman, so he went to the White Sox and then to Detroit, where he caught MacPhail's eye.

No one in either league pictured this guy as anything but an oft-injured fill-in, but MacPhail saw something, so Dixie became one of Larry's reclamation projects, like Allen, Davis and, most of all, Wyatt. Walker had shoulder and knee operations, which made other teams look away, but he was healthy enough in Brooklyn to become a star. And he was loved by the people of Brooklyn, for he willingly signed autographs, kissed babies, went to his fan club meetings, and posed for pictures with the local politicians. He was the People's Choice, a nickname that first appeared in the *Eagle,* but it was changed by the *Daily Mirror's* Dan Parker into "The People's Cherce," typical across-the-bridge condescension.[61]

Dixie got his birthday present the next day as Brooklyn beat Boston 6 to 0 while at Pittsburgh the Cards were beaten 3–1, ending what Rud Rennie of the *Herald-Tribune* termed "the longest and closest pennant struggle in the history of baseball, with neither team ever more than four games out of first place." After the final game, a 7–3 loss, the standings stood: Brooklyn 100 and 54, St. Louis 97 and 56, a 2½-game spread.

Over in the American League it had been over for some time, since the Yankees had the pennant won on September 4, earliest in league history up to that time. At season's end, however, a doubleheader between the Red Sox and the Athletics was of national interest even though Boston was 17½ games out and Philadelphia 37½ behind.

Ted Williams was trying to be the first .400 hitter since Bill Terry had hit .401 in 1930. There was added drama here because that morning Williams was hitting .3995, a figure that rounds out to .400. But Ted, true to form, would not settle for that. It was to be a real .400 or he'd risk sinking back into the .390s.

In the first game he faced three different pitchers and went 4 for 5, including his 37th home run, and then 2 for 3 in the second game, finishing the season at .4057. He could have sat down after his first hit, but that wouldn't have been Ted Williams.

Brooklyn, as might be expected after a 21-year wait, went wild. Not the kind of wildness we have seen in recent years when Detroit and Atlanta, among others, won championships. There were no flaming cars, shootings, looting or any of the other inner city disgraces we have had to put up with. There was joy and what the *Herald-Tribune* called "good-natured rioting" from Prospect Park clear to Borough Hall.

Police estimated the crowds totaled at least 500,000, with any number of people risking their lives by climbing on top of streetcars, heedless of high-power electric wires, jumping onto moving autos and pushing each other and the police around until all were exhausted. Some even dived under the hoofs of prancing police horses for no reason except unrestrained joy.

Some 600 police simply let the crowd blow off steam, the *Herald-Tribune* reported, since there were too many to be controlled and, most important, there were no lootings or muggings, or fires. One police spokesman said it was a miracle that no one in all that crowd, doing all that demonstrating, was seriously injured.[62]

One typical Dodger fan touch: In a Pathe News segment on the celebration there was a group of men near Borough Hall carrying a casket with a name painted on it: Magerkurth. Having him barred from the Series wasn't enough. He had to be ceremonially buried.*

After that pennant race and the exuberance of those Brooklyn crowds, the World Series was somewhat of an anti-climax. One play, of course, will be remembered as long as the game is played, with Mickey Owen unfairly castigated as the "goat" for losing a game supposedly won. But there were eyewitnesses who disagreed.

In game one Durocher played a hunch and started Davis instead of Wyatt in what Drebinger of the *Times* called a "finesse move." Curt was 13 and 7 with a 2.97 ERA that year, more than justifying MacPhail's judgment when he got him from the Cardinals. But Wyatt had five days' rest and was the team's best clutch pitcher.

The move backfired, as Davis gave up six hits and three runs in 5⅓ innings, while the Yankees' Red Ruffing had a no-hitter going into the fifth. The final score was 3–2 with Joe Gordon and Bill Dickey getting the big hits. Medwick robbed DiMaggio of a homer with a great leap near the left-field stands and although his head banged into the concrete, he held onto the ball to the cheers of the crowd.

It was Wyatt the next day and he turned the tables, winning 3–2 on a nine-hitter, giving up just two in the last five innings. The Brooks scored their three runs on four hits in routing Spud Chandler in the fifth, as Camilli drove in Walker for the winning run in the first Series game the Yanks had lost since 1937.

After a day of rain it was Marius Russo against Fitzsimmons at Ebbets Field and it turned out to be a game Marius won not only with his arm, but his bat. Freddie was at his best, shutting out the Yanks on four hits into the eighth inning with his dancing knuckler. Russo was also

---

I could not find a clip on this, but I saw it. I was 14 and remember it like it was yesterday.

pitching shutout ball when he came up with two out in the seventh and hit a hard liner that caught Fitz on the left kneecap, the ball popping into the air for Reese to catch, ending the inning. But Fitz was gone and Casey gave up the winning runs on singles. A bad day but worse was to come.

In game four the Dodgers went into the ninth inning ahead 4–3, having routed Atley Donald after four innings. What should have been the winning Dodger runs came in the fifth inning when Reiser hit one over the right-field screen with Walker on base.

In the ninth Hugh Casey had two out and none on as Henrich approached the plate. Tommy struck out swinging but the ball glanced off Owen's glove and Henrich took first. Then DiMag singled, Keller doubled, Dickey walked and Gordon doubled—four runs in, for a 7–4 Yankee win that put them up 3–1 in the Series.

In the matter of Owen: it's been written countless times that Mickey "dropped" the ball. If he had, Mickey would simply have picked it up and thrown Henrich out by 30 feet. It's also been written many times that Mickey "let the ball get away from him." No, he didn't drop it and he didn't let it get away from him.

Things like that just didn't happen to Owen. He was a superlative defensive catcher, the best of his time. He was a .257 hitter with no power, poor numbers for a catcher. But it was his glove that made him a front-line major leaguer. What happened was that Casey threw a spitter that moved downward with such sweep that it glanced off Mickey's glove and rolled to the backstop. Spitters and knucklers act that way, and Casey never threw a knuckler.

Durocher claimed that the pitch was Casey's "bread-and-butter pitch," a hard, low-breaking sinker, in which Owen loyally backed him up.[63] Let's hear from some eyewitnesses, Tommy Henrich to start: "I was fooled. Casey threw a heck of a pitch. He didn't usually have a good curve, but this one exploded. It looked like a fast ball but when it broke, it broke down so sharply that it was out of the strike zone. I committed myself too quickly. I tried to hold up but I wasn't able to."[64]

Casey threw a good sinker, but nobody's sinker was ever *that* good.

Now from Coscarart, who was playing second that day in place of Herman, who had a pulled muscle: "That was a sad case. We would've been 2 and 2 if we'd won that game. I think Casey threw a spitter. I really think so. Mickey put down his sign for a curve ball, but that thing broke too much to be a curve ball. I really think it was a spitter. He used to throw one once in a while."[65]

Reese, from his shortstop position, thought it a spitter. "It was a little wet slider," Pee Wee told Peter Golenbock, "and the ball kind of broke real sharply to the right and got away from his glove."[66]

And finally, from Hugh Casey himself. Tommy Holmes, who for many years covered the Dodgers for the *Brooklyn Eagle,* writes in his book *The Dodgers*: "Years later Casey admitted that his third strike to Henrich had been a spitball, which may explain why Owen didn't handle it."[67]

The fifth and deciding game was lackluster, especially after the excitement of the previous day. The Dodgers, as described by Drebinger, appeared "wearied," and no wonder. The final score: 3 to 1, with Ernie Bonham outpitching Wyatt, who went all the way, giving up the three runs on six hits. The Dodger run came in the third inning when Wyatt singled and then scored on a triple by Reiser. Series final: Yanks 4, Dodgers 1. In mid-game Red Barber expressed astonishment (in his understated way) as Bonham retired six men on seven pitches.

Thus the season ended, one that saw Williams' .406 average, DiMaggio's 56-game hitting streak and Reiser as the youngest batting champion in the history of the National League. Ask most people today what they remember about 1941 and if they're baseball fans of a certain age they'll say Pearl Harbor, Williams hitting over .400 and DiMaggio's streak.

As for Reiser, his incredible year is mostly forgotten today. In fact, it was overlooked even then. Consider the following vote, supposedly by sports experts participating in the Associated Press annual poll to name the top sports figures of 1941: Joe DiMaggio got 157 votes, Ted Williams 74 and Joe Louis 64. No quarrel with those. But down in the last paragraph Pete Reiser got one single vote. Others who also got one vote included Joe Piatek, handball; Willie Hopp, billiards; Ned Day, bowling; football players Endicott Peabody, Edgar Jones, Billy Hillenbrand and Angelo Bertelli, and Gregory Rice for track.[68]

Imagine, the National League batting champion, who led his team to the pennant, and who led the league in most hitting categories, lumped in with a handball player, a bowler, a pool player and, except for Bertelli, no name college football players.

That would never have happened to any member of the New York Yankees, the boys from across the river.

4

1942: FDR Says the Show Must Go On

As the year 1942 began Commissioner Landis was undecided on the status of baseball with the country at war. He was aware of nationwide doubts that the game would continue, given the projected fuel shortages and transportation problems.

He struggled with the problem for more than a month after Pearl Harbor, then finally decided to write to President Roosevelt, seeking his advice. In his answer FDR termed baseball "a definite recreational asset to at least 20 million citizens" and therefore "definitely worthwhile." This became known as the "Green Light" letter, giving baseball the go-ahead regardless of the military situation.

There would be no blanket deferment for the players, he wrote, knowing that Landis would agree that all of military age should serve. "Even if the actual quality is lowered by the greater use of older players, this will not dampen the popularity of the sport," he added, obviously aware of how Americans love the game.[1]

MacPhail, knowing that baseball would continue, was planning to break up the 1941 Dodger team, heedless of the possibility that with a war on, replacements might be in short supply. The previous November Larry had told John Drebinger of the *Times* that he was ready to trade as many as 12 players because they "can't possibly win another pennant."[2]

MacPhail was venting his displeasure at the loss of the World Series and was taking it out on the entire team. Fitzsimmons' knee, Casey's spitball, or the excellence of the Yankee pitching—he didn't want to hear about any of that. Larry's fuse often burned long and bright and, as Drebinger took notes, he was still fuming and looking for scapegoats.

Weeks after the Series, he hadn't yet calmed down enough to realize what a marvelous collection of ballplayers that '41 club was, how magnificently Reiser and Reese and Camilli and Wyatt and Walker and Higbe—and all the rest—performed down the stretch.

With spring training still months away, MacPhail said he had drawn up a list of "undesirables" and sent it to all clubs in the league who might be interested. Looking back, though, it's obvious that there was no such list. If there had been, at least one club owner would have leaked it to his favorite beat writer.[3]

On the whole, the Dodger president was one of the brightest men who ever ran a ballclub, but on his dark side he was yesterday's George Steinbrenner: ever demanding in victory and graceless in defeat, never realizing that the team he was demeaning gave the country the most exciting pennant race since the beginning of baseball.

After such a race, the Series was an anticlimax, and it was many years before many Brooklyn fans realized that it wasn't an act of God that beat the Dodgers so soundly; it was Yankee power and superlative pitching. And it was clear that after Owen's "passed ball" what happened was not all that unusual.

For, as Henrich led off first, Hugh Casey was pitching into the heart of Yankee power: DiMaggio, Keller, Dickey, Gordon. A four-run rally was nothing to that crew. What is distressing, even today, is Durocher leaving a tired and disconsolate Casey in there while Curt Davis, a money pitcher when rested, was warming up.

As for Yankee pitching, it was never better. For the five games the Dodgers batted .182, and this was a great hitting team. And there was that sequence unheard of before or since: in the fifth game Bonham retiring those six Dodgers on seven pitches, four in the sixth and three in the seventh.

It has been said that losing the '42 pennant was the end for MacPhail in Brooklyn, and the way the Yankees manhandled the Brooks in '41 certainly didn't help his position. To wait 21 years and then go through that infamous ninth inning and lose in five games certainly rankled the Dodgers' owners.

Perhaps MacPhail felt his position had weakened, for as the weeks passed, no "undesirable" list showed up anywhere, and he said no more about it. Instead, he let the team fret all through the winter, and as spring training approached many of the players had no idea where they stood.

Of course there were untouchables—Reiser, Reese, Walker, Wyatt and the like. In fact, for Pete the year started on the highest possible note. Scorned by those "experts" in the Associated Press December poll, he was lionized in January by the Chicago Chapter of the Baseball Writers' Association of America.

They presented him with the Comiskey Memorial Trophy, given each year to their selection as "Rookie of the Year."[4] Baseball's official rookie awards didn't start until 1947 in the National League (Jackie Robinson), and 1949 in the American (Roy Sievers), but those Chicago writers knew what they were doing. What they started, baseball soon copied.

For all of MacPhail's threats, the Brooklyn starting team that emerged from spring training wasn't all that different from the pennant winners. The one big change was the addition of Arky Vaughn. Of the three they traded to get him, the late Pete Coscarart never got over his move to Pittsburgh.

Interviewed almost 60 years after the trade, his first baseball love was still the Dodgers. "Brooklyn to me was the big leagues," he said. "After Brooklyn, Pittsburgh seemed like the minor leagues. That's how I felt and I really missed Brooklyn because they had such good fans and it was the first and best team of my career."[5]

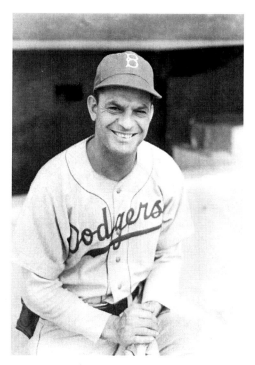

Joseph Floyd Vaughn was 30 years old when he came to Brooklyn, one of the great hitting shortstops of all time. He was a .324 hitter over 10 seasons, but was somewhat of a disappointment for Brooklyn that year, as his average slipped to .277. Plus, the man was never really needed and therefore never seemed to fit in.

With Vaughn coming in MacPhail had to decide what to do with Lavagetto. Cookie was 29 years old and had been a Dodger regular since 1937. He'd been a good-fielding second and third baseman and a very decent .279 hitter over the five years. Would he be made a utility infielder with that level of performance behind him?

Harry "Cookie" Lavagetto, one of Brooklyn's all-time Dodger heroes. It appeared he was through when he enlisted in the Navy's Air Corps soon after Pearl Harbor. He became an Ebbets Field icon, however, when he broke up Bill Bevens' no-hitter in the 1947 World Series, driving in Gionfriddo and Miksis with a double off the wall in the 2–1 victory.

MacPhail didn't have to decide. Cookie, perhaps knowing that he was becoming expendable, or for patriotic reasons, decided to enlist. An amateur pilot, he notified the club on January 31 that he had joined the Navy Air Corps at Alameda, California. Pearl Harbor had been attacked and there was a war on so Harry Arthur Lavagetto joined up. At his age it seemed unlikely that after a long war he would be back in Brooklyn uniform, much less attain mythic stature in Dodger lore.

The big spring training event of that year came out of Daytona Beach when on March 29, Reiser married Patricia Hurst in nearby Titusville with Pee Wee Reese and Dorothy Walton as witnesses. On the same day in Bunnell the situation turned around. Pee Wee and Dorothy were married with Pete and Pat as witnesses.[6]

The marriages weren't made public immediately, the Reeses waiting until April 2 to pose for a *New York Times* photograph. Pete's marriage wasn't disclosed until April 6 when Durocher, in an unduly harsh move, fined Pete $200 for taking a day off and not accompanying the team to Fort Benning for an exhibition game. The last heard of the fine was when Leo was asked if he would rescind it, knowing they were newlyweds: "No, it sticks," he answered.[7]

It's typical of the way Reiser was handled. He was never pampered as many other stars of the day were. Durocher especially, with MacPhail's backing, often played to Pete's fatal instincts, even after he must have realized "the walls weren't there for Pete."

Many years later, in an interview with Donald Honig, Pete said: "They [MacPhail and Durocher] never asked me if I could; they always asked if I would." And Pete, with his competitive fires always ablaze, always "would."[8]

As the 1942 season started, *The Sporting News* saw Brooklyn as stronger than in '41, what with the addition of a hitter like Vaughn. But they questioned the pitching and were proved wrong by unforeseen developments.

First, Larry French reemerged as a front-line pitcher. Larry was 35 and had been around since 1929 but in '41 had arm trouble. In the coming season he was spectacular, with a 15 and 4 record and an ERA of 1.83, second in the league to Mort Cooper's 1.78.

Larry's career ended happily and patriotically: in late September he pitched a one-hitter, beating the Phillies 6 to 0 for his 197th win. Then, in his mid-thirties and after a 14-year major-league career, he joined the Navy, served during World War II and Korea and in 1969 retired as a captain in the reserves.

He was stationed at the Brooklyn Navy Yard in early 1943 when he asked his commanding officer if he could get leave to pitch long enough to get his 200th win, adding that he would donate any baseball salary to the Naval Relief Society. Larry never got a shot at those three wins.[9]

The other pitching surprise was Ed Head, brought up from Elmira at the end of the 1940 season, one of the moves that cost the Dodgers the Elmira franchise. If ever a man was born with the determination to be a major league pitcher, it was Ed Head.

In Selma, Louisiana, he was a lean, fast, left-handed high school pitcher, 6 foot 1, 175 pounds. While riding a bus with a semi-pro team from Pioneer, he was seated with his arm around his boyhood sweetheart when the bus was sideswiped by another bus. Ed woke with his left arm mangled, his girl lying dead next to him.

They just managed to save the arm but he was told he'd never pitch again. With the optimism of youth he began throwing right-handed and became a fastball pitcher from the other side. "It was tough at first, but I had fooled around throwing right-handed. It took me about three years before I could throw with any real speed."[10]

French and Head were a combined 25 and 10 but St. Louis was also stronger than in '41, with added pitching strength and the addition of Musial in the outfield. One of their rookie pitchers proved to be a sensation out of Nashville, Tennessee, Johnny Beazley, a 22-year-old right-hander, who together with Mort Cooper became half of the best one-two pitching combination in the league.

Johnny, like Travis and a number of others, never brought it home from the war. While in the Air Force he pitched in an exhibition game without properly warming up, severely damaging his arm, and was never effective again.[11] While he had it though, he really had it in '42: 21 and 6 with a 2.13 ERA.

The Cardinal outfield was not only stronger with Musial, but also because Moore and Slaughter were fully recovered from the injuries that took them out of the stretch drive in '41. For most of the year, therefore, the Cards' outfield was Musial in left, Moore in center and Slaughter in right—two future Hall of Famers and one of the game's best defensive center fielders. Because of his great defensive ability Moore is overlooked as a hitter. Even though his average fell off after three years in the service, he hit .280 over an 11-year career, and was good in the clutch.

Long before the season started the word was out that Johnny Mize could be had from St. Louis. Big John had been injured part of the past year and his home run production had fallen off to 16 from 43 the year before, but he still drove in 100 runs. Breadon might have been on one of his economy drives or he might have thought Mize was through.

The Dodgers wanted the big slugger and were planning to sell Camilli to the Yankees to make room for him. But Breadon, obviously unwilling to let him go to his closest rival, sent him to the Polo Grounds for Kenny O'Dea, Bill Lohrman, Johnny McCarthy and $50,000. This time, though, Sam's pocketbook outwitted his head, for there were many home runs left in that bat, including 51 in 1947. It was a wonderful trade for Big John. He got to play his last nine years in New York, five with the Giants and four with the Yankees. That long New York exposure is one of the reasons Mize is at Cooperstown.

As the season started there was, naturally, concern about air raids and submarines. The ballparks were declared safe from aerial bombs by Harry Prince of the Office of Civilian Defense, who went along with the consensus was there was no better protection from an air raid than the steel and concrete stands.

Prince, in decreeing that afternoon games go on even during an air raid, said the ballplayers "will be soldiers in that situation. They must stay right out there and take it. The show must go on."[12] Mr. Prince was certainly a brave man.

Within a few weeks night ball was banned at Ebbets Field and the Polo Grounds because, according to Police Commissioner Lewis J. Valentine, the glow from both parks could be seen from out at sea and could therefore silhouette American oilers and freighters for offshore Nazi U-boats.[13] Yankee Stadium at the time had no lights.

Valentine's concern was a real one. Those who walked the beaches at the Jersey shore in the spring and summer of 1942 had to be careful, for along that entire coastline the sands were covered with great splotches of oil from torpedoed tankers.

The Dodgers opened the season at the Polo Grounds by clobbering Carl Hubbell: seven hits and four runs in 2⅔ innings. The day began with the Seventh Infantry band playing the national anthem at the center field memorial to Captain Eddie Grant, a former Giant and the only major leaguer killed in combat during World War I.[14]

Eddie was nicknamed "Harvard Eddie," being a member of the Class of 1905. He was a third baseman and had a .249 batting average over a nine-year career when he left the game to practice law in New York City in 1915. Only 35, he was killed by machine gun fire on October 5, 1918, while leading an attempt to rescue the famous "Lost Battalion" behind enemy lines.

The battalion, part of New York's 77th Division, was down to less than half strength when on October 2, 1918, it captured a German supply depot near Binarville in the Argonne Forest and was then cut off, surrounded by an entire enemy division.

For a week, while out of food, water and medical supplies, they held off against those overwhelming odds while American pilots tried unsuccessfully to supply them by air. They missed on every drop because haze and smoke prevented them from locating the battalion's exact position.

The doughboys held on, under Major Charles Whittlesey, until an Allied attack relieved them on October 7.*

By that time many of Whittlesey's men were dead or wounded. When it was over the battalion was down to 650 survivors.[15] Honors for gallantry came Major Whittlesey's way. He was promoted to lieutenant colonel and then on Christmas Eve 1918 he was awarded the Congressional Medal of Honor in ceremonies on Boston Common.

After the tribute to Captain Grant, the game's beginning was marred by "vociferous" boos against a fan who pocketed a foul ball, refusing to throw it back onto the field, so that it could be added to those collected for shipment to Army and Navy camps. But he stood his unpatriotic ground, obviously a Giants fan.

After the ceremonies the Brooks won the opener 7–5, with Johnny Allen stopping the Giants for Curt Davis in the Giant seventh inning after Mize, in his first game in New York, hit a three-run homer to make it close.

By this time the thrill of beating Hubbell was becoming passé. King Carl was now 38 and past his prime. As he left the mound, with that left arm turned permanently clockwise from 15 years of throwing those reverse curves called screwballs, he was nearing the end of a great 16-year career and five years away from being voted into the Hall of Fame.

On May 4 the Dodgers and Cardinals took up where they left off in '41, starting the second of five furious pennant races. The Brooks lost both ends of a doubleheader, 14–10 and 4–2. The managers started where they left off, too. Durocher was banished in the very first inning for violating the new pitch rule: no arguments over called balls or strikes.

As Durocher left, Fitzsimmons, who wasn't even pitching that day, was thumbed out as he had to be restrained from punching umpire Ziggy Sears for ejecting Leo. The Dodgers were reacting to their manager, as usual, whose real anger in that first inning came after his ace, Wyatt, was knocked out by a grand slam by Kenny O'Dea, a .255 hitter with no power.

The usually calm Camilli was next, ousted after kicking dirt on the plate for the second time after he was warned. The parade off the field continued as Dodger rookie pitcher Chet Kehn was chased, and finally, Cardinal manager Billy Southworth went for protesting a called strike. The double loss was a jolt for the Brooks, knowing the Cards were the team they had to beat. But for Pistol Pete it was the beginning of his

---

*The Lost Battalion was never really lost, but was in the area Whittlesey was ordered to take. He was sniped at for four years as reckless, leading his men into a trap. This abuse finally overcame him, causing his suicide as he jumped off a Havana-bound liner (Doughboys, p. 279).

drive for a second consecutive batting championship, as he went 4 for 7 against Harry Gumbert and Max Lanier.

For the next two weeks, before he went out with a pulled muscle against the Cubs, he went 20 for 53, a .377 pace. The pulled muscle was something that dated back to Pete's Elmira days, where he once swung so hard that he chipped a bone in his elbow. With the Dodgers he was known throughout the league for his vicious cuts, often tough on his upper body when he missed.[16] And, as Eddie Miksis put it: "Pete never got cheated out of a swing."[17]

Translated: Pete was a bad ball hitter, like Yogi Berra, a slasher who sometimes hit any pitch within reach. Brooklyn writer Ed Fitzgerald put into words the feeling generally around the league that if Pete had been more selective, made the pitcher come to him in the strike zone, he'd have gotten more hits and walks.[18] Maybe so, but that type hitter often drives a pitcher crazy, as in "what do I throw this guy?"

On May 19 the Cardinals came into Ebbets Field with the Dodgers in front by seven games and winners of eight straight. Earlier in the month the Cards strengthened their pitching staff by buying 27-year-old Clyde Shoun from Cincinnati. Shoun was a decent reliever, around since 1935, but he was really noted for being part of a trade that, given the value of the dollar at that time, ranks as one of the biggest in the history of baseball.

Branch Rickey sold injured superstar Dizzy Dean to the Cubs on April 16, 1938 for Shoun, Curt Davis, Tuck Stainback and $185,000 to the Chicago Cubs. It was 1938 remember, still the Depression, so that was one load of money. It didn't bother the Cubs that Dizzy's fastball seemed to be gone. Cub manager Charlie Grimm was "elated" over the trade.[19] Dean, after all, was only 27, an age when many injuries heal.

After the trade, and knowing he had a sore arm, Jay Hanna Dean was as cocky and confident as ever. As reports of the payment varied between $150,000 and $185,000, he was asked what he thought of the trade as he hopped into a cab in Chicago.

"I don't think they got enough," he answered.[20]

Dean's left little toe was broken in the '37 All-Star game by a line drive off the bat of Earl Averill. He then altered his motion to the extent that, as events proved, he blew his arm out. But this was not evident at the time of the trade. The Cardinals, in fact, were stunned and saddened by Dean's leaving. "There goes our pennant and World Series money," Pepper Martin said. As to the fastball, Terry Moore told reporters: "Don't worry about that. He'll have his fastball all right when he gets to Chicago."[21]

As the Cardinals took the field that day, Shoun wasn't needed. Mort Cooper took care of the Dodgers and their win streak. In a reversal of their classic duel the previous fall, Cooper beat Wyatt 1 to 0, with Mort giving up just two singles and Wyatt the one run on a Walker Cooper triple, followed by a long fly ball. It didn't have the drama of the fall confrontation, but they all count at season's end.

Brooklyn then dropped two at the Polo Grounds, the first marked by Reese seemingly injured when Ott took him out of a double play. Durocher was up for battle but calmed down when he realized Pee Wee only had the breath knocked out of him.

The Dodgers stopped that mild losing streak up in Boston, beating Jim Tobin 4 to 1, with Reiser back in action with a pinch-hit single in the ninth inning to help win the game. Tobin was a workhorse in '42 with a 12 and 21 record for the seventh-place Braves and, for a pitcher, he was equally active at the plate.

Jim hit .246 that year with six home runs, but two weeks before that 4 to 1 loss to Brooklyn, he went into the record book, and may be there forever, as the only pitcher in the game's modern history to hit three consecutive home runs in a single game. He did it against the Cubs, beating them 6 to 5 and, to make the slugging even more memorable, had homered against Chicago as a pinch hitter the day before.[22]

The Dodgers were in a mild slump when the Cards came in to Ebbets Field on June 19, a Dodger win for Larry French marked by what the *Times'* McGowen called a "free-for-all" in the sixth inning. The two clubs, as we've seen, were always poised for a fight, and this time it came when Medwick tried to take second on a passed ball. The throw beat him so he came in with spikes high at Marty Marion.

They got up and went at it, but Frank "Creepy" Crespi tackled Medwick and was tackled in turn by Dixie Walker. By this time the dugouts had emptied and there was a melee around second base. When the umpires regained control, they threw Medwick and Crespi out and Walker had to leave with an injured leg and what looked like a swollen jaw from an unidentified puncher. Brooklyn's lead was now 5½ games.

Wyatt beat the Cards 4–3 the next day for his seventh win as Pete went 2 for 4 and stole home in the fourth inning. In a year when base stealing was not a major factor in the game's strategy, he led the league with 20 and was starting to make the steal of home his specialty.

On the 21st Medwick, in the midst of a hitting streak, went 4 for 4 against four Cardinal pitchers, lifting his average to .350, past Reiser to lead the league. Pittsburgh came into town on the 24th for a single game. Reiser lined a two-run shot to center for the winning runs, and Medwick followed with a double for two more runs and game number 26.

But that was it as he went hitless the next day against Cincinnati's Elmer Riddle, Joe Beggs and Clyde Shoun. The Reds lost the game on what was baseball's most exciting play, but one seldom seen today: the squeeze bunt. It was tied 4–4 in the 10th when Herman tripled and then broke for home and scored the winner as Reese bunted down the third base line.

Two days later Durocher seemed to be losing his grip, almost totally out of control. In the first inning of a doubleheader against the Reds he ran onto the field to protest Reese being called out on a bunt attempt. Umpire Tom Dunn thumbed him out but Leo refused to go. It took all three umpires almost 10 minutes to get him to leave the game, but before he did he kicked dirt on Dunn three times and, as he was leaving the dugout, threw a towel in Dunn's face.[23]

For this he was suspended for three days and fined $50 "for conduct unbecoming a manager." Durocher would not comment on the punishment but said the umpires "are apparently picking on us." He said he was thrown out in St. Louis under the new rule that a manager could not leave the dugout to protest a called strike, but that Bill McKechnie got away with it several days before.[24] Grammar school time.

With the All-Star game coming up, Bob Feller was preparing to pitch for his service team against whichever team won. The game was scheduled for July 7 in Cleveland for the Army and Navy relief funds. If Bobby was telling the truth the week before, he had developed a pitch that would drive batters crazy for the rest of time.

Feller said he had developed a pitch he called the slider to show the home folks the next week. The idea, a fast ball that breaks at the last instant, came to him "in his sleep" while he was stationed at the Great Lakes Naval Training Station.[25]

Maybe Bobby didn't work hard enough on the pitch. In any event, he started against the American League All-Stars and was pounded for three runs in the first inning, and then driven from the mound in the second before he could get a man out.

Bobby contradicted himself some nine years later. Writing for MacFadden Publications in 1953, he said pitcher George Blaeholder of the St. Louis Browns of the late '20s and early '30s originated the pitch "as we know it."[26]

If so, Blaeholder should be famous, having invented a pitch that has joined the curveball in driving many a rookie back to the minors. But he pitched in obscurity, being with the St. Louis Browns from 1928 to 1935. And not too bad either, a 104–125 won loss record with a 4.47 ERA for his meaningful years. Nothing to be ashamed of, considering he worked for mostly second-division clubs on the worst field in the majors.

That ERA would no doubt have been lower had George pitched for better teams, for a hitter as great as Jimmy Foxx said he was the toughest pitcher to hit in the American League.[27] That from one of the toughest outs in baseball history.

After the All-Star game the Dodgers went on a western swing that would prove one of the most tragic in the team's history. It started well with three out of four at Cincinnati, and two of three from the Pirates. Then it was on to Chicago where one of their three wins was marked by more knockdown pitches than had been seen in years.

Higbe got it going by throwing a pitch behind Bill Nicholson's back, enraging the entire Chicago bench, since hitters usually back into a pitch like that. Then there was retaliation time and again. Cub pitcher Hi Bithorn not only decked Higbe but, frustrated as he was being relieved, threw at Durocher in the dugout, where Mickey Owen deflected the ball.[28]

The team left Chicago with an eight-game lead over St. Louis, its next destination. In hindsight we can see that it was there in Sportsman's Park that they lost the pennant and their budding superstar on July 19 when Pete again crashed into a wall, this time never to fully recover.

Pete was in a mild slump when he hit the wall and was at .350, not the .380 often reported,[29] when Pee Wee Reese helped him off the field and on the way to the hospital. The circumstances of that tragic game were much more mundane than has been written.

Slaughter hit one on a line above Pete's head and with his speed Pete caught up with it, but dropped it as he hit the wall at the same time. Slaughter then scored the winning run. Pete has been quoted as saying he hit the wall in the thirteenth inning of one of those Wyatt-Cooper scoreless duels.

The *Times'* McGowen, however, reported that "by the time the half-stunned youngster recovered the ball and started it homeward, Slaughter had rounded the bases for a home run to give the Cardinals a 7 to 6 triumph" with "Johnny Allen, the fourth pitcher for the Dodgers, the loser after facing Slaughter and pitching only four balls before Enos hit his homer."

The *Brooklyn Eagle* gave Medwick's close-up view:

> ST. LOUIS, July 20—Joe Medwick, closest to the scene as the ball, Reiser, and the fence met in joint collision, was still shaking his head this morning. "It might have been the greatest catch I've ever seen," said Joseph. "I'll swear that Slaughter hit that ball beyond Reiser and that Pete overtook it. He was traveling like a bullet when he hit the fence."[30]

There it is, Reiser's speed, once again his enemy. But there is no scoreless tie with Wyatt pitching. It was the second game of a double-header and Whit had been knocked out of the opener. The box score shows Allen, not Wyatt, the loser.

In any event, in that inning Reiser the batting champion, Reiser the

.350 hitter, disappeared forever. He had some major league years left, but would never again take the field completely injury free. The dizzy spells started then and were with him on and off for the rest of his career.

After he hit the wall, Pete got up groggy and weaving. At St. John's Hospital Dr. Robert Hyland, St. Louis club physician, announced that he would be out for up to a week. On hearing that, Durocher said to the *Eagle*'s Tommy Holmes: "Betcha a hundred dollars we'll have a tough time keeping him out of center field tomorrow night."[31] Leo, blind as ever to Pete's blind spot, would have let him play that next night.

Privately, Dr. Hyland was much more worried than he let on to the press. Pete said he woke up the next morning and had a talk with Hyland, who was a good friend of his. "He told me I had suffered a severe concussion and a fractured skull. He recommended I not play anymore that year. When MacPhail heard about it he went through the roof. He began screaming that Hyland was saying that just to keep me out of the lineup."[32]

Sounds like MacPhail with a few in him. Someone once said that with no drinks MacPhail was brilliant, on two drinks he was a genius, but on three drinks he was a maniac. He was then probably in his three-drink persona, suspicious of everyone and always looking for ulterior motives. That Dr. Hyland wasn't going to put anything over on *him*.

Durocher was even more to blame. He was the field manager and saw the players day by day, and should have seen that none of them played when injured to the point where a career might be at stake. But Leo was incapable of that. Even though Pete was his boy, he could not see beyond the next game. And sure enough, three days after hitting the wall Pete was in Cincinnati on the field working out. Then on July 25, less than a week after the injury, he was back at Ebbets Field and got two hits in a 4–1 loss to the Pirates.[33]

After reading extensively about Pete, talking to his teammates and noting how his injuries occurred and his reaction to those injuries, it becomes apparent that his problem wasn't just intensity or fearlessness. Many ballplayers are intense and fearless, but Pete was fearless to the point where he lacked the sense of self preservation. Had he been fit for combat he would have been another Audie Murphy or John Basilone. His drive was so intense, the aggressiveness so acute, that he had nothing in reserve, no sense of the self that makes most of us wary of danger, of wanting to live another day.

The comment by Eddie Miksis that "the walls were never there for Pete" could have been Reiser's epitaph, for that was his basic problem. No other player has ever played so single-mindedly. Cobb maybe, but Cobb was crazy, Reiser wasn't. And even Cobb, as psychotic as he was, never ran into a wall hard enough to seriously injure himself.

Gene Hermanski, who played alongside Pete for three seasons, had to play those same Ebbets Field walls and knew how dangerous that tiny ballpark could be. "I remember balls hit over my head and I could feel that wall, you know, by some sixth sense I knew the wall was there. The hell with it. I wasn't going to run into it." When reminded that all outfielders play that way, realizing that there is a tomorrow, Hermanski, like Miksis, expressed the crux of Pete's problem: "He was oblivious of the walls."[34]

A key factor in Reiser's ruin was one MacPhail deal too many. Arky Vaughn was never needed and, in fact, never played an important role in Brooklyn. When Lavagetto enlisted in early '42 it was the perfect time to bring Reiser in to play third, next to his buddy Reese and away from those walls. But Vaughn was there and Leo had to use him.

Rickey knew at once that Pete shouldn't have been playing after that July 19 injury, because, as the Cardinals' team doctor, Dr. Hyland worked for him. After Rickey came to Brooklyn as team president he always blamed MacPhail, letting Durocher off the hook, probably because he had to deal with the Dodger manager almost daily.

Once he confided in Harold Parrott, by then Dodger road secretary. "Larry had wasted Pete Reiser, the perfect ballplayer," Parrott wrote in *The Lords of Baseball,* "and in St. Louis, Rickey anguished over it. What MacPhail had done to Rickey's superbaby galled the Old Man deeply. 'That character never should have been entrusted with anything so fine,' Rickey said with tears in his eyes."[35]

The bitterness never left Rickey. MacPhail, in his opinion, had ruined the finest young baseball player he had ever seen and he never forgave him for it. After the 1947 Series, Larry approached Branch to shake hands and forget their differences "for old times' sake." Rickey rebuffed him, saying: "I will be civil because people are watching, but I don't want you to ever speak to me again."[36]

Pete played just one week after hitting the wall and then was forced back to the bench again by dizzy spells that would hit him sporadically for the rest of his career.[37] One of the games he missed was headlined in the *Times* as a Boston "Bean Ball Battle" with pitchers Wyatt and Manuel Salvo "throwing more dusters" than hits allowed. Not just that; they were throwing at each other.

It started in the third inning, with Wyatt throwing one "high and tight" at Salvo. When Wyatt came up Salvo didn't just come inside to him. He made Wyatt hit the dirt. The two almost came to blows several times, with both dugouts emptying but no punches thrown. In the eighth inning Salvo hit Wyatt in the ribs and an enraged Wyatt threw his bat at the mound but his control was bad and he missed.

Both pitchers were fined $50, with an extra $25 from Wyatt for throwing the bat. At that time tight inside pitching had been a concern throughout the National League for several years. Frick used the words "bean ball battle" in levying the fines, but left it at that. The next day Tommy Holmes of the *Brooklyn Eagle,* one of the league's ultimate insiders, editorialized that the situation was chaotic and that Frick wasn't dealing with it because of a "powerful umpiring bloc" that was content with things as they were.

Bill Klem, the league's umpire emeritus, Holmes wrote, believes an umpire has enough to do without adding mind reading to his duties. The umpires could have stopped it. Holmes added, if they were empowered to do so as they are in the American League.[38]

On the 24th the Dodgers went into Sportsman's Park and dropped three out of four. Lanier beat them 7–1 and then Wyatt and Cooper hooked up in another one of their classics, this time Cooper up 2–1 in 14 innings. Mort went all the way and Whit went 12⅓ in another example of how those two went at one another so consistently and artfully.

As August ended MacPhail announced the purchase of Louis Norman (Bobo) Newsom, who back in 1929 started his career with the Dodgers under Uncle Wilbert Robinson. He was known at the time as the most traded man in baseball, having played in eight leagues with 13 teams.

Bobo was one of those outspoken guys who wear on their bosses. Worse, he had a great sense of humor, a gift sadly lacking in most baseball front offices. But he certainly could pitch, winning 211 games over a 20-year career and, although he lost 222, he worked mostly for second-division teams. And he was always good for a quote. When his trade to Brooklyn was announced he sent a telegram to Durocher: "Congratulations on buying pennant insurance. Will report tomorrow in fine shape, rarin' to go."

Bobo backed up his words while with the club only two days. On a stifling night at Crosley Field he beat Cincinnati 2–0 as Vander Meer gave up a single unearned run while striking out eight in eight innings. Newsom, his uniform heavy with sweat most of the game, gave up four hits, also striking out eight.

On September 12 Lanier won a 2–1 pitching duel with Max Macon, bringing the Cards up into a tie for first place. The Brooks had led the league since April 20, a total of 144 days. As Durocher was snarling and shouting in the clubhouse trying to rally the team, worse was to come.

The *Eagle*'s Tommy Holmes wrote in *The Sporting News* that all of Brooklyn was dazed by what had happened to the "bewildered Dodgers." They were up by 10 games on August 5 and then lost 18 out of 35 in a "painful plunge into second place."

Holmes had covered the Dodgers for years, a marvelous sports writer who had lost an arm in an accident during his youth. It didn't faze him in the least, his friend Dave Anderson recalled of the days they both worked sports on the *Brooklyn Eagle*. "He typed with that one hand and was a great reporter," Anderson said. Like most of the really good beat men, Holmes was a fan but never a "homer." His Dodgers coverage was comparable to Red Barber's broadcasting: fair and unhysterical. Even in this darkest hour Tommy paid tribute to the "terrific fight" the Cards were putting up. "These are real men from Missouri," he wrote. "By all the rules of psychology, they should have realized they were beaten long weeks ago."[39]

During that week the Dodgers had two off days during which the Cards built their lead to three games. Then the Brooks came alive, playing with the verve that later carried them into their final eight-game winning streak. On the 16th they broke out with 19 hits to rout the Pirates 10–3. There was a price, however, perhaps brought on by the pressure of the pennant race.

Just before game time Walker and Owen and some unidentified teammates hopped into the stands and "soundly thrashed" two of four people who had been beating up an usher. Then Walker, with bruised right knuckles, went 4 for 4, Camilli 4 for 5 and Reiser 3 for 5.

The next day Dixie and Mickey were charged with assault by the alleged usher beaters, who also charged the usher and co-workers with disorderly conduct. The case was heard on October 5 and ended peacefully as both sides withdrew the charges. It turned out the fight started when the four went down to the field railing to get autographs and started throwing punches when told to get back to their seats.[40] The tension, it seems, was getting to everyone.

Two days later the Dodgers lost 7–3 to the Phils' Tommy Hughes and Nick Etten's three-run homer, but then Newsom went all the way to win the second game 4–2, the first of the eight straight wins ending the year. That final string was cherished by the Brooks because it removed any taint of "choke," that they had blown the pennant, as many who don't know baseball have believed ever since.

Those games were won under the most intense pressure imaginable, with each Dodger knowing that any loss during that stretch would mean the end. The winning pitchers, Newsom, Higbe, Head, French, Wyatt and Head, French and Higbe again, knew they could not afford to lose even one game. So they won the eight straight, waiting for the Cardinals to crack. They never did.

Years later, Pete blamed himself for "costing" the Dodgers the pennant by volunteering to play the month of September. "Leo kept me in there," Pete said, "but I probably shouldn't have played. Fly balls I could stick in my hip pocket, I didn't see them until they were past me. I went

[down] to .310. But the big thing wasn't the batting average; it was the fly balls I couldn't run down. That's what hurt us. So we blow the pennant. I say blow—we won 104 ball games. But there's no question in my mind that by being stubborn, I cost the Dodgers the pennant in 1942."[41]

On September 24 the MacPhail era came to an end as Larry, preparing to enlist in the Army, resigned as club president. It was a strange time for him to go, with the team in a desperate and what looked liked a losing fight for the pennant. Two days later the players gathered in their clubhouse and gave Larry the traditional watch while wishing him good luck in the Army.

As they gathered around him, Durocher on one side and Camilli presenting him with the watch, they all knew that he was the one who brought them together to form the first of the great Dodgers teams of the '40s, who brought night baseball and television to the major leagues, developed the first batting helmets and rescued Ebbets Field, turning it into one of the gems of the National League. Read Harold Parrott as he escorted MacPhail on his first visit to the park after Larry took over back in 1938: The entrance rotunda, with its mildewed, peeling ceiling, resembled an aging Italian opera house, Parrott wrote. "There was something symbolic about that dreadful lobby, which curved inward almost to the home plate area, enmeshing the fans" as they tried to leave the park.

"As we stood there that day, I felt this depressing spell working on MacPhail. Larry waved at the chipped paint on the splintered seats that surrounded him. 'We'll paint every seat in the park, every girder, every post, every wall.'"[42]

And he did, starting with a $200,000 renovation financed by the Brooklyn Trust Company. As he looked around the dilapidated ballfield that day, the Dodgers owed Brooklyn Trust a total of $600,000. When Larry entered the Army, the club had $300,000 in the bank, had paid off the $600,000 debt and was in a position to pay off a $320,000 mortgage.[43]

MacPhail had done so well, in fact, that it was now possible for Brooklyn Trust, holders of the mortgage, to attract new ownership. George McLaughlin, the bank's president, was able to persuade John L. Smith, president of Pfizer, to buy 25 percent. Then Rickey bought 25 percent and McLaughlin sold 25 percent to his stooge, Walter O'Malley, a director of the Dodgers since 1932.[44]

McLaughlin was a political power, having been police commissioner of New York City, state superintendent of banks and vice chairman of the Triborough Bridge and Tunnel Authority.[45]

O'Malley, ever conscious of the bank president's influence, knew what he wanted and how to get it: play up to McLaughlin, be his gofer, see to his needs. McLaughlin, for example, was quite a drinker so O'Malley made it his business to be on hand to drive him home on the many nights he was too drunk to drive himself.[46]

For all this fawning O'Malley finally got his reward. With his 25 percent he was part of baseball's elite. The fox was now not only in the henhouse, he was part owner of it. From that day, the Brooklyn Dodgers Baseball Club had 15 years to live.

One anecdote from Harold Parrott, when he was road secretary after Rickey was long gone, is all it takes to show the meanness and pettiness of Walter O'Malley. The Dodgers were going on a tour of Japan in 1956 and Parrott was organizing it. He got a call from Mrs. Harry Hickey saying she and Harry would like to go along. Hickey was not only a member of the Dodgers' board, but also a close pal of O'Malley.

Hickey had been very ill but was recovered and well enough to make the trip, so Parrott, knowing of the close relationship through many years, told O'Malley he had added the Hickeys to the travel roster.

"Take their names off the list," O'Malley ordered.

"But ... but...." was all Parrott could get out when O'Malley added: "Have you stopped to think what it would cost to send a body home from Japan? We just can't take that chance."[47] Poor Brooklyn, with its team at the mercy of such a man.

MacPhail in leaving reminded the press of his accomplishments, the money he spent, and the overriding fact that he was leaving the club in sound financial shape, with money in the bank and star ballplayers on the field.

The writers were sorry to see him go, aware of the fact that Larry had also installed the first press lounge and started the tradition of free drinks for the press. His final official statement: "I've talked enough. Let's have another drink."[48]

As he left for the Army, the Cardinals clinched the pennant with a double win over the Cubs at Sportsman's Park, 9–2 and 4–1. The first game was all that was needed and when it was over the entire Cardinal team surrounded winning pitcher Ernie White and carried him off the field while the crowd cheered for several minutes.

The final standing of the clubs appeared in the *Times* of September 28 showing the Cardinals winners by two games in a pennant race like only one other in terms of wins. The Cards were 106 and 48, the Dodgers 104 and 50. Those who say the Dodgers blew that pennant overlook 104 wins. Only one other team in modern baseball finished second with 104 wins: the Chicago Cubs of 1909 were runners-up to Pittsburgh's 110–42 total. Further, only one other team with 100 wins had ever lost out: Detroit with a 100–54 to Boston's 101–50 in 1915.

So it would be much more accurate to say the Cardinals won the pennant rather than the Dodgers lost it. No team "blows" a pennant with

Lt. Colonel Larry MacPhail (left) confers with his successor, Branch Rickey, after he enlisted in the Army in late 1942. Brooklyn was fortunate in having these two as general managers, both seen by many as the best in baseball history. Rickey replaced MacPhail after being fired by Cardinals owner Sam Breadon because of disputes over money.

104 wins. The Cards simply played superb ball in September and took it away from them. On September 1 the Brooks were 88 and 40, the Cards 85 and 44. In the final standing the Cards were 106 and 48, Brooklyn 104 and 50. That September the Cardinals were 21 and 4, repeat, *21 and 4*. So that 106 wins was the result of one of the great stretch drives in history.

And in the next week they blew right by the Yankees, beating them four games to one, the final three at the Stadium. The lone Yankee winner was Red Ruffing by a 7–4 count. Then the Cards beat Ernie Bonham, Spud Chandler, Atley Donald in relief of Hank Borowy, and then Ruffing.

As the series ended, the Branch Rickey era began in Brooklyn. The Dodgers' Board of Directors had received permission from Sam Breadon to talk to him and the deal was sealed. Rickey was said to be somewhat reluctant to leave St. Louis after 24 years with the Cardinals but the truth is he was fired after a rift had developed between him and Breadon.

The trouble involved the percentage that Rickey earned on players he sold to other teams, a good amount of money since St. Louis, with its extensive Rickey-developed farm system, always had a surplus of players other clubs wanted. This eventually rankled the always money-conscious Breadon and led to the dismissal.[49]

Rickey, known for years as baseball's best judge of talent, immediately began to expand the Brooklyn farm system. Because of the war, it took awhile for it to become evident that the Dodgers were most fortunate in that, having lost one of the finest executives in the game, they picked up another equally gifted.

As the MacPhail stars aged and retired, Rickey developed or traded for players who dominated the league for the decade before the team was stolen away. In his obituary, the *Times* on December 11, 1965, described Rickey as the "master trader" of his day, who used shrewd judgment in trading away top stars, sometimes past their peak. He usually didn't wait that long, however, often saying that it is better to trade a man a year too soon than a year too late.

When he arrived in Brooklyn, one of the first things Rickey did was sit down with Durocher to discuss the coming year. But he didn't sign him until November 19, even though it was something he just about had to do in light of Durocher's success. But they did make an odd couple: the woman-chasing, gambling Durocher and Rickey, the pious Methodist who refused to play ball on the Sabbath when he was a catcher with Cincinnati back in 1905, Rickey, the professor who taught English, German, Shakespeare and Greek drama as a professor at Allegheny College.[50]

With a background like that Branch could never be your typical baseball executive. In fact, soon after his arrival in Brooklyn he was dubbed "The Mahatma" by *PM* sportswriter Tom Meany. Tom had run across the title as it applied to Mohandis "Mahatma" Ghandi in the book *Inside Asia,* where author John Gunther likened Ghandi to a combination of "God, Tammany Hall and my own father." This, Meany thought, was Rickey, and the name caught on.[51]

Rickey used all his Mahatma wiles on Durocher, signing him to a one-year $25,000 contract with the understanding that he would be a playing manager. One verbal stipulation Rickey included was a 15-cent poker limit, prompting Durocher to state publicly that he and some of his players had played for high stakes.

But, he added, there wasn't any more gambling than there was in the '41 pennant year. "In fact, I can name you seven players—Vaughn, Camilli, Medwick, Reiser, Walker, Wyatt and Reese—who never touched a card and never bet a nickel."

He then defended himself against the persistent rumors that he won large sums from his players. "Writers who traveled with the club know I never [kept] any of that money. I used to let the players owe it to me and I'd pay it back to them in the form of bonuses whenever they turned in exceptional work on the field."[52]

Before the signing, Rickey was in Brooklyn a month or so when Frank Graham of the *New York Sun* made *The Sporting News* roundup with a column in which he pointed out that Rickey was the antithesis of MacPhail.

"Branch Rickey doesn't raise his voice, lose his temper, bawl out umpires, wear loud checked sports jackets or spend money recklessly," Graham wrote. "Now all he has to do is get the results that MacPhail did. That he will do so is likely, his record as a baseball executive being a bright one. That he will endear himself to the Brooklyn multitudes as the colorful MacPhail did is doubtful."[53] Graham was a hell of a sportswriter but he was only half right in this instance.

Rickey sure produced: a playoff in '46 and championships in '47 and '49. And the fans responded with affection for the old man and his big cigars. After all, he was a winner and that's all they wanted.

5

The Dodgers Are Not for Sale

With O'Malley now part owner, the Dodgers' days in Brooklyn were numbered. This need not have been, for down through the years offers to buy the team were made by local people and organizations. All were blocked by Mrs. James P. (Dearie) Mulvey, who would not give up her Dodger shares.

The best offer, from the point of view of the fans and Brooklyn in general, was announced on February 9, 1945: the Kings County Chapter of the American Legion wanted to buy the team and would immediately put a $50,000 deposit on the purchase.[1]

Legion Commander Lawrence Wiseman told the *New York Times* that a committee had met the previous night to negotiate with the club but that Dodger representatives had failed to appear, as scheduled, with a statement of the team's financial condition.[2]

Dodger President Branch Rickey said he knew nothing of the meeting. "I don't know a thing about it," he said. "I have been hearing that they want to buy the club for some time, but other than that I know nothing."[3] Sure Branch.

The next day Wiseman said that in "preliminary discussions" two sale prices had been informally discussed—$2.5 million, which the legion considered "way out of line"—and $2 million. "However, until we see the books and know what we are talking about it will be useless to discuss prices," he said. "I understand all the stockholders are agreeable to selling," adding that the legion would be interested in the sale only if 100 percent of the stock was available.[4]

If only that had been so, we would still have the Dodgers, today and forever, somewhere in Brooklyn and probably playing in a new Ebbets Field or American Legion Stadium, whatever the name. Neither the legion nor Kings County have gone away.

The sticking point, as it had been in other sale offers, was the continued refusal of Steve McKeever's niece and heir, Dearie Mulvey, to sell her 25 percent of the stock, a situation unacceptable to the legion. In the face of Wiseman's assertion that all stockholders were agreeable, Mulvey insisted her stock was not for sale.[5]

The legion, with its 20,000 members, certainly had the money for the deal but, as Wiseman kept repeating, was interested in purchasing the entire block of stock and thus sharing ownership with no one. The last mention of the matter came eight days later, with Wiseman saying the legion was still definitely interested in the deal but that no agreement had been reached with the stockholders. That was it. No deal, no further word.[6]

Five years before that, two solid offers were made, one by a syndicate headed by boxing promoter Mike Jacobs, and the other by a group of five men led by George M. Cohan, star of Broadway, and George Jessel, star of Broadway and Hollywood.

The Jacobs offer of $2 million was made on August 7, 1940, and seemed on solid ground, since it had the backing of the Brooklyn Trust Company, at that time owner of 51 percent of Dodger stock. In fact, the impetus for the sale came from the bank, which had been looking for some time to sell the team.[7]

George McLaughlin, the bank's president, approached Jacobs saying that if the bank could get the 49 percent owned by the McKeever heirs Jacobs would acquire full ownership. The boxing promoter, according to the *Herald-Tribune,* then rounded up a group of wealthy "sportsmen" and said they would buy if all the stock was available.[8]

Jacobs denied this, stating the next day that he had no partners, that he would buy the team himself, and that he would own the club before season's end.[9]

Apparently Mike hadn't been reading the papers, for Mulvey had told the *Tribune* she would block any sale, even if the National League approved the deal. "I've stuck with them all through the hard times," she said. "Why should I sell now when things are going good."[10]

Obviously Mulvey was taken at her word by McLaughlin, for within hours he did a complete about face, announcing: "I don't know much about it, but I can assure you nothing will ever come of it." End of negotiations.[11]

Two months later the Cohan–Jessel group came forth, represented by the New York law firm of Golenbeck and Brand. The firm seemed to have a deal in mind that included all properties of the club, including its minor league franchises.

Here MacPhail stepped in to deny everything. "There have been no discussions with anyone concerning the sale of the Brooklyn club."

He was joined in the denial by George Barnewall, the club's vice president.[12]

Knowing the prejudices of Baseball Commissioner Landis, it is likely that he expressed opposition to both the Jacobs and Cohan–Jessel offers. Think of how he must have viewed the Jacobs offer: linking the Brooklyn club and by extension the National League with the sordid world of boxing, with its gangsters, gambling, and fixed fights. He would never have permitted that.

As to the other, Landis could probably accept Cohan, one of America's national symbols of patriotism with his songs "Grand Old Flag," "Over There" and all the rest, but never Jessel. Cohan represented the bright lights of Broadway and the patriotism of the Great War, while George was Hollywood, with its loose women and drunken and debauched men like John Barrymore.

Jessel, true to the breed, had just married a 16-year-old showgirl, after divorces from Florence Courtney and Hollywood star Norma Talmadge.[13] Nothing ever surfaced on this, but you can be sure Landis would never permit a 44-year-old man who married a 16-year-old to own any major league team, let alone a showcase team like the Brooklyn Dodgers. The offer died quietly, with never an explanation.

Another serious offer to surface was made by a man with a fascinating name: Colonel L'Hommedieu Tillinghast Huston. There was nothing Landis could have objected to in this offer, Huston being very rich, very respectable, and once the partner of Jacob Ruppert as half owner of the New York Yankees.

Huston, according to the *Times*, had pulled a group together that was ready to buy "anytime the owners indicate a willingness to sell at a fair price." One of Huston's aims, John Drebinger wrote, was to own the club and restore his lifelong friend, Wilbert Robinson, to his former position as president and manager of the team.

The offer stayed on the table for a while but died when Stephen W. McKeever, 79-year-old Dodger president, said the sale would not take place at any price "as long as I live."[14] As we know now, even if he had died soon after, his brother's daughter, Dearie Mulvey, would have opposed the sale, as she did others for many years.

After her father died Dearie held on to her stock for the rest of her life. After she died in 1975 her heirs sold out to Walter O'Malley, making him sole owner of his beloved Los Angeles Dodgers.[15]

6

The War Years

For one brief afternoon, on August 4, 1945, the Washington Senators had a pitcher with one foot, and the St. Louis Browns an outfielder with one arm. Such was the state of major league baseball two days before the atom bomb was dropped on Hiroshima.

The wartime game's long slide through mediocrity into that carnival atmosphere started on March 8, 1941, when Hugh "Losing Pitcher" Mulcahy of the Philadelphia Phillies was the first major leaguer to be drafted. Later that year Hank Greenberg went in, followed by a number of lesser names. They were the trickle that later became a flood as more and more ballplayers were called up or enlisted.

That '41 season seemed unaffected by the coming war and was as exciting as baseball can be, since many of the stars were still playing. Although the younger and unmarried players started disappearing into the draft, there was a tight pennant race, the DiMaggio streak, and Ted Williams hitting over .400. After Pearl Harbor, however, there were those doubts that baseball would continue during a war that was global rather than confined mostly to Europe, as was World War I.

They disappeared after Roosevelt wrote his "Green Light" letter calling baseball, in effect, indispensable, even during a time of war. Landis, however, remembered 1917 and knew that even with backing from the highest level, the game would have to adapt to wartime conditions. There would be, for example, no long spring training trips for any team, since fuel and transportation facilities would be military priorities. As a result, the Dodgers would train at Bear Mountain, New York, the Yankees in Asbury Park and the Giants in Lakewood, both in nearby New Jersey.

As more and more players were drafted or enlisted, the game looked for survival to has-beens or those too young or too old for service. It was three years into this ersatz baseball before Bert Shepard, with one foot, took the mound for the Senators and Pete Gray, with one arm, was a part-time outfielder for the Browns.

It was 1943 before wartime ball really started, since many players waited until the '42 season was over before they enlisted, and many draft boards didn't toughen up their deferment standards until then. As we entered that second war year the dominant teams were the Yankees and the Cardinals, since both had stars not yet drafted or classified 1A. The Yankees had lost DiMaggio but still had Gordon, Crosetti, Dickey and Keller in their lineup, with Spud Chandler and Tiny Bonham heading their pitching staff.

The next year the Cardinals maintained their superiority because even that late in the war, midway through 1944, they still had Musial, Marion, the Cooper brothers, Johnny Hopp and Danny Litwhiler. By then the Yanks had slipped as the likes of Bud Metheny, Mike Milosevich and Mike Garbark took the place of those off to war (or service baseball).

With 1942 already covered, this chapter deals with the rest of the war, but not in the usual way. For the years '43 to '45 there will be no batting champions or strikeout pitchers lauded here, since, given the level of play, such exploits were meaningless during those years. Consider: the St. Louis Browns won the only pennant in their history with what a writer in *Colliers* described as "a rickety-looking pitching staff and an outfield that has the appearance of something discarded from the Salvation Army."[1] Red Barber, when asked years later to compare wartime ball with normal years, said: "It's like comparing apples and oranges, you can't compare it. It was just a matter of playing anyone who was breathing."[2]

In short, you will read of no glorious feats of valor here. Those were taking place in Europe and the South Pacific. This chapter covers those terrible baseball years through the experiences of seven people: Pete Reiser, Ben Chapman, Bert Shepard, Pete Gray, Babe Herman, Joe Nuxhall and Ray McLeod, a Newark, New Jersey, high school catcher.

Pete Reiser is a perfect example of how the military often exploited star athletes for their name value and, for reasons that baffle reasonable people, to field winning teams. Pete was inducted into the Army on January 13, 1943, although he had been previously rejected when he tried to enlist in the Navy.*

He was told he was wasting his time, that his baseball injuries would

---

*The public relations staff at Fort Riley, Kansas, where Pete spent almost all of his service time, has virtually no record on Pete. Therefore, much of this section is from interviews by Donald Honig for his Baseball When the Grass Was Real and W.J. Heintz for his The Man They Padded the Walls For.

prevent any service from accepting him. But a number of Army officers thought otherwise even though he was rejected again after a physical at Jefferson Barracks in Missouri.

Doctors, viewing him as a soldier and not a baseball star, knew that he was unfit for combat and therefore of no real use to the military. But after the second rejection he was approached by a captain who asked: "Aren't you Pete Reiser the ballplayer?"

Yes, was the reply. Then the question: "What will you do if we let you go?"

"Play ball, sir."

The captain turned to a sergeant, saying: "Fingerprint this guy and induct him."

Pete was sent to Fort Riley in Kansas for basic training where things didn't get any better. He collapsed on a 50-mile hike with full pack, probably from the recurrent dizzy spells. When he came to, the doctor asked: "How did you ever get in the Army?"

"They fingerprinted and inducted me," Pete answered.

"You'll be out in two weeks," the doctor said, walking away.

As he was waiting for his discharge he was ordered to report to headquarters. There was a colonel waiting for him, telling him of his love for baseball. "You know I've always wanted to meet you," he said. "They want to discharge you, but I'm not going to sign this," he added while ripping up Pete's discharge papers.

Pete sat there helpless as the colonel, while ripping the papers, was telling him how he looked forward to having "a hell of a baseball team" at Fort Riley. And he did, with major leaguers including Joe Garagiola, Lonnie Frey, Creepy Crespi, Harry Walker, Al Brazle, Murray Dickson, Rex Barney and Ken Heintzelman.

Pete's next stop was Camp Lee in Virginia where he played the outfield with Johnny Lindell and Dave Philley. And, true to form, he soon suffered the serious shoulder injury that affected the rest of his career. Ebbets Field, Sportsman's Park or an Army base, they were all the same to Pete. This time he went though a fence and down 10 feet into a ditch.

Finally he was discharged after another physical, this one for a trip overseas with other celebrities to entertain the troops. He had to see another colonel who looked up from his desk and said: "For three years you've been putting up with this crap? You come with me." He signed some papers and told a sergeant: "I want this man discharged within 24 hours." The next day, November 30, 1945, Pete was on his way home.

Through it all, however, he said he had no complaints "considering what a lot of guys did in the war." True, and with all those guys getting killed and wounded over there it's hard even now to figure how a colonel or general would think a winning baseball team at Fort Riley or Camp Lee had anything to do with defeating Germany or Japan.

Ben Chapman was a fine outfielder and hitter for the Yankees in the 1930s, but became known to a later generation as one of most vociferous and nastiest of Jackie Robinson's tormentors during the 1947 season.

Ben had 12 years in the majors before the war, a speedy outfielder and a .302 hitter, with 287 stolen bases. He was never popular, always arguing with opponents, umpires, and even his own teammates. He once told Babe Ruth, who at the time was the highest paid player in baseball at $80,000 a year: "If you were paid as much as you're worth you'd be making less than I am." And, wrong as he was, he meant it.[3]

Along with that attitude he had an uncontrollable temper, as in 1942 when he was banned from organized baseball for the entire 1943 season after punching an umpire while he was player-manager of Richmond in the Piedmont League.[4]

Chapman was still hitting well when the Yankees traded him to Washington in 1936 to make way for DiMaggio in centerfield. That was the publicized reason for the trade. In reality the Yankees shipped him out because of his blatant and public anti–Semitism (covered in chapter nine). He drifted to Boston, then to Cleveland, then to the White Sox, where he was down to .237 when the Sox cut him after the 1941 season.

With his skills so eroded it appeared he was through as a player. It's one thing to be nasty and unpopular when you're hitting .300 but at .237 many were glad to see him go, hoping they'd never see him again. But then came the war and rejuvenation when Chapman was 35 and managing at Richmond.

It was June of 1944 when Ben, aware of the conditions in the majors, decided to try a comeback as a pitcher. Speaking to a *Sporting News* writer, he declared himself the equal or better than most wartime big leaguers, adding: "If I get a chance I will show them that I'm far from done and that I'm a changed man when it comes to respecting the other fellow on the field."[5]

And scouts, hard up for bodies, were watching as he ripped through the Piedmont League, hitting .348 as a part-time infielder-outfielder, and 7–0 as a pitcher after he developed a decent curve and change-up. The fact that the competition was even more dismal than the majors made no difference. Nor did Chapman's year-long suspension or his reputation for nastiness. They apparently believed that he was "a changed man," as he claimed.

The Brooklyn Dodgers needed bodies, especially experienced ones, so Ben was called up to Ebbets Field on August 4, 1944. Both Brooklyn and the Philadelphia Athletics bid for "fiery Ben," as *The Sporting News* described him, but the Athletics dropped out when the price went over $8,000.[6]

He was impressive in his pitching debut. On the night of his arrival he faced the Boston Braves and was the winner, 9–4, giving up eight hits and one run in seven innings and driving in two runs on 2 for 4 at the plate. In the lineup facing him were only two recognizable names: Tommy Holmes and Clyde Kluttz.

Roscoe McGowen's account of the game in the *Times* described the fans cheering the various deliveries Chapman had added to his curve and change-up, particularly what he called his high "slow ball," described by McGowen as resembling the "Eephus" pitch made famous by Rip Sewell of the Pittsburgh Pirates.

Ben hung on with Brooklyn for most of two seasons, winning 8 and losing 6 and hitting .297, mostly as a pinch hitter. He was traded to the Phillies on June 15, 1945, and became their manager for the next four seasons. By mid–July of 1948 Phillies owner Bob Carpenter had enough of Chapman. Some said he was fired because of public reaction to what he called his "bench jockeying" of Jackie Robinson during the 1947 season.[7] But no one was fooled. Everyone knew the taunts shouted at Robinson were racist insults.

They started during spring training in '47 and within a month had reached the point where Commissioner Chandler summoned Chapman and chastised him for his racist baiting of Robinson.[8] Not even a public hand-shaking with Robinson could save his job. After his dismissal he would never manage again in the big leagues, since he was obviously a man who could not control himself when confronted with anything that displeased him. He was not a "changed man" after all, but still the man who slugged that umpire back in the Piedmont League in 1942.

Bert Shepard, a former minor-league pitcher, was 25 years old when he took the mound for the Washington Senators against the Boston Red Sox, the only man with but one foot to ever appear in an official major league game.

Bert was on a combat mission over Germany in May of 1944 when his P-38 was shot down by Nazi groundfire that also shattered the lower portion of his right leg. He was able to radio in that he was wounded but was unable to control the plane as he lost consciousness.

He woke up in a German prison camp hospital with his lower leg amputated eleven inches below the knee.* Five months later, in Sep-

*Shepard is invariably referred to as one-legged, but if that were true he could not have pitched again anywhere. Monte Stratton, truly one-legged, could not make it, great as he once was with the White Sox.

tember of '44, he was part of a prisoner exchange program and after arriving back stateside was transferred to Walter Reed Army Hospital for further treatment and recuperation.[9]

Baseball had been his life when he pitched in the White Sox farm system before being drafted in the spring of 1942, and would remain so. This very determined young man never gave up hope, as impossible as it seemed, that he would pitch again. While still a prisoner in Stalag IX-Z he had started working toward that goal after a makeshift limb was fitted to his leg.[10]

Within a month after strapping on the new leg he was running steadily and starting to play baseball. When he got back home and was recuperating in Walter Reed, his dream of pitching again started to take shape.

First, he got lucky. Somehow Undersecretary of War Robert Patterson heard of his hopes and called Larry MacPhail, who had been one of his military aides. With Larry's help Bert reported to the Senators' training camp in nearby College Park and went through a three-hour pitching drill.

"This is the one thing I've been dreaming about over there for months," he told reporters afterward. "Sure I'm serious about playing ball. I can still take a good cut, throw well, and when I get a special leg instead of this temporary one, I'll do okay."[11]

Shepard said years later that Senators owner Clark Griffith felt obligated to give him the tryout in the spirit of the war effort because he was a veteran amputee. In the same spirit, the Senators let him pitch some exhibition games and in the spring of 1946 kept him on as a batting practice pitcher and coach.[12]

But it was on the previous August 4 that he made history as the only amputee to ever pitch in an official major league game. The Senators were being blown out as the Red Sox were scoring 12 runs in the fourth inning, so with the score 14 to 2, manager Ossie Bleuge figured what the hell, and gave Bert his chance. Against the Sox' wartime lineup he did an impressive job. He ended the 12-run inning by striking out George Metkovich and then gave up just three hits and one run in the remaining 5⅓ innings.

The wonder is that after such an effort Bleuge didn't give him a couple more starts through August and September. But he didn't and Shepard's major league pitching career was over, but, understandably, has never been forgotten.

In later years Bert explained that he could pitch with only one foot because he had most of his leg and was a left-hander, noting that the right leg of a left-handed pitcher is not the all-important "push-off" leg. "I wouldn't get out on the field if I couldn't do everything the other person could."[13]

Bert stayed on as a coach with the Senators, and a month after his historic performance Undersecretary of War Patterson, his old sponsor, arrived at Griffith Stadium to honor him for his war record. In a public ceremony on the field Patterson awarded him the Distinguished Flying Cross and Air Medal as Generals Jacob Dever and Omar Bradley looked on.[14]

Like Shepard, Pete Gray made history as an amputee: the only one-armed man ever to play in the major leagues—the 1945 season with the St. Louis Browns.

Gray, a lean 6 foot 1 and speedy, was 6 years old when he fell off a farm wagon and had his right arm caught in the spokes. It had to be amputated above the elbow. As he grew up he loved baseball and taught himself to field fly balls and grounders by catching them in his glove, tucking the glove under his right armpit, and then withdrawing the ball for the throw.[15]

Gray must have known he was being exploited as a gate attraction, but there was some ability there. He was a sensation in the low minors, batting .381 with Three Rivers of the Canadian-American League, and .333 with Memphis in 1944. With that average he also hit five home runs, stole 68 bases and was named the MVP of the Southern Association. The Browns then purchased his contract for $20,000.[16]

Pete stayed with the Browns for the entire '45 season, playing in 77 games and batting .218 with six doubles, two triples and 13 runs batted in. Given that average and the extra moment's edge his fielding gave baserunners, it wasn't an easy year for him, especially in the clubhouse where some of his teammates resented him being on the team.

Third baseman Mark Christman wrote years later: "He cost us the pennant in 1945. We finished third, only six games out," adding that hitters singling to center "could keep on going and wind up at second base. I know that cost us eight or ten ballgames."[17] His manager, Luke Sewell, was quoted in *Even the Browns* by William B. Mead as saying: "He didn't belong in the major leagues and he knew he was being exploited. Just a quiet fellow, and he had an inferiority complex. They were trying to get a gate attraction in St. Louis."[18]

But there were other opinions, such as that of second baseman Don Gutteridge. "I certainly marveled at him," he told the *St. Louis Post-Dispatch* in 1944. "He could do things in the outfield that some of our other outfielders could not."[19]

Whatever his skills, his mere presence in baseball was viewed as an inspiration for handicapped youngsters and for thousands of veterans maimed in the war, many of whom looked forward to seeing him as he toured Walter Reed Army Hospital.[20]

But that year was it for him. The following spring he announced from his home in Nanticoke, Pennsylvania, "The pitching is a little bit too tough for me up there," adding, "The competition will be even keener now that a lot of former ball players have been discharged from service."[21]

Pete was once asked how good he might have been if he had not lost an arm.

"Who knows," he said. "Maybe I wouldn't have done as well. I probably wouldn't have been as determined."[22]

Floyd (Babe) Herman came back to Brooklyn during the last year of the war and the fans fell in love with him all over again. And so did the beat writers.

The fans loved him because they remembered him as one of the best hitters Brooklyn ever had. The writers loved him because he was great copy, never denying even the most outlandish things written about him.

And those who knew the game and didn't pay attention to "the outlandish things" remembered him as a great right fielder, contrary to the mythology. All of his managers played him in right, knowing he was fast and had a great arm. Consider: no manager in his right mind puts a cluck in right, a position that takes judgment and arm, the position of Ruth, Kaline, Furillo, Walker, Bauer and the like.

Getting hit on the head, doubling into a triple play, lit cigar in his pocket. None of this ever happened but Babe didn't care. After he retired he was asked why he put up with stories so obviously false. He smiled and replied: "I don't care what they write about me. They have to make a living too."★[23]

Unlike many of the wartime old-timers, Babe didn't need baseball or the money. He was wealthy, the owner of a California poultry farm that prospered year after year.[24] He reported to Ebbets Field as a favor to an old friend.

"Babe," Branch Rickey said, "I've been looking for a pinch hitter for weeks. I want a man who can drive in a run instead of strike out. Can you still hit, Babe?"

"Yes I can Mr. Rickey," was the reply. "But I haven't been playing at all this year and I can't run a lick."

"You won't have to run much," the Mahatma told him. "Just hit the ball. We'll pay you $7,500."[25]

Sportswriter Tom Meany welcomed Herman back in his column

One example: Babe buys a cigar on a sultry day and the countergirl tells him how cool he looks. "Thanks," says Babe, "and you don't look so hot yourself." Forward into the age of Yogi Berra, standing next to Mayor John Lindsay's wife, who says, "You certainly look cool." Yogi's reply: "Thanks, you don't look so hot yourself." Was somebody making things up here?

with the truth about him, for a change, saying that he was paying the penalty for becoming a legend. Fiction pays better than the truth, he wrote, "which may explain the many tall tales flooding the press about Floyd Caves Herman," back with the Dodgers 13 years after he was traded away.[26]

It was 13 years but he wasn't forgotten. McGowen of the *Times* wrote that in his first game back, on July 8, he was "cheered so vociferously that the announcement of his appearance was entirely inaudible." The old Brooklyn favorite was back, the man with the .324 lifetime batting average, the man who once hit .381 and .393 in 1929 and '30 for the Dodgers.

And in that first appearance he didn't disappoint the Faithful. As he got to the plate he saw that he wasn't facing some kid or somebody over-the-hill. That was Red Barrett out there, a genuine major leaguer, 30, and in the league since 1937. (Barrett would pitch in the National League until 1949.)

Babe waited for his pitch and, with Luis Olmo on third, hit a line single to right, driving in Luis with the third Brooklyn run, just as he was paid to do. McGowen wrote that the crowd reacted as though the Babe had driven in the deciding run in the seventh game of a World Series.

After being out of the majors for seven years Babe hit .265 that year on 34 hits, including one home run and nine RBIs. Not at all bad for a 42-year-old. But from the day he came back he knew things hadn't changed from the old days.

On that very first hit the writers got on him, claiming that he tripped going round first base. "Same Old Herman" was one headline.

"I rounded first base and Durocher shouted go, then yelled get back," Babe explained. "I slipped because my spikes were too short. I had to crawl back to the base. Well, you can imagine what the papers wrote about my falling down."[27] Babe was right. Nothing had changed.

Not even years later when John Lardner wrote one of the classic lines in all of sport on Babe's baserunning: "Herman never tripled into a triple play but he doubled into a double play, which is the next best thing." Untrue, but who can resent a line that clever.

They were both 16, Joe Nuxhall and Ray McLeod, when they met at the Cincinnati Reds training camp at Bloomington, Indiana, in March of 1945. Joe was a high school pitcher out of Hamilton, Ohio, and Ray a catcher for Central High School in Newark, New Jersey.

They spent two weeks at camp and, although only one of them was to make the major leagues, the moment they put on those Cincinnati Reds uniforms they made history. Never before or since, in regular season or in training camp, has there been anything close to the youth of that battery: a combined 32 years in age.[28] It was the only time one 16-year-old pitched to another 16-year-old in organized baseball.

But, such was the war. Kids of 16 were draft-proof and might prove valuable, if not right away then during some later years.

Joe had been up the previous year when on June 10, 1944, at age 15 he became the youngest player ever to appear in a major league game. The Cincinnati scouts had been watching him even in junior high school, where he was 6 foot 3, 195 pounds, and what sports writers used to call a "phenom." They signed him in February 1944 for $175 a month plus a $500 bonus, stipulating that he attend classes during the day but show up at Crosley Field for night games and weekends.[29] Then came that June 10.

Manager Bill McKechnie had a bad one going, losing 13–0 in the ninth inning, so he figured it was a good time to test his 15-year-old. Joe took the mound, probably scared to death but game, and experienced what if made into a movie would be called "Nightmare on the Mound."

He pitched two-thirds of an inning and gave up five runs on five walks, two singles, and a wild pitch before McKechnie showed mercy and replaced him. Those five runs in just two-thirds of an inning made the youngster's ERA 67.5, not to be lowered until years later. Many a youngster would have been ruined by that but not Joe. He came back.

Ray McLeod was smart in class and smart behind the plate, a slim 5 foot 10 catcher who caught Cincinnati scout Frank O'Rourke's eye even before he made Newark's All-City team.

O'Rourke knew what he was doing. He spent 14 years in the big leagues as an infielder. And he knew what he was looking for—a catcher with a head for the game. Ray, he saw, could be improved as a hitter, but behind the plate no 16-year-old called a game better or fielded better. The year before he made All-City, the sports staff of the *Newark Evening News* felt that "catching is the only position where the [Central High School] coach has few problems. He has Ray McLeod, a first-class receiver." O'Rourke, a *Newark News* reader, started watching.[30]

He was soon impressed enough to approach Ray with an offer: two weeks at the Reds camp, all expenses paid. Ray had two hurdles, his parents and his high school principal. The parents agreed on the promise he would return and finish high school. Principal Stanton Ralston, knowing Ray's classwork, thought it a great idea.

That spring training was wonderful, Ray recalls, and Nuxhall, big and friendly, was an ideal companion, both then and in later years when they were battery mates at Columbia down in the low minors. "Joe was a great guy, the kind of guy you liked to hang around with," Ray later remembered.

Nuxhall came back from his nightmare, proving that with proper handling a player can recover from too much, too soon. Cincinnati, aware of the potential, was patient. They sent him down to mature, bringing him back in 1952 when he was 24.

Their patience paid off. Joe had a fine 16-year career: 135 and 117 with an ERA of 3.90 as a starter and reliever. The figures are actually better than at first glance, since Joe didn't exactly pitch for the Big Red Machine. During his 14 seasons in Cincinnati the club won one pennant but was in the second division most of the other years.

Ray gave it nine years and figured that was enough . He realized he wouldn't make the majors, but with a wife he met in high school and their children he knew there were plenty of good years ahead. Unlike many others he didn't hang around until it was too late, until baseball in the minors would be his only life. He went back to his roots in New Jersey and became a stockbroker.

"I've no regrets," he said. "Baseball was good for me." There were his memories of all the good people he met through the years and all of the Brooklyn Dodgers he met during two spring trainings down in Vero Beach.

"I remember facing Don Newcombe once," he recalled.

"Did he brush you back?" he was asked.

"He was so fast he didn't have to brush *me* back," was the answer.[31]

How many stockbrokers in this world can sit back between sales and remember a Don Newcombe fastball flashing by them?

With the war over, gone were Pete Gray, Danny Gardella, Bud Metheny and their like. But also gone were the skills of many who put in three or four years in uniform and returned older, out of shape for baseball, and with no future in the game.

Among them were stars: Johnny Beazley, never to repeat that glorious 1941 season with the Cardinals; Cecil Travis, in 1941 the best shortstop in the majors, whose frozen feet at the Battle of the Bulge would end his career; Hugh Mulcahy, through because of a disease he caught in the South Pacific; and Howie Krist, a reliever who was 23 and 3 with the Cardinals for the years 1941 and '42, and 0 and 2 and gone in 1946.

But, those casualties aside, the real major leaguers were returning, replacing the replacements. Of the 132 players who were starters during the 1945 season, just 32 were regulars during post-war 1946.[32]

As the veterans came back they didn't realize that the baseball world they left was gone forever. In 1944 Commissioner Landis had died, thus freeing Branch Rickey to look for a black man to play on the Brooklyn Dodgers. No more of the clandestine stuff. There was no Landis to stop him.

So the boys were discharged and came home and, to the surprise of many and the horror of some, saw that a black man, Jackie Robinson, was playing with the Montreal Royals. The logic for his playing, though mostly unstated, was irrefutable. How could we keep Jackie Robinson, who served as a lieutenant in the Army, from playing major league baseball?

We couldn't and now we're all the better for it.

7

1946: Baseball's First Playoff

The 1946 baseball season turned out to be one of the most important and exciting in the history of the game. For those who doubt, consider the following: the American Baseball Guild was formed, the Mexican raids on the major leagues proved unsuccessful and the Dodgers and Cardinals were tied at season's end, resulting in the first playoff ever.

The Dodgers were a particular target for the Mexican raiders, who during the spring probably offered contracts to almost every man on the Brooklyn squad. Mickey Owen was one of the first to go south, causing the management concern that escalated to alarm when Reiser was offered $100,000 to follow Mickey across the Rio Grande.[1]

It was the latest move by the Pasquel brothers in their campaign, backed by what was said to be a $60 million fortune, to lure players to Mexico and thus break what they termed United States monopoly control of major league baseball.

Jorge and Bernardo Pasquel had, in effect, declared war on the majors back in February when they signed Dodger outfielder Luis Olmo, wartime Giants outfielder Danny Gardella[2] and then the following month, Owen, one of the bigger names involved. Three days after Owen's defection Baseball Commissioner Albert B. Chandler announced that any player not reporting back by opening day would be suspended from the game for five years.[3]

On May 7 Rickey decided to act. Spurred by Owen's move and the offer to Pete, the team's lawyers obtained a temporary restraining order in federal court prohibiting the Pasquel brothers from "unlawfully interfering" with the Brooklyn Dodgers by persuading its players to break their contracts. Owen was cited as a player of "unique and outstanding performance" who was so persuaded.[4]

Rickey's concern was a real one for, in addition to Owen and Reiser, offers had been made to Stan Rojek, Cookie Lavagetto, Herman Franks, Johnny Rizzo and Mike Sandlock back in March at their Daytona Beach training camp, and Augie Galan and Hal Gregg later in New York. Harold Burr of the *Brooklyn Eagle* reported that other Dodgers were approached but no additional names were revealed.

Most of the Dodgers turned the offers down, with Lavagetto expressing the mood of the majority when he said: "I just wasn't interested."[5] But Reiser and utility infielder Rojek considered the proposals, Pete saying he'd be crazy not to consider such a huge amount, and Rojek because of a $10,000 bonus and an $8,000 annual salary.

Pete, still considered a potential star if he could heal and stay away from the walls, had the club so concerned that Rickey immediately took a chartered plane to St. Louis where the team was scheduled to play. He arrived the day after Pete announced that he had started considering a move to Mexico when the Pasquel offer reached $100,000.

"The first offer they made was for $15,000 a year for five years and a $15,000 signing bonus, and then $75,000 for three years, both of which I refused," Pete said. "But they came right back with the $100,000."

The Mahatma's persuasive powers worked, as usual, and within a day Pete and Stan announced they had decided not to jump, Pete saying: "I've told the Mexican representative that I'm not going to leave the Dodgers."[6]

Meanwhile, baseball was in turmoil. The *Times* in the next couple of months carried any number of stories on players jumping their contracts and, eventually, players disillusioned with life in Mexico and, finally, with the Pasquels' failed promises.

Among name players in addition to Owen, Max Lanier, Sal Maglie and Alex Carrasquel went south, as did Vern Stephens and Ace Adams. Among the number of others who jumped was Hooper Triplett, and, even though he was the Sally League batting champion, it was here that the Pasquel brothers drew the line.

Triplett, 27, signed with the Nuevo Laredo club, having nothing to lose since he'd been banned for life for betting against his own team. Evidence showed that he'd bet $20 that his Sally League Columbus team would lose to Columbia on August 3, 1946. He said he had just been fooling around.

No one believed him, including Jorge Pasquel, who on August 28 ordered the Nuevo Laredo club to remove Triplett from their roster in order to "preserve the prestige of the Mexican Baseball League."[7] Baseball officials in the United States saw this as a possible move toward peace. They weren't wrong.

For some of those who left for Mexico disillusionment set in very early. Vern Stephens, for example, stayed in Mexico just two days before returning to the St. Louis Browns, setting up the first of a number of what proved to be unsuccessful Pasquel lawsuits charging various players with breach of contract.*

With Owen down in Mexico, the Dodgers had to come up with a catcher, preferably one from their farm system. They had tried Ferrell Anderson and Mike Sandlock, but neither could hit on the major league level. Then, up from Mobile came Bruce Edwards, and right from his first game on June 23 it looked like Brooklyn had a catcher for the next decade.

Bruce was a favorite from the start. They called him Bull and at 5 foot 8 and 180 pounds he was rugged, and a hitter. That first season in 92 games he hit .267 and in 1947 a solid .295 in 130 games. Then that fall his arm went and only occasionally came up to full strength again.

It was a tough break for Edwards and for all the Dodger Faithful. Two fine ballplayers, Edwards and Spider Jorgensen, went down almost at the same time, both with arm trouble, which is supposed to be a pitcher's problem. Instead of a decade the Dodgers got one great year out of both, although in each case the potential had been so great that they hung on for a number of years as various managers hoped they'd come around.

As the team was heading north from spring training Reiser was having trouble making the long throws from center field, causing Durocher to open the season with Pete at third base and Furillo filling in for him in center field. Why Durocher didn't keep him there, safe from the outfield walls, is unanswerable. Moving him back made no sense, especially since Augie Galan was a fine outfielder and a consistent .285 to .300 hitter.

Part of the problem was that Leo wasn't worried about lineups at this particular time. He was defending himself against a felonious assault charge filed against him by John Christian, a medically discharged soldier. The complaint alleged that during a game against the Phillies on June 10, 1945, Christian had heckled the Brooklyn team and when the game ended was asked by Dodger special policeman Joe Moore to accompany him to a place under the stands where, it was charged, he was beaten severely by Durocher and Moore.

Christian, released by the Army because of a damaged knee, identified both Durocher and Moore as his attackers as he lay in Kings County Hospital with a broken jaw and other injuries. He told police

*Jorge Pasquel was especially bitter at Vern Stephens for staying just two days in Mexico. Of interest was the byline on the Times' account of the Pasquel interview: Camille Cianferra, years later the Times' Rome correspondent killed when the ships Andrea Doria and Stockholm collided (4/1/46, p. 36).

Moore hit him with a blunt instrument and when he got up he was hit with the same instrument by Durocher.[8]

There was conflicting testimony during a two-day trial of the case. On April 24 Jake Garfinkel, a former basketball player at St. John's University, corroborated Christian's story, saying he witnessed the attack. Durocher, asserting his innocence, said he "never laid a finger on Christian," did not "take a blackjack from Joe Moore to hit him with," and that Christian must have suffered the broken jaw when he slipped on a wet walkway.[9]

In what would have been a damaging admission in other circumstances, Leo admitted that he paid Christian $6,750 in settlement of a civil suit dealing with the alleged assault.

The jury, apparently heeding Judge Louis Goldstein's charge to them that the $6,750 payment had no bearing on the case, acquitted both Durocher and Moore on the first ballot in just half an hour. There was jubilation in and outside the courtroom as Judge Goldstein thanked the jury "for a just verdict" based on the evidence.

"I am glad for the sake of the Brooklyn baseball team," he added, "that their manager has been vindicated, and that no discredit has been placed on the great American game of baseball."[10] Was he a judge, or a fan?

Jury nullification has been with us always, but John Christian, though he didn't get justice, at least got the $6,750, a good amount of money in the spring of 1946. Leo always had his darker side, but this assault was a new low for him, hitting a guy with what the *Eagle* called a blackjack owned by Joe Moore, another obvious lowlife.

As things were getting back to a semblance of normality the postwar Dodgers powerhouse was starting to form. Rex Barney, just out of service, reported on May 10, with Reese, Stanky, Hermanski and Furillo already on hand. Ralph Branca, who had pitched some during the war, would come later, in time for his annual year-end damage. Barney arrived as the Brooks were walloping the Phils 13 to 4 and awaiting the arrival of the Cardinals.

The Dodgers were two games ahead when the Cards came in and were soon tied, as Lanier got away with one, 7–5, and Pollet needed only a Whitey Kurowski single and a triple by Dick Sisler for a 1–0 complete-game win. Shades of Mort Cooper, who by this time was with the Braves.

On the 18th they took the lead back again with a 16–6 rout of the Pirates, Pete 3 for 5 with a three-run homer. Then after an off day they were shut out by Cincinnati veteran Ed Heusser. Pete threw a scare into the entire team as he hit the wall again, this time chasing a triple by rookie Grady Hatton, a $25,000 bonus baby off the University of Texas.

For once Pete ran into some luck in that he stumbled just before he reached the wall. Never off scot-free, however, he left because he suffered a slight muscle pull throwing the ball in off balance. Leo, as usual, was undaunted by the wall.

After an off day, the Brooks arrived in Chicago for what proved to be one of the most violent two-game series since before the war when the Frey-Coscarart fights set off those Cincinnati-Brooklyn battles. This Chicago series was even worse, with players punching, choking, and rolling around on the field.

The first game went 13 innings, with the Dodgers winning on a Whitman single followed by a Walker triple. In the 10th inning Stanky and Cub shortstop Len Merullo tangled at second base. Both fell, with Stanky wrapping his legs around Merullo's throat, both punching away. They were separated by other players and ejected.

The trouble continued into the next day when before the game started Merullo approached Reese and accused him of punching him when he was on the ground the day before. Pointing to his bruised eye, Merullo was quoted as saying: "Next time you take a sock at me, hit me when I'm looking and I'll break your neck." Walker, passing by, heard the remark and, before Pee Wee could react, punched Merullo and walked toward the Dodger dugout. Merullo followed and soon both he and Walker were on the ground, punching and kicking at one another.

Both benches joined in, the Chicago crew led by Phil Cavaretta and coach Red Smith. Things looked so bad that the Brooklyn batboy grabbed all bats within reach and put them into the batrack, out of reach until park and city police finally got between the two teams. Dixie and Len were fairly well matched, with Walker slightly taller. But when order was restored, Dixie had gotten the worst of it, with one tooth knocked out and half of another missing.[11]

The game proved to be as tense as the combatants and just as close. But there was no further trouble as Hank Wyse, a wartime star good enough to pitch into the 1951 season, went 11 innings, giving up two runs on seven hits. Art Herring was the winner when Reiser tripled and scored the deciding run on Reese's single to left.

All involved in the violence drew fines, with Merullo suspended eight days and Walker and Smith five days. The suspicion here is that Lenny was on edge because of the miserable year he was having. He was mediocre at the plate even during the war, but now in 1946 he hit just .151 in 65 games and by the end of '47 he was gone.

During the next week the Dodgers swept a four-game series at Philadelphia, the 16th time in a row they had beaten the Phillies at Shibe Park. Brooklyn was playing one pennant-winning strategy perfectly: stay even with the top three and stomp all over the second division. The trouble was that the Cardinals were doing the same thing, and the Brooks weren't staying even with the Cardinals.

On the 28th the Washington Senators beat the Yankees 2–1, with knuckleballer Dutch Leonard going all the way. But the big news was that the game was the first under lights at Yankee Stadium. The weather, however, didn't cooperate. The *Times* reported that the 49,917 first nighters "shivered in the wintry gales that swept across the brightly illuminated arena."

Four days later Babe Ruth returned from a trip to Mexico, where he and his family had been the guests of the Pasquel brothers, and announced on his arrival that Larry MacPhail had refused to appoint him as manager of the Newark Bears.[12] There had always been great sympathy for Ruth as the great slugger baseball turned its collective back on. Well, baseball has a long memory, and those in command did not forget Ruth's performance as a Brooklyn Dodgers coach back in 1938.

He and Durocher had almost come to blows after Leo told the press that the Babe couldn't pass on signals from his coaching box because he couldn't remember them. Ruth as a player had been undisciplined and as a coach still seemed to be. Or perhaps he really couldn't learn and remember the signals. Either way, the word went out that he lacked the skills needed to manage.

Now on June 2 he's getting off a plane from Mexico and, in an amazing display of gall, is saying that he wants to get back into baseball again. This is a man who, when he left for Mexico, had nothing but praise for the Pasquel brothers, saying they were "doing a fine thing for baseball and for their country."[13] At the time the raids were still going on and men like Mickey Owen were playing in Mexico and Max Lanier was soon on his way.

In his worst move during his Mexican stay, Ruth had betrayed his own interests by siding with the Pasquels in their charge that major league baseball was a monopoly. "Just read the contract," he told reporters when he got back.[14] Whether it was monopoly or not is beside the point. Even though the Babe had only two years to live, if he had lived another fifty he would never had been hired by anyone after siding with the Pasquels. Baseball was built on the monopoly called the reserve clause and Ruth, Bambino or no Bambino, was considered a traitor by the owners.

The week after Ruth got back a union of sorts was being formed that within weeks would, for the first time, succeed in winning meaningful concessions from the owners. Player organizations under various names had been started since as far back as the 1880s, but none had lasted for any significant length of time or ever become strong enough to force the owners into even thinking of pensions and other benefits.

Robert Murphy, a Harvard-trained labor relations specialist, started the organizing movement by trying to persuade the Pittsburgh players to go on strike if Pirate officials did not agree to an election on whether the team would join Murphy's American Baseball Guild.[15]

The team, according to Pete Coscarart, had seemed fertile ground for a union but it was not so. Pete, the regular second baseman for four seasons, had been outspokenly for the union, prompting team President Bill Benswanger to ship him to the Pacific Coast League on June 1 as union sentiment seemed to be developing on the team.[16] The blackballing of Pete Coscarart had begun. He did some scouting later on but never managed in the minors or again wore a major league uniform either as player or coach.

Coscarart was wrong about the players' feelings, for on Friday, June 7, they voted against a strike, and later on August 20 they voted against joining the guild by a tally of 15–3.[17] Veterans like Truman (Rip) Sewell, who was making a comfortable $15,000 a year, led the opposition. But, unlike such movements in the past, this one was gathering strength behind the scenes.

By June 10 it was becoming obvious that Reiser's arm problems were affecting the team's pennant chances. They lost a game 3–2 against the Cardinals when the winning run scored after Red Schoendienst fell rounding second but scrambled back safely when Pete couldn't throw strongly enough to trap him. A loss like that, especially against the Cardinals, would haunt them later.

The Brooks left St. Louis leading by two games after beating the Cards 10–7 with a four-run rally in the ninth. Pete led off with a double followed by two outs and then four straight hits, with Ed Stevens driving in Reese with the winning run. Wins do not come any sweeter than that.

As they arrived back at Ebbets Field to play Chicago, Billy Herman, in a senseless trade, was sent to Boston for Stewart Hofferth, a 31-year-old, .216-hitting wartime catcher who was gone after 20 games and a .207 average. Billy was aging at 37 but he was still hitting .288 and would have been valuable down the stretch.

The following week a syndicate headed by Bill Veeck, with Bob Hope in a minor role, bought the Cleveland Indians for $2 million. Veeck was a master promoter whose Cleveland teams set attendance records yearly while he was there. He sold out and later bought the St. Louis Browns, where he set up the most bizarre at-bat in major league history. On August 19, 1951, he sent a midget up to pinch hit, a move that would stay with him till the day he died.

Eddie Gaedel, 26, was 3 feet, 6½ inches tall and had been signed to a one-day contract that morning for $100. He walked on four pitches, all high, from Detroit pitcher Bob Cain. Umpire Ed Hurley had been doubtful of the move until he was shown Gaedel's contract.[18]

The next day American League President Will Harridge ruled Eddie ineligible for further play "in the best interests of baseball." Eddie died in Chicago on June 18, 1961, at age 36. He was with Veeck to the end, however. When Bill, with 45 years of baseball promotions behind him, died at age 71, the first line of his obituary included "who once sent a midget to bat" for the St. Louis Browns.★[19]

On the 22nd the Dodgers suffered a 5–1 loss to the Cards at Ebbets Field that saw Musial go 3 for 5 to take the batting lead away from Dixie Walker. The Man's .365 that year would be his first of six peacetime batting championships. During the game, Augie Galan was out with a leg injury and saw the action from the press box, saying: "Boy, I'd go crazy watching a game from up here. I can't judge anything at this height." If a pro like Galan couldn't judge how do all those broadcasters tell a slider from a curve?

During the next 24 hours Teletype messages clicking out of the Seattle Associated Press bureau alerted the country to what has been called baseball's darkest night:

Spokane—
Seattle State Patrol says chartered bus has gone off the road at Snoqualmie Pass and that it may be the Spokane baseball team. Please check club there soonest.
Seattle

Two hours later the answer came:

Bulletin
Ellensburg, Wash. June 24 (AP)
A chartered bus carrying the Spokane baseball team of the Western International League went over a bank at Snoqualmie pass tonight and the State Patrol said at least five players were killed.

Thus it was the Spokane bus and it turned out that nine members of the Spokane Indians were killed as the bus plunged 500 feet down a drop in the Snoqualmie Pass in the Cascade Mountains near Seattle.

Survivors of the crash said the driver was doing only 35, since the road was slippery from rain, but had to swerve away from an oncoming "wrong side" driver and then could not avoid the plunge. On the way down, they said, the bus hit a large boulder, turned over, and as it came to rest the gas tank exploded, spewing flaming gasoline down the length of the bus.

*Frank Saucier, the player Gaedel pinch hit for, was an outfielder who played in just three major league games. He hit .071 and was gone. A very tough trivia question (New York Times, 8/20/51, p. S1).

Jack Wayne Lohrke, the Spokane third baseman, was nicknamed Lucky Lohrke because two hours before the crash he received a message that probably saved his life. San Diego of the Pacific Coast League had traded Jack to Spokane and they wanted him back, right away. The message went from a highway patrolman to the roadside restaurant where the team was eating. Lohrke called San Diego and then got his bag off the bus.[20]

Jack went up to the Giants the following year and had a seven-year career as a utility infielder, finishing with a lifetime average of .242. His luck held in New York where, in his fifth and last year before being traded to the Phillies, he was a member of the "miracle" 1951 Giants.

All of baseball responded to a fund drive chaired by a Spokane lawyer. Dixie Walker helped get things started when he suggested that the families of the Spokane injured and dead receive a portion of the receipts from the All-Star game coming up in July. Commissioner Chandler agreed and a check for $25,000 was sent after the game.[21]

The following week Pete showed some sense when he was selected for the All-Star game but withdrew from the squad on Durocher's urging. For once, he took himself out of a game on the sound logic that his arm and shoulder needed all the rest they could get. The only other Dodgers to make the team were Walker, who was leading the league again at .368, and Higbe.

The game had resumed that year after being cancelled in 1945 because, although the war in Europe was over, the railroads were clogged with troops returning home and others being shipped to the West Coast in anticipation of the invasion of the Japanese Home Islands.

The result was an embarrassment for the National League, a 12–0 rout that included two homers by Ted Williams, the second in the eighth inning off Rip Sewell's "Eephus" (nothing) ball. Ted had four hits in this, the most one-sided game in All-Star history.

After the All-Star break the Dodgers split two with the Cubs, then went on to St. Louis and a dismal a four-game sweep by the Cardinals. In the opening doubleheader the first loss hurt but the second game was a 2–1 crusher. Vic Lombardi, all 5 foot 7 of him, pitched all the way into the 12th inning when Musial hit one out for the ball game.

The next game was simply a thumper, a 10–4 Card win with three wasted Dodger runs in the ninth. Then came the getaway game, an even more bitter loss than the Lombardi game. Brooklyn was ahead 4–2 when Marty Marion was hit by a Joe Hatten pitch, Clyde Kluttz singled over Lavagetto's head, and pinch hitter Erv Dusak, after a failed bunt attempt, lined one deep into the left field seats. The Dodgers had headed West with a five-game lead. They left St. Louis a scant half game ahead of the Cards.

It was at this low point that somebody, a sportswriter most likely, came up with the phrase "Miksis'll Fixus," as Eddie, just out of the Navy, joined the team. With him came Cal McLish and all his names. Cal, a Native American, was probably the most named player ever to hit the major leagues: Calvin Coolidge Julius Caesar Tuskahoma Buster McLish.

As bad as the St. Louis series went, things got even worse in Cincinnati. Higbe lost 4–2, dropping the team into second place as the Cardinals beat the Phillies 5–4. The Brooks were jittery behind Kirby, with Reese, Reiser, Galan and Anderson making errors in the first three innings.

Then they headed for Forbes Field and the second-division Pittsburgh Pirates, now in seventh place and one of those have-not teams the Dodgers fattened up on all season. They took three straight at Forbes Field, beating Fritz Ostermeuller, Rip Sewell and Kenny Heintzelman, three good pitchers who rarely, if ever, worked for contenders.

That same day a group of Missouri English teachers took off on Dizzy Dean, claiming that Ol Diz's broadcasts of the Cardinals and Browns' games were having a bad influence on their pupils. In a complaint to the Federal Communications Commission, the teachers said Dean's game descriptions were replete with busted syntax and grammatical errors.

The fans, however, felt otherwise. Letters and telegrams poured into Dean's radio station telling him not to change his style, and condemning the teachers as elitists and faultfinders. The Associated Press reported Diz as unfazed, continuing with phrases such as: "Slaughter slud safe into second." "Marion thowed Reiser out at first." "The runners held their respectable bases." "Musial stands confidentially at the plate." "Don't fail to miss tomorrow's game."[22]

Diz admitted this sort of thing was somewhat put on, unlike his spiritual descendant, Yogi Berra. Like Dean, Yogi is no fool, but he's not a homespun philosopher either. He's wise enough to play his role and thereby make a lot of money, something we can all envy. But the publicist who came up with "If you come to a fork in the road take it" should own up. That's too good to have someone else take credit for it.

Diz counterattacked through the United Press, telling the teachers: "So I say Stan Musial or Chet Laabs is in a hitterish form at the plate. What's the difference? They hit. But I ain't dumb. I know most of the folks listening are from my part of the country—mostly from the Ozarks. They like it. A guy's got to do that sort of thing in this business."[23] He kept his job and was at it almost until he died on July 17, 1974, too soon at 63.

Meanwhile, the Dodger-Cardinal seesaw battle for the lead went Brooklyn's way until, with July ending, the Cards came into Ebbets Field and took two out of three. The Brooks won a close one 2–1, got hammered 10–3, and then were beaten 3–1, with Reiser again carried off the field after hitting the wall in the fifth inning.

Pete went after Whitey Kurowsk's long double, cracking his head so hard against the left field wall that he lost consciousness as Furillo, racing from his center field position, was waving for stretcher bearers to carry Pete into the dressing room. From there he was taken to Peck Memorial Hospital for observation. The attending doctor, finding no concussion, said that Pete would be able to play soon.

Cincinnati came in the next day for what proved to be another Brooklyn heartbreaker. Losing in the ninth inning was becoming a habit, and in hindsight if just one of those last-inning defeats could have been avoided—just one—there would have been no tie at season's end.

The Brooks behind Higbe were leading 2–1 after eight. Then in the top of the ninth Kirby walked second-baseman Benny Zientara. Eddie Lukon followed with a pop fly to short right that Walker had a bead on, but Stanky tore after the ball and dropped it while colliding with Walker and Whitman, Zientara scoring the tying run. The winner scored after a deliberate walk to Grady Hatton followed by a clean single to left center by Al Libke, a .208-hitting outfielder who was shipped out the next year.

Pete came back against the Giants with his usual heavy hitting after an injury. He was practically the whole offense in a 3–1 overtime win. He hit a homer on the first pitch to him in the first inning, and then in the 10th he won it, tripling with two men on.

The next day in Philadelphia he did it again. Higbe had a five-hit shutout into the eighth inning. Then Pee Wee hit a double to center and Pete followed with a single, driving in Reese with the winning run for a 1–0 Higbe win. The Brooks again had a 2½-game lead.

But not for long. On August 11, the Cards won their Sunday doubleheader in Cincinnati but the Dodgers lost theirs to the Phils as the Magerkurth-Durocher feud broke out again. Brooklyn had beaten Philadelphia 12 straight and should have won the opener but for four errors. Durocher, knowing the Cards had won their first, was ready for anything to set him off. It came in the first inning of game two.

Stanky started back to the bench after being called out on strikes. There's a touch of vaudeville here with Eddie walking into Maje's arm as he was signaling strike three. Eddie kept walking, insisting that Magerkurth lower the arm. Magerkurth insisted Eddie walk around him. When neither would budge, out came Leo.

Logically Maje should have used better judgment and simply let his arm fall rather than let Stanky bait him. But logic was overshadowed by the hatred that existed for years between this umpire and that team, especially this umpire and that manager, whose protest blocked him from umpiring in the 1941 World Series.

By the time Stanky had shaken loose it was too late—the George and Leo show had started. The *Times'* Louis Effrat was sure a fight would break out as the two became more enraged, Magerkurth at one point shoving Durocher out of his face. But Effrat didn't know his man. As Durocher started to charge he got his temper in check. Leo was not known to exchange punches with a man as large and tough as Magerkurth, and there was no blackjack handy.

When 10 minutes went by with Durocher still jawing, he was thumbed out. After that the insults from the Brooklyn bench became so that Stanky, Branca and Hank Behrman were banished and then, finally, the entire bench. Only coaches Charlie Dressen and John Corriden were left to manage the team and the bullpen. This Black Sunday ended with Brooklyn losing the second game also and heading home with their lead again down to one-half game.

While all this ruckus was going on Mickey Owen was making his way back from Mexico, traveling with his wife under an assumed name because, he said, he felt his life would have been in danger if the Pasquel brothers had found out.

After landing in St. Louis, he told the press that he had "escaped" to the United States. "The natural route would have been through Laredo but I would never have made it there. One of the Pasquel brothers, Alfonso, is located there and everyone there knows me, for I have played there several times.

"So you see, I doubt if the government officials would have permitted me to cross the Rio Grande without an okay from Alfonso," he said, adding that no other players could return at the time because all passports except his had been collected by the Pasquels. "Those Pasquels are the real power in Mexico, no matter what anybody tells you."[24]

During this *Sporting News* interview Mickey told of bad playing conditions and broken promises, the major reasons for his returning. But between the lines of his comments, and those of other jumpers, there is simply homesickness. Much of the talk had to do with feeling isolated in not knowing the language, and missing friends and the glamour of playing in the major leagues.

Of the name players, Owen and Lanier stayed in Mexico longest, Mickey about four months and Lanier through 1947. The day after he returned Owen appealed to Commissioner Chandler to have his five-year suspension reduced, saying that if he were reinstated other players would stream back across the border. "They're waiting to see what happens to me," he told reporters.[25]

There was, however, bitterness against the jumpers among players back home, much of it stemming from resentment that men with the skills of an Owen or Lanier abandoned them for a quick dollar, thereby hurting everyone's chances for a World Series share.

The Philadelphia Phillies, for example, held a team meeting and voted unanimously against lifting Owen's suspension. Infielder representative Roy Hughes announced that the team felt "it would be unfair to players who remained loyal to American baseball" to let Owen come back.[26]

The strangest condemnation of Owen came from Vern Stephens, the St. Louis Browns' shortstop. "He got the dough, I didn't," Stephens said. "If they let him come back, anybody can jump a contract anywhere."[27] The logic is stunningly flawed; Stephens forgot that he jumped his Browns' contract and returned in two days without his bonus only because he found conditions in Mexico unacceptable.

Chandler turned down Mickey's plea and, given the bitterness of the time, it seemed the five-year ban would hold. That it didn't was the result of an anti-trust suit filed in late 1947 by Danny Gardella against major league baseball when he wasn't allowed to return from Mexico. Gardella, a wartime Giants outfielder, had skipped south early, knowing he had no real future in the big leagues.

The owners mounted a token defense, not really thinking the suit had a chance until, almost belatedly, they realized that it could threaten baseball's reserve clause, the structure on which the game at that time was based.

Under the reserve clause once a player signed with a team he was theirs for rest of his professional life. If he didn't play for that team he didn't play for any team. Gardella's suit described the clause as "monopolistic" and in its restraint of trade a violation of both the Sherman and Clayton anti-trust laws.[28]

The suit was dismissed, as the owners had expected. After all, the reserve clause was inviolable—they all thought. None other than Justice Oliver Wendell Holmes, in a suit involving the Federal League in 1922, wrote the U.S. Supreme Court's majority opinion that baseball was exempt from the anti-trust laws because it was "not trade or commerce in commonly accepted use of those words."[29]

The owners were therefore complacent in the face of Gardella's suit until on February 9, 1949, they were stunned when the United States Court of Appeals reinstated it, with one judge making it clear that he regarded the reserve clause as illegal, and another, Judge Learned Hand no less, saying the clause would have to go if baseball should be declared a monopoly.[30]

The owners finally realized that this wartime ballplayer was a major threat and could not be laughed off any longer, but must be bought off. Which is precisely what they did.

Gardella withdrew his suit on October 8, 1949, and some months later announced that he had been paid off by the owners, telling reporters: "You may say in the papers that Gardella was paid something to drop his suit. That is all." Danny would not reveal the amount but said he had to pay his attorneys half the proceeds.[31]

Months before this, however, Chandler was so worried about the Gardella suit he announced that the ban on all major leaguers who had jumped to Mexico would be lifted and they would be welcomed back.[32] All the owners now realized they could no longer depend on the ghost of Oliver Wendell Homes to preserve their reserve clause. This little-known outfielder, working as a hospital orderly in Mount Vernon, New York, had humbled them all, including the commissioner of baseball.

The bribery of Gardella bought the owners time, many years in fact. But even without the anti-trust threat there was Bob Murphy's American Baseball Guild, the first time since 1912, except for a weak and brief try in 1922, that ballplayers got together in any kind of solidarity. The guild failed, perhaps because it was too soon after the war. But the unrest that brought it about did not go away.

Almost 20 years went by until the arrival of Marvin Miller as head of the Major League Baseball Players Association with offices on Park Avenue in New York. Miller took advantage of the unrest with a strike threat in 1969 and the real thing in 1972, a work stoppage that forced the cancellation of 86 regular-season games and ended when the owners increased their contributions to the players' retirement and health plans.[33]

The reserve clause survived the Curt Flood challenge but then came the bombshell ruling that opened the way for free agency. It was 1975 and pitchers Dave McNally and Andy Messersmith went to arbitration on the automatic renewal clause. They played a year unsigned and then demanded their freedom.

Arbitrator Peter Seitz, part of a three-man panel, cast the deciding vote in the case, ruling that both McNally and Messersmith were free agents, that the reserve clause was binding for just one year instead of perpetuity.[34] The Lords of Baseball, as Dick Young used to call them, were in a panic, knowing their hold on each of their players was virtually over. The protective umbrella provided by Oliver Wendell Holmes was gone.

As for the Pasquels and the rest of the Mexican owners, they had long since surrendered, admitting on October 28, 1947, that they were in deep financial trouble and would therefore make no further attempts to raid the major leagues. "I am going to let the United States club owners know that we will not steal one single player from them," the Mexican head of baseball, Alexander Aguilar, told a press conference, adding that his league is "ready for friendship" with all of organized baseball.[35]

On the day Chandler turned Owen down, Rickey revived an old idea for increasing attendance: for the first time the phrase "day-night doubleheader" was heard, with fans asked to pay for a game in the afternoon and another at night. Naturally, the fans resented this and some writers sided with sportswriter Jimmy Powers in calling Rickey "El Cheapo."

The idea was a mistake from the fans' viewpoint, but resulted in a paid attendance of 57,224 for the split doubleheader that brought the year's attendance to a record-setting 1,236,162 on this, only the 14th day of August, in the smallest park in the majors.

Powers was probably unaware that the split doubleheader idea was not new, that it was not uncommon back in 1912 among National League teams. According to Horace Stoneham the New York Giants charged separate admissions for two games played on July 4th of that year.

He told *New Yorker* writer Roger Angell that those who owned the team before his father bought it in 1919 had come up with double admission idea. The first half of that split bill was the first time he saw the Giants play, he said. "The Giants' battery was Christy Mathewson and Chief Bender," he recalled. "They opened with their stars in the first game because they charged separate admissions for the morning and afternoon games, and that way they got the crowds out early."

Presumably Matty would pitch his usual fast game, clearing the ballpark for the afternoon crowd. It didn't work that day, however. The *Times* account has Christy gone by the third inning as the Dodgers went on to sweep both games of what was, as far as we know, one of the first split doubleheaders imposed on the paying customers.[36]

Split doubleheaders apparently weren't that rare back then. Just a week before, on May 31, the Giants were in Philadelphia for a morning and afternoon game. The morning "pre-breakfast" game drew some 20,000 and about half that in the afternoon.[37]

The day after Rickey revived the idea Brooklyn beat the Phillies, but the win was marred by Medwick being taken to Peck Memorial after being hit by a wild curve ball thrown by lefthander Frank Hoerst. Joe had remained conscious on the field but passed out in the clubhouse.

What is unbelievable here is that Medwick was struck on the left side of his head and probably would have been only shaken up if he had been wearing the MacPhail protective helmet. This was the man whose serious beaning in 1940 prompted MacPhail to develop it in the first place, and there he was, not wearing one. Luckily he was not seriously injured, but even so he was out almost two weeks with a concussion.

There was a four-game series with the Cardinals coming up over the weekend that both teams were looking forward to, but first there was a sweet win in Cincinnati. The Dodgers were down 4 to 2 in the eighth when Pete hit one out with Stanky on to tie the game, making Dick Whitman a happy rookie when he homered for the win in the ninth.

Brooklyn then went into St. Louis tied for first place, and after a four-game series, left the same way. They opened with a doubleheader, the first game decided when Lavagetto singled in the winning run in the ninth inning off Cards' ace Howie Pollett—a euphoric win, coming in that manner in Sportsman's Park. But they got killed in the nightcap, 14–3, as six Dodger pitchers got knocked around.

The next day Murray Dickson won a 2–1 squeaker as the Cards scored both of their runs in the first inning on Slaughter's two-run double. Murray had just turned 30 the previous week and was one of the Cardinals' three leading pitchers that pennant-winning year: 15 and 6 to lead the league in winning percentage at .714, and an ERA of 2.88. He was shipped to the second division Pirates in 1949 where two years later he was 20 and 16 with a *seventh place* team. A terrific pitcher.

That Thursday, July 18, baseball's owners, in an unprecedented and historic move, agreed to player demands that included improved contracts, representation on baseball's governing body, formation of a grievance committee and a pension plan.[38] As the *Times* pointed out, all this was spurred by the owners' fear of unions, so Bob Murphy's American Baseball Guild wasn't a failure after all.

September opened with an exclusive story in the *Times* that the Dodgers were switching their spring training quarters from Clearwater, Florida, to Santa Ana, California. The story stressed that the announcement was not official, but could be regarded as "authoritative." The switch, according to the paper, was being made because Jackie Robinson had not been welcome in the South the previous spring. The California site, it was thought, would present no such difficulties.

The figure of Robinson seemed to be already looming over the team, even though he was still with Montreal. The switch, however, never took place. The Dodgers, without explanation, trained in Cuba in 1947 and the Dominican Republic in '48 before buying their Vero Beach training site the following year.

As the minor league season was ending Dodger Secretary Harold Parrott announced the recall of 18 players from the Dodgers' farm teams, among them Gil Hodges, Erv Palica, Gene Mauch, Clyde King and Harry Taylor. They arrived in time for a game that no one at the ballpark would ever forget. Higbe retired 27 out of the 28 he faced and didn't even get a shutout. He won, 4–1, and but for one pitch to Ernie Lombardi, who hit it out in the second inning, he would have had a perfect game.

Walter Kirby Higbe is mostly forgotten today, for he spent just four seasons with Brooklyn, but he was one of the most effective pitchers to ever wear the Dodger uniform. He was 70 and 38 from 1941, when he and Wyatt pitched the team to the pennant, through 1946 for a winning percentage of .648. Only Preacher Roe at .698 and Don Newcombe at .657 had higher percentages. Higbe was also a money pitcher, usually up for the big one, like Wyatt and Casey.*

Kirby was traded to Pittsburgh in May of '47 for what were termed personal reasons. But everyone knew the real cause was Robinson's arrival. Kirby liked to drink but that wasn't the problem for, unlike Mungo, he was always there for reveille, always ready to pitch. And he was another of Brooklyn's fearless, with an inside pitch there for anyone digging in too much.

But, again, he did love to drink, and with Casey as his roommate there were plenty of opportunities as they bar-hopped through the seasons. Often after a shower, two sandwiches from room service, and two quick shots, he and big Hugh were ready for the town.[39] Unlike many other ballplayers, though, Kirby's

Kirby Higbe was one of the most effective pitchers in Dodger history, a hard and fearless fastballer who compiled a 70–38 record in his four years at Ebbets Field. Higbe, a South Carolinan, was traded to Pittsburgh after he told Branch Rickey he didn't want to play ball with Jackie Robinson. He never backed down, as some others did, so was soon gone.

drinking never really got out of hand and he was 70 when he died in his hometown of Columbia, South Carolina. As he admitted in his book, the Southern mores he was weaned on were the primary factor in his not accepting the arrival of Robinson.

A players' nightmare hit Ebbets Field when Cincinnati and Vander Meer came in on the 12th: a nineteen-inning scoreless tie, four hours and

---

*Higbe was drafted in '43 and fought across Europe. When Germany fell he was sent to the Pacific and was in on the invasion of Leyte and recapture of Manila (Philadelphia Inquirer, 5/8/85, p. 10E, Obituary).

40 minutes, with Vander Meer going 15 innings and Hal Gregg 10. Dog-tired as they were, especially team elders like Dixie Walker on his 36-year-old legs, the locker room brightened when word came that the Phils had beaten the Cardinals 9–4, thus evening up the loss column: the Brooks 51, the Cards 51. It was this kind of game: three of the team's best hitters, Walker, Furillo and Reiser, went 2 for 21 among them.

Another Cardinals series was starting, with each game crucial as it became obvious that the first playoff in history was a possibility. This one opened in Brooklyn and Pollett won again, 10 to 3, his fourth over the Brooks that year. Joe Garagiola started it by hitting one into Bedford Avenue with two on in a five-run first inning.

Dixie got three hits in this one but his dream of a second batting title was long dead. He was down below .320 and Musial was above .350, driving toward the .365 that would lead both leagues and result in the first of his six peacetime titles. (Stan had hit .357 to win the title in 1943 but that was against wartime replacement pitching.)

The Dodgers won the next day 4–3, but the Reiser curse struck again when Pete came up with a charley horse so severe that it kept him out of the next 13 games. Durocher said it cost the Dodgers the pennant, coming so late in a two-team race.

True, it came at a bad time, with but 15 games to play and the Dodgers just 1½ games out. But it was just one of a series of injuries that limited Pete's play to just 122 of the 156-game schedule. That was the key statistic for, as Leo and the whole team knew, Pete was missed during those absences because when healthy he was a factor in just about every game.

Like Robinson after him, Pete had an unsettling effect on the pitcher once he got on base. He led the league with 34 stolen bases that year, not that much today, but a lot during those years. And whenever Pete got to third the pitcher had to be wary, for among the 34 steals seven were of home. The seventh was against Bill Voiselle in a Dodgers win over the Giants on September 8.[40] This set a record for steals of home equaled only by Rod Carew when he was with Minnesota in 1969.

The Dodgers stayed in the race by beating the Cardinals the next two games, Higbe and Branca doing the job. Kirby, after being bounced around the day before, pitched 2⅔ scoreless innings to save a 4–3 win for Hatten. Branca pitched a three-hit shutout to close out the series, 5 to 0, one of the few times in his career he delivered in a really clutch game.

Chicago came to town at this time, to the writers' delight. They dredged up their clippings from the fights that lasted through two games back in May when Merullo tangled first with Stanky and Walker the next day. Unlike most baseball fights there were punches thrown and teeth knocked out, so the beat guys predicted, and probably hoped for, more of the same. There's no struggling for a lead when a fight is going on.

The *Brooklyn Eagle* had a five-column headline: "Fists That Flew in May Come Back to Haunt Dodgers in September," with a subhead: "Feud Makes Cubs Try Twice as Hard to Cost Flock Flag." Well, perhaps the players weren't reading the papers that week. They split four games peacefully, with the Cubs of course wanting to play spoiler, the normal incentive for any club out of it.

When the Cubs left, Brooklyn was still two games out as the Cards beat the Giants 10–2 for Pollett's 20th win. Howie was 21 and 10 that year, so two years in the service hadn't hurt him as it did so many others.

Branca came up with another shutout, this time against the seventh-place Pirates, after the Brooks had lost the first game, for a 3–2 and 3–0 split. His win cut the Cards' lead to 1½ when they lost to the Braves. Ralph now had two important wins in a row, but, sadly for him and for the team, the playoff games were but days away and Dodger fans would see the Branca swoon for the first, but not the last, time. Then on September 25 there was a heartbreaker in Philadelphia, a loss so unexpected and at such an inopportune time that it would have broken most other teams.

Brooklyn had a three-run lead going into the ninth inning against a team they usually beat handily, but couldn't hold it. They were ahead 7–5 after five innings and 9–6 with just three outs to go. Then the bullpen blew up.

Taylor, the starter, had been blasted early but those that followed could do no better. Behrman, Branca, Art Herring, Higbe, Hal Gregg, Casey and Lombardi each failed in turn, with Little Vic taking the loss. There were four hits in that ninth: singles by ex–Dodger Charlie Gilbert, Ron Northey, Jim Tabor and Emil Verban. Dixie committed a key error that allowed Northey to go to third, where he scored the winning run on a sacrifice fly by another ex–Dodger, Dee Moore. The eight pitchers the Brooks used were a record at that time.

The locker room was like a tomb until two announcements penetrated the gloom. The Cardinals had been beaten, shut out 6 to 0 by Bucky Walters, thus keeping the lead to one game—not insurmountable with each team still having three to play. The second good word came from Branch Rickey: each member of the team would be given a new Studebaker of their choice from a display on the field that coming Saturday, two days away.[41] So much for the "El Cheapo" nonsense.

It was when Rickey announced the car gifts that Walter O'Malley started his public campaign to get rid him. Walter had been making fun of Rickey behind his back for some time, especially among his cronies and political friends. In undermining him any way he could, O'Malley had been privately ridiculing Rickey's "slovenly appearance," complaining of his "exorbitant" salary, criticizing his handling of players, and began calling him a "psalm-singing" fake.[42]

It had all been behind the scenes until this, since O'Malley previously never had the guts to come out against a man of Rickey's stature. And there was an air of "psalm singing" about the Mahatma, but is wasn't fake, and it was something that Walter O'Malley could never, never understand.

How could a man like O'Malley ever comprehend Rickey's attitude toward the church and the Bible? Walter was probably unaware that as a young catcher Branch was released by the Cincinnati Reds because he refused to play or even appear at the ballpark "on the Sabbath."[43] Had O'Malley known he would have laughed at the thought of

The man Brooklyn loves to hate: Walter O'Malley took the beloved Dodgers to Los Angeles in 1958. There are those now who defend him, blaming Robert Moses for the move, but those who lived through it know better. As sportswriter Dave Anderson put it: O'Malley would have broken through a brick wall to get his team into Los Angeles.

anyone giving up a major league job because of a moral principle.*

The free Studebakers smoked O'Malley out. He finally went public, complaining to the press that in giving the Studebakers Rickey was wasting money that should have gone to the Dodger stockholders. The team declared a net profit of $451,000 that year, thanks in great part to the Mahatma's sale of so-so ballplayers to other teams, yet O'Malley still complained.[44]

*After his release by the Reds Rickey played a total of 119 games in the majors, but never on Sunday. The Sporting News described him as "high strung with ability and enthusiasm" during his time with the St. Louis Browns and New York Highlanders. He had arm trouble and retired after setting a major league record by allowing 13 stolen bases in his final game (Branch Rickey, p. 46).

Walter was a master at behind-the-scenes intrigue, but Rickey was no fool. He knew what was going on, and he still had enough influence to fight O'Malley off at the time and get a contract for 1947. But within a few years he was on his way to Pittsburgh. One of the great baseball minds of our era was banished from Ebbets Field by a man not worthy to be in the same room with him.

But no matter what O'Malley was saying, or what Rickey hater Jimmy Powers wrote in his *Daily News* column, the Mahatma had the team's loyalty and they showed it. In appreciation of the Studebaker gifts each Dodger contributed $300 towards the purchase of a Chris Craft boat, the *Dodger's Skipper*, for Rickey.

When Dixie Walker approached home plate for the presentation, Rickey was overcome and found it difficult to speak. "Everybody on the team contributed on an equal basis," Walker said. "We thought he deserved it." Furillo said he was especially glad for Rickey's sake. "One thing I always liked about him," Carl said, "when he gave his word that was it."[45]

The day after the bullpen blew up in that crucial Philadelphia loss the team got hit again when Reiser's season ended as he suffered a broken leg sliding back into first base in the first inning. Before the game Pete, just returning to action, had told Leo that his charley horse hadn't completely healed and that he therefore couldn't run with his usual speed. Durocher played him anyway and after Pete drew a walk in the first inning he flashed the steal sign. What could have been in his mind, telling Pete to steal when he knew he couldn't run all that well?

Roscoe McGowen wrote in his *Times* account that Pete slid back to first base after taking a lead, caught his foot on the bag and suffered a fractured fibula in his left leg and, as had happened to him before, was carried off the field on a stretcher and taken to Peck Memorial Hospital.

That couple of days showed the cohesion and spirit of that '46 team. After losing a three-run lead in the ninth inning one day and then losing their star player the next, they never gave in. They scored eight runs behind Higbe, as Kirby gave up eight hits and two runs to the Phillies in one of the most important games of his career. A big game pitcher in a big time game: Kirby Higbe, who defiantly wore number 13, now 17 and 8. The Card lead was down to one-half game.

On the 26th it is likely that glasses were raised throughout Brooklyn to the Cubs' Hank Borowy and Hank Wyse after they teamed up to beat the Cardinals 7 to 2, dropping the Redbirds into a tie with the Dodgers. They were 95 and 57 with two games to play.

They split the two remaining games, so for the first time in baseball history there would be a playoff for the pennant. While Brooklyn had won two of its last three games, the Cardinals lost two of their last three.

This was not typical of that Cardinal team, but they were playing a Chicago club that was fighting for third place money, which they got by edging the Braves by one game.

On the last day neither team grabbed the brass ring. Mort Cooper, now with the Braves, was still poison to the Dodgers as he shut them out 4 to 0 on a four-hitter, giving up only four hits. The gloom in Ebbets Field was so intense during the shutout that the stands were unusually quiet, until at mid-game the scoreboard keeper put up a "5" for the Cubs in the sixth inning against the Cardinals. The ballpark erupted "as the crowd went wild," knowing the Cubs had a 5–2 lead. At day's end the season was over with the Dodgers and Cards tied and preparing for a two-game playoff, the first in baseball history.

Durocher was asked after the game who he would start against the Cards at Sportsman's Park on October 1. "I'll pitch either Kirby Higbe or Ralph Branca, probably Branca," Leo answered.

There was some question at the time over whether the coming playoff was really the first. A few of the older writers cited the 1908 post-season game between the Giants and the Cubs as the actual first.

The *Eagle*'s Tommy Holmes did some research and found that the 1908 game was not a playoff but rather the replay of a regular season game that had been protested, the game of the famous Fred Merkle so-called "boner" that cost the Giants the pennant.[46] Merkle, on first base, had gone into the dugout after Al Birdwell's single drove in the winning Giant run, and was called out for not touching second, negating the run.

But it wasn't a boner at all. David W. Anderson points out in *More Than Merkle* that because of the rowdy fans it was the custom up until that time to run to the dugout rather than second on a game winner. The rule called for it to be done but it was never enforced until that game. Johnny Evers, knowing the rule, got the umpire's attention and tagged second for the third out, negating the run.[47] It was a terrible call, against tradition, especially with a pennant at stake.

The playoff centered around pitching: the Cardinals had it, the Dodgers didn't. Howie Pollett, Murray Dickson and Harry Brecheen did their jobs. Most of the Dodger pitchers didn't, starting with Branca.

Here was a man Brooklyn had for the prime years of any pitcher's career and he finished up at 80 and 58 as a Dodger, with excuse after excuse for blowing big games. He was 6 foot 3 and 220 pounds, with a great moving fastball, slider and changeup and he won 88 career games.*

---

*Years later Branca told writer Rick Westcott that he never mastered his curve ball, a "big overhand downer" that he never learned how to shorten and control because the team "had no pitching coach in those days" (Splendor on the Diamond, p. 189). Today pitching coaches are invaluable and paid accordingly.

With that kind of physical equipment he should have been a 150-game winner, at least.

When he was going good there would be an occasional important win from him, but only during the season. Unlike Wyatt or Higbe, when the money was on the line in the really big games, goodbye Ralphie, as they used to say along Flatbush Avenue.

However you put it, he got the ball three times with the pennant at stake, and one World Series game, and his fastball, control, and poise went out the window.* There was always one overriding flaw in Ralph Branca: with all that God-given talent and size there was something missing. As the song goes, "You Gotta Have Heart."

He was 3 and 1 when Leo gave him the ball for the first playoff game. Higbe, Brooklyn's gamer with 17 wins, had

A somber Ralph Branca stares at the camera wearing number 12, which replaced 13, the number he defiantly wore until his pitch to Bobby Thomson resulted in "the shot heard 'round the world," that won the '51 playoff between the Dodgers and the Giants.

four days' rest, but Durocher goes with this 20-year-old kid. He was up against Howie Pollett, 21 and 10 with a league-leading 2.10 ERA.

Pollett went all the way for a 4 to 2 win while Branca struggled from the start. He loaded the bases in the first inning, got away with just one run, and then couldn't even get past the third inning. He moaned after the game that he was beaten by cheap hits and lucky bounces. But this is what John Drebinger of the *Times* had to say: "The Cards bestirred themselves again and this time drove Branca to the showers with a two-run splurge on a pass and a trio of singles that included no infield taps." The sequence: Musial walked, Slaughter singled and Kurowski forced as Musial scored. Harry Walker singled, and Garagiola singled as Kurowski scored the second run of the inning. That was it for Branca: six hits, two walks, three earned runs in 2⅔ innings.

*The Series in 1947 and the pennant races of 1946, 1949, and 1951.

The next day another magnanimous gesture by Rickey was announced, despite O'Malley's complaints about the free Studebakers. The Mahatma decreed that all proceeds from the playoffs would go to the Dodgers' employees. He stressed that no executives or players would be involved, just the 50 everyday working people employed by the club.[48] El Cheapo indeed.

Two days later it was all over at Ebbets Field as Hatten, facing 15 and 6 Murray Dickson, was belted for seven hits and five runs in 4⅔ innings, and Brooklyn never caught up. Three runs in the last of the ninth were useless in an 8 to 4 game with five Brooklyn pitchers following Joe to the mound. As the pennant headed west there were no bright spots in Ebbets Field that day. The hitting had come too little and too late.

There was justice to the St. Louis win. It was simply that the Brooks, murder on most clubs in the league, just couldn't handle the Cardinals that year. Against the team they had to at least stay even with, they were 8 and 14, so with the playoff wins the Cardinals took 16 of the 24 games against them. The reason there was a playoff at all was that the Dodgers pounded teams like the Phillies and Pirates.

In the face of that disheartening ending to such an historic season, there were two things that brightened Brooklyn Dodger–National League souls: the Yankees didn't win it that year, and the Cardinals took the Red Sox in seven, with Slaughter scoring from first on a weak hit, his "Mad Dash" the deciding run.

The play was so daring and happened so quickly that different versions have come down to us over the past 50 years or so. The main one blames Johnny Pesky for "freezing" with the relay as Slaughter rounded third and kept going on a "dying seagull" hit to left-center by Harry Walker. True to the code of his generation Pesky never blamed anyone else for the play, but recent analysis of film clips show that, though surprised, he made the relay without pausing or freezing, and that the throw from center fielder Leon Culberson was almost a lob, since he never expected Slaughter to go in.

Glenn Stout and Richard Johnson write in their *Red Sox Century* that the films prove Pesky made the play called for in a "situation that was already lost" because of Culberson's throw. Ordinarily Dom DiMaggio, one of the top center fielders in the game, would have been out there but Dom had pulled a hamstring earlier and was replaced by Culberson, a part-timer left over from the war.

Slaughter, one of the fastest men in the game, had an edge in that with the steal sign on he had broken for second and therefore had a great jump on the play. He was six strides from the plate as Pesky's throw drifted about eight feet up the baseline away from catcher Roy Partee.[49]

Enos later told sportswriter Bob Broeg of the *St. Louis Post-Dispatch* that he had no doubts about the play. "I knew I was going to score before I hit second base," he said, "because I knew Culberson was in center, not Dom DiMaggio."[50]

Bobby Doerr, watching the play from his second base position, added another dimension: the field. "The thing that no one remembers is how terrible the field was," he told David Halberstam. "It was just brutal, as bad a field as I've ever played on. So bumpy and rough. Dom was accustomed to it by then but Leon was very tentative."[51] It was the field where, as Slaughter once said, "the ball comes at you ever' which way."

As the game ended Bob Broeg chided the official scorers for ruling Walker's "dying seagull" a double when under most circumstances it would have been seen as a single looped over the infield. "Gentlemen," he told them, "by scoring that as a double, you've taken the romance out of a great play."[52]

After the Series, as the year closed out, many Dodger fans were aware that down in Montreal a second baseman had won the International League batting championship and had stolen 40 bases. Some were frightened by this, others, more tolerant, were not.

Whatever their reaction, they knew that Jackie Robinson was on his way to Brooklyn and that baseball would never be the same again.

8

1947: Jackie Robinson Arrives

The year of Jackie Robinson, Durocher's suspension, and the most exciting inning in World Series history, 1947 was also Pete Reiser's last season as a full-time major leaguer. He would be carried off on a stretcher for the third and last time at Ebbets Field, for the time would come when if he hit a wall again he would be playing for a different team.

But as it turned out, Rickey kept Pete for two more years during which he went to extraordinary means to save his career, padding the walls and laying a warning track and even offering to pay him full salary if he would take 1948 off to rest and recuperate.[1]

At contract time the Mahatma continued to show his regard for Pete, signing him for an estimated $18,000, probably the best contract of his career, especially since he was coming off a season during which he played only 122 games because of injuries.

Rickey also showed his appreciation to the fans, spending more than $300,000 to improve Ebbets Field by painting the stands, installing a new men's room and adding 1,400 more box seats in the outfield area.[2] The added seats reduced the distance from home plate to left field by 14 feet, from 357 to 343.* Thus the small park became even smaller and had almost fatal results for Pete later in the year when, chasing a fly ball, he thought he had room he didn't have.

As the ballpark work was starting, the Catholic Church, unhappy with Durocher's conduct on and off the field, started a drive to get rid of him. The first move was a letter from the Rev. Vincent J. Powell, director of Brooklyn's Catholic Youth Organization (CYO), to Rickey protest-

*This reduction was spelled out in the press. By comparing the left field distance figures of 1947 and 1948 in books like Green Cathedrals (p. 117) it is clear that 14 feet was taken: 1947—357 feet, 1948—343 feet.

ing that Durocher's overall conduct was "undermining the moral training" of the borough's Roman Catholic youths.

The CYO, Rev. Powell wrote, would not "continue to have our youngsters associated with a man who is an example in complete contradiction to our moral teachings." He added that the 50,000-member organization would resume its association with Dodger baseball if the club replaced Durocher.[3]

There was no immediate comment from the Dodgers, since all of their front office people were in Cuba at the club's Havana spring training camp. Meanwhile, Father Powell remained busy attending his night classes at St. John's University. So all seemed quiet for the time, but it was obvious this would not go away.

Many Brooklyn fans thought the entire matter a sham, but to the Catholic hierarchy of Brooklyn it was not. It set out to get Leo and had the backing of the numerous Irish, Italian and Polish parishes, among others, behind it. Perhaps the parishioners were divided on the matter, but the parishes, the neighborhood units of the church, stood as one behind the diocese.

As the situation developed, it was the things that Rev. Powell's letter did not mention that were being written about in the press, making it apparent that, far from being a sham, the church's move had a moral authority behind it, given the extent of Durocher's many, as the church would put it, transgressions.

The movie star Laraine Day's divorce was messy enough, with Durocher named correspondent, but it was just the latest in a pattern of turmoil and violence that were part of Leo's daily life: the constant brawling, often with people in no position to fight back, the daily umpire baiting, with its foul language often heard in the stands, and there was the John Christian blackjacking.

Not everyone in Brooklyn, and particularly the churches, was happy with Durocher being found innocent in this case on his flimsy assertion that Christian's jaw had been broken when he slipped and fell. Just because a jury of fans and a nitwit judge combined to find him innocent didn't make him so in the eyes of those not mesmerized by his Dodger aura. It was bad enough that two men jumped Christian, but the use of the blackjack gave the case a particularly brutal gangland touch. What was the manager of the Brooklyn Dodgers doing using a weapon associated with the lowest of thugs?

Commissioner Chandler was aware of Leo's activities from the day he took office. "I read Landis' file on Durocher so I knew what I was up against," he told Arthur Mann, his personal troubleshooter. But he was shocked at the not guilty verdict, saying the trial "was a fix."[4] And, as a former governor and senator, he lived by public opinion and was sure it would eventually go against Durocher, even though he was found not guilty.

Another major problem Leo was facing was his association with gamblers and the underworld figures involved with them. At one point it got so bad that the beat writers started complaining to Rickey and his staff that they were banned from the clubhouse while bookies, touts and assorted gambling celebrities were not.[5] Chandler knew all about all this from the Landis files and from reading press accounts of Durocher's friendship with people like the movie actor George Raft and his gangland connections.

Rickey had been concerned about such Durocher associates for some time, to the point where the previous fall he had asked Chandler to meet with Leo to warn him to stop seeing people like Raft. Chandler agreed and met secretly with Durocher, ordering him to avoid Raft and mobsters like Bugsy Siegel and Joe Adonis, two of the most famous thugs in the world.[6] Adonis was bad enough, but Siegel, underworld glamour or not, had the smell of Lepke Buchalter and Murder Incorporated still about him.*

At one point, according to Arthur Daley in his *Times* column of April 10, Durocher was asked by Chandler if he knew certain gamblers and Durocher repeatedly replied, "I have a nodding acquaintance with him." Finally the commissioner snapped, "Stop nodding."[7]

Before the meeting ended Leo promised Chandler he would avoid bad company, saying: "They'll call me a louse but I'll do it." He immediately moved out of Raft's house, where he had been staying temporarily, but it was too late. He had gotten away with too much over the years and too many people had looked the other way. The church was onto him now and there was no star-struck jury to save him this time.

Chandler revealed years later that Raft, his movie star ego obviously bruised, called him to protest his name being used. The conversation, Chandler said, was brief:

Raft: "I want to talk to you Commissioner."

Chandler: "What about?"

Raft: "Well, I got a bum rap."

Chandler: "You didn't get it from me George. Do you have a baseball contract?"

Raft: "No."

Chandler: "Take your business someplace else, because I don't give a damn what you do. I don't have to be responsible for you."[8]

They wouldn't have to worry about Siegel much longer. On June 20, 1947, he was slain gangland style in the Los Angeles home of his then girlfriend, Virginia Hill (New York Times, 6/22, p. 7).

To make matters even worse for Durocher, just two months after he met with Chandler the biggest gambling scandal since the Black Sox of 1919 hit baseball. In January five members of the Houma club of the Evangeline League were accused of throwing a game against Abbeville in a post-season series between the two Louisiana teams. All were declared ineligible for further play as the alleged fix was being investigated.[9]

Major league owners reacted immediately when it appeared the investigation might take in many more players than the original five. Backed by Chandler, they adopted resolutions with essentially the same goals:

1. Any player who fails to report a bribe offer to his manager or league president immediately would be banished for life.

2. All known bookmakers, touts, or other undesirable characters, to be barred from all ballparks. This would be done through the Ed Barrow system of making lists of undesirables and employing a staff to see that such persons are kept out of the ballparks.

3. All visitors, before, during, or after a game to be barred from clubhouses, dressing rooms, and dugouts. Exceptions: accredited persons such as the press.[10]

This spotlight on gambling came at a bad time for Durocher, given his past activities and association with known gamblers and bookies. And then, as he was supposedly trying to heed Chandler's advice, another scandal of his own making erupted when the Laraine Day divorce case made headlines throughout the country, she being a movie star and Leo charged by her husband with stealing his wife while posing as a friend.[11] There was even an account, described by Durocher to Chandler, in which he and Day's husband, Ray Hendricks, argued about sleeping arrangements in front of Laraine in her bedroom.[12] It was becoming apparent that behind that sweet face there was more femme fatale than Mormon maiden in Laraine Day.

This was the stuff the New York tabloids lived on, and there was worse to come. The divorce was granted on January 20, but instead of waiting the mandatory year required by California law before Laraine could marry again, she and Leo flew to Juarez for a quickie Mexican divorce.

Obviously none of this was missed by the Catholic Diocese of Brooklyn, for after the next development, the couple's marriage in El Paso in defiance of California law, the church finally had enough and Rev. Powell sent off his letter to Rickey.

Chandler made his move on April 9, banning Durocher from baseball for one year because of "conduct detrimental to baseball." There were public outcries that Durocher had done nothing wrong, that he was the victim of a feud with Larry MacPhail. But Chandler brushed these aside, saying in the text of his decision that "Durocher has not measured up to the standards expected or required of managers of our baseball teams." He was suspended, the commissioner continued, "as the result of an accumulation of unpleasant incidents in which he has been involved."

The press in the main came down on Chandler's side, except for those who were always blind to Leo's thuggish ways, like Walter Winchell and Bill Corum. Shirley Povich of the *Washington Post* was undecided, but he knew the real Durocher, as he wrote: "Maybe the punishment was in excess of the crime, but who can shed a tear for Durocher?"[13]

At first many Brooklyn fans regarded Leo as a hero and burned Chandler in effigy. But this didn't last, and the turning point came on April 27 in Yankee Stadium when Chandler took the microphone to pay tribute to Babe Ruth during ceremonies honoring him that day.

Before he could speak the crowd was noisy and hostile, its boos preventing him from saying anything. Chandler stood his ground as announcer Mel Allen repeatedly called for silence. When he was finally allowed to speak he began his tribute to the Babe, and at that point a ripple of applause grew into roars of approval that drowned out any opposition.[14]

After that it was just about over as far as pro–Durocher demonstrations went. A few surfaced here and there, but there were other things for fans to worry about, principally, who would be the new manager and would Pete Reiser be fit to play a full season, if at all.

Reasonable people knew that Chandler was right, and there were many who agreed, but thought he should have acted sooner, that Durocher should have been banned after the bludgeoning of John Christian two years before. Chandler knew the trial had been a farce. He also knew things that didn't come out in the courtroom, the rumors, for instance, that Christian was held by Moore as Durocher blackjacked him. Baseball insiders knew this and that is one of the reasons Shirley Povich, and many others, wouldn't shed a tear for Durocher.

Amidst all this storm and stress Clint Hartung, the most ballyhooed rookie in the history of baseball, reported to the New York Giants training camp. He was 6 foot 5, 210 pounds and, coming from the Texas town of Hondo, he was soon called the Hondo Hurricane. And the numbers he brought to spring training, even though they were service ball numbers, were awesome: as a pitcher, 25 starts, 25 wins; as an outfielder, a .567 batting average with 30 home runs.

All during spring training the tabloids went wild over this kid day after day. He would be the next Babe Ruth, he could be the next Christy Mathewson, and on and on all through March and April. His home runs were measured, with the readers never reminded that this was spring training, that he wasn't facing pitchers like Pollett, Higbe or Raffensberger.

Hartung's problem was that he thought service ball was the equivalent of professional experience. As he was being discharged the Giants signed him for $35,000, intending to send him down to Minneapolis for seasoning. But young Clint, thinking he was too good for the minors, threatened to go back into the Army if they sent him down. The Giants went along with him, unmindful of that old baseball cliché "the flowers that bloom in the spring."

Hartung never did bloom in the summer. Over the next six years he played in 196 games, 122 of them as a pitcher. Over six seasons this "next Babe Ruth" hit .238 with 14 home runs, and this "Christy Mathewson" was 29 and 29 with a 5.02 ERA. Hondo thus turned out to be just another example of how on-the-job training seldom works on the major league level. Not everyone is an Al Kaline.

For Pete the spring looked promising after Dr. Hyland told him the operation was a success, that he would soon be throwing with power again. Durocher, however, decided to go easy with Pete by not playing him much during spring training, preferring to test rookies such as Ed Stevens. And, although the storm aroused by Rev. Powell's letter was still a week away, Leo had other things on his mind, mainly Jackie Robinson.

Even though Jackie was still with Montreal he was the main topic while both teams were playing exhibition games in Panama and Cuba. There was a survey in *The Sporting News* that showed Dodger reaction "mainly antagonistic."[15] Some players were apprehensive enough to circulate an anti–Robinson petition, even though Jackie was still not on the Dodger roster. Robinson had been the batting champion of the International League, hitting .349 with 40 stolen bases, so they had no doubts he would make the team, at least until he played himself onto the bench or back to Montreal.

The situation got so tense that a week into spring training coach Clyde Sukeforth reported to Durocher that an anti–Robinson petition was being circulated. Robinson wrote years later that the ringleaders were Casey, Bragan, Walker and Furillo.[16] Other sources had Stanky involved. Among the first who refused to sign were Reiser, Hodges, Snider and Barney, all of whom had befriended Robinson from the first day he arrived in camp.[17]

Durocher recalled that after Sukeforth's report he got out of bed and called a night meeting to stop the petition before it made the rounds and was presented to Rickey or some other official. The players arrived in pajamas or half dressed. "I hear some of you fellows don't want to play with Robinson and that you have a petition drawn up," he told them. "Well boys, you know what you can do with that petition. I'm the manager of this ball club and I'm interested in only one thing: winning. I'll play an elephant if he can do the job, and to make room for him I'll send my own brother home. This fellow is a great ballplayer. He's going to win pennants for us. He's going to put money in your pocket and mine."

Durocher then told them Robinson "is only the first," with many more right behind him—great athletes, hungry ballplayers. "Unless you fellows look out and wake up," he said, "they're going to run you right out of the ballpark. So I don't want to see your petition and I don't want to hear any more about it. The meeting is over. Go back to bed."[18]

It seemed to be over, but it wasn't quite. Higbe was the first of the petitioners to go. After he appeared in just four games he was traded to the Pirates, along with Behrman, Gene Mauch, Dixie Howell and Cal McClish for Al Gionfriddo and a sum *The Sporting News* of May 14 estimated at $200,000, although other sources put the figure at about $100,000. It was announced that Higbe went for "personal reasons" but everyone knew the truth.

"If I could have looked ahead and seen all the change that was coming," he said many years later, "I still think I would have done what I did. I was brought up a Southerner, and I was brought up to stand by what you said and believed in even if you were the last one standing there."[19]

Higbe's leaving didn't make much difference in the overall picture, for as Robinson signed his Dodger contract on April 11 his troubles were just beginning. The petition faded away but as the season started there were constant racial insults from other teams, and a threat from the St. Louis Cardinals that they would strike if he played.

The strike was averted after Cardinals owner Sam Breadon went to New York to warn Ford Frick, National League president, that the Cardinals would strike if Robinson were to play in an early May series at Sportsman's Park. The *Herald-Tribune* of May 9 reported that the strike was called off after Frick took a strong stand against it, telling the Cardinals that if they carried it through they would be suspended from the league and that his office would "go down the line with Robinson, no matter the consequences."

The instigators were never publicly identified. In fact, the great second baseman Red Schoendienst in later years denied the whole thing, saying there never was a reason for a strike and that he never heard mention of it.[20] Robinson, however, knew of the plot and credits *Herald-Tribune* sports editor Stanley Woodward for exposing it and averting what would be a "chain reaction throughout the baseball world, with players agreeing to unite to keep baseball white."

As the season went on little changed, but Robinson kept a promise he made to Rickey before he signed with the Dodgers: that he would keep his temper under control, no matter the provocation. Given Jackie's combative nature it must have been extremely difficult, but he stuck by it through the entire year.

It could never have been easy for him, especially since the most vicious attacks on him came from a most unlikely team—the Philadelphia Phillies, representatives of William Penn's "City of Brotherly Love." In his autobiography *I Never Had It Made* Robinson recalls the first game against the Phillies at Ebbets Field, saying it "brought me nearer to cracking up than I have ever been." It started with Ben Chapman, Phillies manager and Yankee center fielder of the 1930s. The hate language poured out of the Phillies dugout: "Hey nigger, why don't you go back to the cotton field where you belong." "They're waiting for you in the jungle, black boy." "We don't want you here nigger."

The abuse, Robinson knew, was being orchestrated by Chapman, a Southerner. "Perhaps I should have been inured to this kind of garbage,' he said, "but I was in New York City and unprepared to face the kind of barbarism from a northern team that I had come to associate with the Deep South."

Later that spring the Dodgers made their first trip to Shibe Park, where things got even worse. After an afternoon of continued racial taunts from the Phillies dugout, Robinson arrived at Philadelphia's Benjamin Franklin Hotel with his teammates and was refused a room.[21] This in *Philadelphia*, one of the main stations on the Civil War's Underground Railroad.

Jackie got a measure of revenge against the Phillies when he was told that because of all their racial taunts and insults, Chapman, object of a flood of negative publicity, was in danger of losing his job. Therefore, would he pose for a picture shaking hands with Chapman to quiet things down? At the urging of many, including the baseball commissioner, he consented, admitting later "having my picture taken with that man was one of the most difficult things I had to make myself do." There are varying accounts of this, some writers claiming that the handshake never took place. But in the next sentence Jackie writes: "There were times, after I had bowed to humiliations like shaking hands with Chapman when thoughts as to whether it was all worth while would seize me."[22]

There were times also during that early season when conditions went beyond taunts and insults—the time in Cincinnati, for example, when Jackie received death threats. As Duke Snider tells it: "Gene Hermanski had a unique suggestion in view of the death threats—give every player Jackie's number, 42, so anybody thinking of trying something wouldn't be able to tell which one of us was Jackie."[23]

Hermanski elaborated: "It was a Sunday game at Crosley Field and the park was jammed. Shotton came into the clubhouse and told us that a serious situation had developed, that Robinson had received death threats. He said there were FBI agents scattered all over the ballpark. I was worried. I liked and admired Jackie, especially for all he went through.

"After Shotton spoke there was a lull and I came up with this idea about Jackie's number for all of us. That broke up the room, relived the tension. We all relaxed a bit."[24]

All of the threats and abuse finally got to the rest of the Dodgers. Even Eddie Stanky, who had opposed Robinson's arrival, gave vocal support to his first baseman. Finally, during a game in Boston, Brooklyn Captain Pee Wee Reese signaled to the baseball world that the Dodgers were united behind Robinson, that the team had, in a sense, become color blind.

As Duke Snider remembered it: "Some of the Braves players began to heckle Pee Wee being a Southerner and playing ball with a Negro. Pee Wee didn't answer them or even look at them. He just walked over to Jackie and put his hand on his shoulder and began to talk to him. That shut the Braves right up.[25]

As Jackie recalled: "He put his hand on my shoulder and began talking to me. I don't even remember what he said. It was the gesture of comradeship and support that counted."[26] And it wasn't lost on anyone that Pee Wee was born and raised in Louisville, Kentucky. It was a magnificent gesture and it certainly helped Robinson maintain his composure as the race baiting and insults continued. Through it all he somehow kept his vow of silence no matter how maddening the provocation. Rickey had counted on this from the day Jackie first walked into this office.

That day didn't just happen by accident. It was, in fact, the end of a three-year Rickey search for the right man to break the color line, a search he referred to back in January of 1943 at the New York Athletic Club. He told a meeting there that it was possible that a "mass scouting might possibly come up with a Negro player or two."[27] Landis, you can be sure, was not pleased.

Rickey had come up with any number of possible candidates before Robinson, but all lacked something. Some too old, some too set in their ways, some too flighty and unsophisticated. It had to be someone with qualifications for success, for failure would have been a deadly blow to baseball integration. He finally made his choice known to Dan Dodson, an NYU professor who headed New York's Committee on Unity, a group that had been working toward integrating baseball.

At a meeting in his office Rickey told Dodson that he had spent more than $5,000 scouting black players. "I feel now that I have spotted the player most likely to succeed," Rickey said. "The player I have in mind is Jackie Robinson. He is college-educated. He is intelligent. He is playing in the Negro Leagues right now." Branch also knew that Jackie had been a second lieutenant in the Army and had starred in four sports at UCLA.[28]

The last hurdle was Robinson himself, to sound him out personally and then to judge whether the man matched the seemingly perfect background. In August of 1945 Dodger scout Clyde Sukeforth persuaded Robinson to take a leave from the Kansas City Monarchs and go to Brooklyn, with all expenses paid, to meet with Rickey.[29]

There were, of course, things that Rickey didn't know. That Jackie's childhood, for example, was far from perfect or that his early manhood wasn't all UCLA and California beaches. Things had turned tough early, just after Jackie's first birthday when his father deserted his mother for another woman. It was then Mallie Robinson decided to leave Cairo, Georgia, where Jackie was born on January 31, 1919, for sunny Pasadena.

Mallie worked as hard as she could, going out to do washing and ironing, but with four sons and a daughter to raise she couldn't make it without help from welfare, and even then, according to Jackie, she had a hard time keeping the family adequately fed.

"Sometimes there were only two meals a day," Jackie remembered, "and some days we wouldn't have eaten at all if it hadn't been for the leftovers my mother was able to bring home from the job. My mother got up before daylight to go to her job, and although she came home tired, she managed to give us the attention we needed."

Mallie's dream was schooling for her children and in Jackie she was doubly blessed, for her youngest not only had brains but was the best athlete in the area,* often earning his lunch at age eight by playing on teams where he was rewarded through shared sandwiches.

Multiple letters in high school and Pasadena Junior College led to the University of California at Los Angeles, where he became the university's first four-letter man, starring in basketball, baseball, football and track. He left the college after two years, however, convinced that no amount of education would help a black man get a job. UCLA literally begged him to stay, even offering financial support, but he was determined. Not even the pleading of fellow student Rachel Isum, the future Mrs. Robinson, could sway him.

Jackie wanted to play football but because of segregation the only job offer came from the Honolulu Bears where during the week he would work for a construction company near Pearl Harbor. He played through the season and headed back home.

*Athleticism ran in the family. Jackie's older brother Frank, a noted West Coast sprinter, finished second to Jesse Owens at the 1936 Berlin Olympics. He was killed in a motorcycle accident as a fairly young man.

A young and svelte Jackie Robinson on the athletic field at UCLA, where he became the first four-letter athlete in the school's history, starring in basketball, baseball, football and track. Despite pleas from university officials and his future wife, Jackie quit after two years because he felt "no amount of education would help a black man get a job."

"We saw the crew painting all the ships' windows black," he remembered. "The captain told us Pearl Harbor had been bombed. When I got home being drafted was an immediate possibility." Four months later he was at Fort Riley, Kansas, having passed the test for Officers' Candidate School. With the help of Joe Louis, also stationed at Fort Riley, he was admitted and was a second lieutenant by January of 1943.[30]

Jackie's first brush with trouble on racial grounds came when he was invited to play on the Fort Riley football team and then quit after the University of Missouri refused to play a team with a black player on it. He was ordered to play but persuaded the coach that his heart wouldn't be in it. He was soon transferred to Fort Hood in Texas.

A more serious problem arose when Jackie, an Army officer, ignored the driver's order that he sit in the back of a bus taking him back to Fort Hood. "I didn't even look at him," Jackie said. "I was aware that recently Joe Louis and Ray Robinson had refused to move to the back of buses in the South, with publicity that caused the Army to bar racial discrimination on any vehicle operating on an Army post."

Later, during an interview about the incident with one of the Fort Hood duty officers, Jackie refused to back down from his position and was ordered court-martialed. "My black brother officers wrote letters to the black press," he wrote in his autobiography. "The *Pittsburgh Courier,* then one of the country's most powerful weeklies, gave the matter important publicity."

Jackie was acquitted but, probably because of the court-martial, might have been seen as a potential trouble-maker and was subsequently given an honorable discharge in November 1944. "I guess someone was really anxious to get rid of me fast," he said.[31]

Rickey knew about the court-martial but didn't care, nor did he worry about reports that Jackie had been a racial agitator at UCLA. As Robinson entered his office for that first meeting and then sat across from Rickey, the Mahatma's first question was: "Have you got the guts to play the game no matter what happens?" Jackie said yes, of course, and Rickey continued, citing the troubles ahead.

"Branch Rickey had to make absolutely sure that I knew what I would face," Jackie recalled years later. "Beanballs would be thrown at me. I would be called the kind of name that would hurt and infuriate any man. I would be physically attacked." Then the second, and last, key question: "Could I take all this and control my temper, remain steadfastly loyal to our ultimate aim?"

"Mr. Rickey," I asked, "are you looking for a Negro who is afraid to fight back?"

"Robinson," he said, "I'm looking for a ballplayer with guts enough *not* to fight back."[32] Two months later, on October 25, 1945, Jackie reported to Montreal and signed what probably is the most historic contract in the history of sport.

Although never expressed publicly, there were mixed feelings among Negro League ballplayers about Jackie's signing. Hall of Famer Monte Irvin, who at that time was starring for the Newark Eagles, revealed them years later. "I was delighted," he told the writer Harvey Frommer, "but there was a certain amount of jealousy. I knew it would give us all a chance to make it, but there was a certain amount of envy that he had been picked. There were real stars in the Negro Leagues—Josh Gibson, Satchel Paige, Roy Campanella. But they said Branch Rickey wanted a guy with talent and a college education, able to express himself with the press and in other situations. Jackie was perfect for all this.

"And we knew that if Jackie made it there was a chance for all black athletes, not only in baseball, but for all other professional sports. We were truly for him one hundred per cent, but there was also a certain amount of jealousy."[33]

Irvin proved right, of course. As it became obvious that Jackie was going to make it, Larry Doby joined the Indians in early July and Dan Bankhead was bought by Brooklyn in late August.

As the Dodgers got deeper into spring, the anti–Robinson faction on the team seemed to relent, especially after Higbe was traded to Pittsburgh. Everybody seemed to quiet down, including Dixie Walker. There was even a widely circulated photo of Stanky with his arm on Jackie's shoulder on the steps of the dugout. But it was too late for both. By the time spring training came around Dixie had joined Higbe with the Pirates and Stanky went to the Boston Braves.

No doubt Durocher meant what he said to his players about Robinson, given his approach to winning. But it wasn't long before Leo was gone and Rickey was looking for a new manager. The *Times* ran a page one story on April 13 saying the Dodgers tried to lure Joe McCarthy out of retirement and when Joe refused went after Bill Terry. The paper questioned whether the man who asked if Brooklyn was still in the league in 1934 would be acceptable to Dodger fans. It became moot when Terry later declined.

The Brooks opened the season by beating the Braves 5 to 3. In a surprise move, Clyde Sukeforth, interim manager for two days, started Spider Jorgensen in place of Lavagetto, the first of his 128 games at third base that year. The next day Spider topped all hitters with six RBIs on a homer and two doubles in a 12 to 6 rout of the Braves. Johnny was off on his great .274 season.

Arthur Daley pointed out in his *Times* column of April 16 that the opener was the first game that the left and center field stands were extended out to make room for the 1,400 new box seats. He also quoted, anonymously, a Dodger veteran about Robinson's first game during which he had a bunt single in three times up. "We just don't know how to act with him. But he'll be accepted in time, you can be sure of that. Other sports have Negroes. Why not baseball?

In Brooklyn's opener at the Polo Grounds, a 9–4 loss, Burt Shotton took over the team. Shotton was 62 and started in the major leagues as an outfielder with the St. Louis Browns in 1909, hitting .270 over a 14-year career.

Speculation was that he'd be merely a fill-in for Durocher, especially when it was announced that he was working without a contract, that he didn't think one was necessary. Several things had been in his favor in getting the job: he had managed the Phillies for six years and the Reds for one and he was an old friend of Rickey. And Branch probably never forgot that it was Shotton who stepped in and broke up his fight with Hornsby back in 1923.

What proved to be a disturbing note later in the season was that he would be wearing civilian clothes at all times and thus not allowed on the field. It was generally agreed throughout the league that this was tough on Robinson, not having a Durocher-like manager to fight for him. During that rough first year Jackie was virtually alone out there. For the umpires, Magerkurth for example, it was a lot easier handling a delegate from Shotton than a raging Leo Durocher.

Burt never got the kind of respect the players had for Durocher, and not just because he seemed to be an interim manager only. There were lapses from the bench during his years, the most glaring one during the final 1950 game the Brooks lost to the Phillies, a loss that cost them the pennant.

Let Eddie Miksis tell it as he was asked about Abram's wide turn around third: "Abrams practically went into the dugout and got a drink of water [before heading for the plate]," Eddie said. "And that dumb son of a bitch Shotton. I'm the fastest man on the ballclub. He forgot I was on the bench and he let Abrams run."

When reminded that Richie was perfectly positioned, playing somewhat in for Snider's single, Eddie said: "I don't care where he was playing. He would never have thrown me out. Abrams was slow."[34]

The week after Shotton's arrival, on May 3, the Dodgers made the Higbe deal. It must have hurt Rickey to give him up, but the team had to have peace in the clubhouse and Kirby, unlike Walker and Stanky, never softened his position on Robinson. Still, it had to be a blow to lose a man who at only 31 the previous season was 17 and 8 with a 3.03 ERA in 42 appearances.

A few days later there was another Magerkurth show, this time without Durocher. It had been a good day for Brooklyn, blasting Mort Cooper off the mound in an 8 to 3 win. Although Coop's career was almost over it must have been satisfying, routing the man who had beaten them in so many crucial games over the years.

Maje blew up early in this one, clearing the Dodger bench—again—in the second inning when they started screaming over a called fourth ball instead of the strike Branca thought he had thrown to Cooper. When things quieted down only Shotton, coach Jake Pitler, trainer Doc Wendler, and the batboy were left in the dugout.

Two days later the Dodgers faced one of the most awesome righthanders in the game's history—Ewell Blackwell, 6 feet 6 and a stringy 195. Like Reiser, he was the best while he had it but he didn't have it long enough. Today the name Blackwell means nothing to those weren't around in the 1940s. But to those who go back far enough he is remembered as the most feared righthander of his era, Ewell "The Whip" Blackwell.

He came in sidearm, all 6½ feet of him, with what became known as his bullwhip curve. The best righthand hitters in the league bailed out game after game as the ball came whipping in from what seemed like third base, with the batter leaning away as it clipped the corner.

Let's look at his '47 season before the arm problems. And remember, those were the days before expansion, when each league had but eight teams. There were no clubs like the '62 expansion Mets and their 120 losses.

This was the year he was 22 and 8 with a 2.74 ERA as he led the league in strikeouts with 193. His mark of 16 straight wins is still the National League record, and at one point he came within two outs of equaling Johnny Vander Meer's two consecutive no hitters. On June 18 he no-hit the Braves and in his next start, against the Dodgers, he had another no hitter with one out in the ninth when Stanky got a single up the middle. And he did this with a team that never got out of the second division.

As they faced him on that May 15 the Dodgers did no better than most teams against him that year. He beat them on a six-hit shutout 2 to 0, with Joe Hatten the loser.

When the Brooks arrived at Pittsburgh two days later they got their first look at the "Greenberg Garden" and faced Higbe for the first time since they traded him. Branca beat Hig 3 to 1 in the opener, but the next day Hank put one into his "Garden" with one on to win the second game.

The "Garden" had been Greenberg's idea. When Hank was traded from the Tigers to the Pirates on January 18, his demands included more money and that a bullpen should be built in left field to shorten the distance. His salary went from $55,000 to $110,000 and the left field distance was reduced from 365 to 335. It didn't help Hank that much. He retired at the end of the season after hitting .249 with 25 home runs that brought his final homer total to 331, despite injuries and almost four years in the Army. His "Garden" later became "Kiner's Korner."

Back in New York, the Dodgers had a hitter's day in beating the Giants 14–2 at the Polo Grounds, as Edwards had the best day of his career with a two-run homer and a bases-clearing triple. With the win the Brooks took over first place for the first time.

The next week the Pirates came into Ebbets Field for a night game that saw the further disintegration of Pete Reiser as a major league star, and this time it wasn't his daring that did him in. Pete was chasing a line drive by Pirate outfielder Cully Rikard when he crashed into the center field wall and dropped to the grass unconscious. He may have thought he had more room than he had, apparently forgetting Rickey's new box seats in center field.

Gene Hermanski in 1949, a good year for him and the team. Gene came off the bench hitting, compiling a .288 batting average in his five years at Ebbets Field. Eddie Miksis claims the trade that sent him and Hermanski to the Cubs destroyed the locker room spirit that held the Dodgers together, causing the 1951 loss to the Giants.

The *Times'* McGowen saw Pete hit the wall as the ball "nestled into his up-flung glove, and miraculously stayed there for one of the most dramatic putouts in the game's history."[35]

The miraculous catch, as described by Gene Hermanski: "I'm playing left, Pete's playing center," Gene said. "Someone hits a shot to left center. His catch. I couldn't get it. He runs toward the wall, jumps up and kind of smothers the ball. He went down with the ball and hit his head on the concrete and was out cold. Boom. The ball was between his body and the wall—this is a true story—and I ran over to check on him. As I was waving in for a stretcher I slipped the ball into his glove with my right hand. The umpire runs out, checks, sees the ball in Pete's glove and calls the guy out. That was the last time he hit the wall. They padded it the following year because of that incident."[36]

Hermanski came up with the Dodgers after several years in the Coast Guard during the war and it seemed the team's perennial left field problem was solved. New Jerseyans loved him because he was from Newark, where he was All State for East Side High School. And the man could hit.

The *Daily News'* Dick Young thought his fielding was uncertain but it's likely that Young was unconsciously comparing him to Reiser and Furillo, unfair since they were two of the best ever. Brooklyn fans didn't see anything all that wrong with his fielding and loved his hitting. And he was known around Ebbets Field for his sense of humor and wit.

And again, the man could hit. Until he was traded to the Cubs in 1951 he averaged .288 over five seasons with Brooklyn. In the last three years before he left, his averages were .290, .299 and .298. That is not easy to do as a part-timer coming off the bench. In 1948, the one year he had virtually full-time status, he got to bat 400 times and hit .290 and led the team in homers with 15.

Reiser was taken to Swedish Hospital where an examination showed no fracture. In its report on his condition the *Brooklyn Eagle* chided Rickey for not giving Pete some protection out there in the outfield. "Either the wall should be rubberized or a gravel path constructed at the base of the stands," the paper editorialized. "He would feel the gravel under his feet and be warned that he was in the danger zone."[37] It was the first mention of things that were to come the following spring.

They followed it up the next day with a five-column headline: "Ponder Rubber Walls for Ebbets Field." The story made it obvious that the Dodger people had been giving the idea some thought, since they told the paper of a sponge-like rubber called Koylon, with the explanation that it would cost approximately $15,000 to complete the job.

These developments, important as they would prove to the future of the game, were virtually ignored by the rest of the metropolitan press. Even today there is no mention of them in books and articles about Rickey, including his biography, or even an "inside" autobiography such as Parrott's book, *The Lords of Baseball*. It wasn't until the padding was up that other papers followed the *Eagle*'s lead, and even then with only a paragraph or two.

With Duke Snider taking his place in center field, Pete spent the next 10 days in Swedish Hospital. He came back to the team on June 15 in St. Louis but didn't play in a double loss. "I still feel a little groggy," he told the *Times'* McGowen. From then on Pete suffered periodic headaches or dizzy spells for all of the baseball time left him.

While Reiser was laid up Blackwell pitched that memorable game against Brooklyn, going into the ninth inning trying to equal Johnny Vander Meer's double-no-hit feat. He was pitching in daylight, whereas Vander Meer's second no hitter was played under the lights at Ebbets Field, the first night game in Dodger history. Pete Coscarart played in that game and later recalled, "None of us had ever played under the lights before. We weren't used to them and they made a difference."[38]

Blackwell was pitching under a bright sun, the first game of a doubleheader at Crosley Field. He had his second straight no-hitter going with one out in the ninth inning when Stanky hit a pitch that "skittered between Blackwell's long legs into center field" for the game's first hit.

"I might have blocked it," Blackwell said in the clubhouse, "but the ball hugged the ground and I felt it touch the right knee of my pants as it went by." Jackie Robinson looped one into right for a second hit, but Blackwell then settled down to win 4–0, his 11th straight on his way to his National League record 16 wins in a row.[39]

The Dodgers left Cincinnati for Pittsburgh where they opened by beating Higbe again, with Jorgensen having another great game, driving in five runs. The medical news, however, was not good. Reiser would not be playing for another two weeks, Johns Hopkins neurologist Dr. James Arnold told the press, as he suggested that Pete go home to St. Louis for a total rest. The headaches and dizzy spells must have been extreme, else Pete never would have consented. He would not return to action until July 13.

It was now obvious that Pete was no longer the core of the team's offense. Without him they took over first place that week with a five-game winning streak, led by the nucleus of the team that would dominate the league for the next decade: Robinson, Hodges, Snider, Furillo, and Reese.

As July began, history was being made in the American League as Larry Doby was bought from the Newark Eagles by the Cleveland Indians, thus becoming the first black ballplayer in the league's 47-year history. Larry's debut, like Robinson's, was not auspicious. He got a rousing welcome from the more than 18,000 fans at Comiskey Park but went down swinging against White Sox righthander Earl Harrist as a pinch hitter with two men on. It was the start of a 13-year career that would lead to the Hall of Fame.

Bill Veeck said he received some 20,000 letters protesting his signing of Doby,[40] so from the start it was obvious that Larry would experience the same prejudice that greeted Robinson, though not so extreme. Robinson had gotten people somewhat used to having a black man on the major league level.

Doby, however, was much more his own man than Jackie had been, since he had obviously made no promises to Veeck or anyone else that he would keep himself under control. Veeck pointed out in *Veeck As in Wreck* that Larry would sometimes throw his bat at the mound after being knocked down and, in an action bordering on whining, would point to his hand after an umpire's call as if to say: "You called that on me because I'm colored."[41]

Before things settled down Cleveland was no different than Brook-lyn. Players who objected to Doby were sent elsewhere by Veeck. Then, once Tris Speaker converted Larry from second base to center field, the rest of the team realized, as the Dodgers had about Robinson, that this man Doby was going to put World Series money in their pockets. In Cleveland as in Brooklyn, money made men colorblind.

At All-Star time five Dodgers made the team: Stanky, Reese, Walker, Edwards, and Branca. Those were the days when the American League won almost every year and 1947 was no exception. It was 2–1, Spec Shea beating Johnny Sain.

With Reiser out, Furillo was leading the club and becoming the great outfielder everyone thought he would be, with an arm feared through-out the league. Robinson was also becoming a team leader, batting near .300 and a constant threat on the bases.

It was now mid–July and the Brooks got a jolt as the last-place Pirates beat them badly in a double-header at home 12–4 and 7–3. Outfielder Wally Westlake, Pete's old teammate in Elmira back in '39, had eight RBIs on the day, including a grand slam in the first game. Even with the double loss the Brooks had a 2½–game lead, but might have been look-ing over their shoulders as nemesis St. Louis was now just 4½ games away, finally starting to play up to the Musial, Slaughter, Moore level.

In their next home series they beat those Cardinals by 7–0 and 3–2, the second game a beauty. The Dodgers came up with three runs in the ninth with Miksis driving in the winning run on a single to right. The game was played under protest, however, when Cardinal manager Eddie Dyer argued that what he thought was a Ron Northey home run was ruled in play and Northey was thrown out at the plate by Stanky. The Brooks' first-place lead now seemed to be three games with the Cards 5½ out.

Not so. Five days later league president Ford Frick upheld Dyer's protest, ruling that the umpires admitted mishandling the play as Beans Reardon signaled home run, causing Northey to slow down, while Jocko Conlon ruled the ball in play, causing Ron to be thrown out. Frick ordered the game replayed August 8 at Ebbets Field.

Reiser missed the intervening Cincinnati series because of that old shoulder injury he suffered in the Army. It recurred when he hit the grass trying for a lunging catch of an inside-the-park homer by first baseman Babe Young. Miksis, filling in for him in left field, drove in the winning run for the second straight game as Brooklyn beat Cincinnati 5 to 2 in a single away game on the 23rd.

Eddie, who grew up in rural Burlington County, New Jersey, was 17 when he came up with the Dodgers in 1944 before he went into the Navy. He came back in mid–'46 and was with Brooklyn until traded to the Cubs in June of '51, a hard-nosed, tough, six-footer who was basically a second baseman but could play the outfield.

He never hit for average, just .236 over a 14-year career. But a man who hits in the .230s doesn't stick around for 14 seasons unless there's a lot more to his game. Eddie's assets, in addition to his fielding, were his versatility, durability, great speed, and delivering in the clutch more often than his average would indicate.

The Cub trade also involved Hermanski, Hatten, and Edwards for Andy Pafko, Rube Walker, Wayne Terwilliger, and Schmitz. Eddie said years later that it destroyed the "locker-room camaraderie" that held the Dodgers together, causing the 1951 loss to the Giants.[42] Who's to say he's wrong? No matter how well the Giants played, a 13½–game lead is a 13½–game lead, especially as late as August.

Home from Cincinnati, Brooklyn ran into a hitting slump for a few games, but their lead was

"Miksis'll fixus" was coined when Eddie returned to the Dodgers in 1946 after his discharge from the Navy. He scored the winning run when Lavagetto broke up Bevens' World Series no-hitter. Of Pete Reiser's daring outfield play, Eddie, who played with Reiser for three seasons, said as far as Pete was concerned the walls were never there.

still 3½ after Robinson laid down two bunt singles to start two five-run innings for a 10 to 5 win over the Braves. They were perfect illustrations of Robinson's "superlative bunting skill," Tommy Holmes wrote in the August 14 *Eagle*. "And in each case the effect was far greater than the intrinsic value of two one-base hits."

Robinson had come into his own by this time, frightening pitchers as he did for the next decade. "Robinson has the quality of upsetting the opposition," Holmes went on. "His antics on the basepaths, the ever-present threat that he will steal prevents the pitcher from devoting full concentration on the men who follow him at bat."

He didn't have to tell that to Jim Hearn or any of the other National League pitchers Jackie harassed right up through 1956 when his legs were 36 years old. He didn't steal much by that time but the threat was still there, a residue in the minds of those pitchers he had tormented season after season.

Carl Furillo stepped up the next day for a win against Warren Spahn, who was having the first of his many great years. A group of admirers had presented Carl with a Buick convertible before the game as Lombardi and Spahn were warming up* Lombardi pitched a four-hit shutout, beating Spahn 1 to 0. And who should drive in the winning run but Furillo, scoring Stanky from second in the eighth inning.

The following week Brooklyn got its second black ballplayer, the pitcher Dan Bankhead from the Memphis Red Sox of the Negro American League. Dan just didn't have it. Maybe it was the pressure of being the first black to pitch in the majors, or maybe he should have been given some time at Montreal, as was given Robinson. Whatever, Dan got really rocked in his first appearance. He started well, hitting a home run off a good pitcher, Fritz Ostermeuller, his first time up, but in relief of Hal Gregg he gave up 10 hits and six earned runs to the Pirates.

Dan never made it. In 14 appearances over three seasons he was 9 and 5 with a 6.52 ERA. The problem might have been his age. He was judged to have a good fast ball, curve, and control, but looked like he was up there in years. They gave out his age as 27, but he seemed a very old-looking 27.

The team took a chance on him because the pitching had gone bad. Joe Hatten was going through a wild spell and, worse, Harry Taylor went down with arm trouble. Bankhead seemed worth a look, since the rest of the league would never give Brooklyn a first-rank starting pitcher.

Brooklyn went into September up by seven, thanks to the bats of Jorgensen and Furillo. Spider drove in four runs with a double and single against Chicago for a 6 to 2 win. The next day Carl drove in the winning run in a 3 to 1 win over the Giants.

They had just rested Jorgensen for a week, so he had come off the bench rejuvenated. This was necessary, for he did not have the physique for a 154-game grind. He was 5 foot 9 and 155 pounds, small for a third baseman. In contrast, Lavagetto was 6 foot, 170, a size that enabled him, in his younger days, to play a full schedule, first as a second baseman and then at third.

Jorgy had sense enough to rest on occasion, but that year, even with the week off, his average, although a very decent .274, dipped at the end. "I kinda flopped out at the end there in '47," he said. "I just ran out of gas."[43]

As September began, Vic Lombardi, the "Giant Killer," shut out the

---

*This kind of craziness is always a puzzlement: everyday working people giving expensive gifts to athletes making 10 times as much money as any of them.

Giants 2 to 0 at the Polo Grounds to run his record to 11 and 1 against the Ottmen, as some New York writers called them.

His next time out Vic lost the kind of game that a team driving for a pennant must blot out, just as a golfer must forget that missed putt on the previous hole. Lombardi had a shutout going into the eighth, leading Chicago 3 to 0 at Wrigley Field. Then the unexpected, twice. First Pee Wee, one of the top shortstops in the league, messed up a double-play grounder trying to get rid of the ball before he had it, thus loading the bases. Then rookie Cliff Aberson, who had played halfback for the Green Bay Packers the previous fall and who lasted just 63 games in the majors, pinch hit for Johnny Schmitz and hit a grand slam for the ball game. With that loss the lead went down to 4½ as the Cards' Murray Dickson shut out the Phils.

Two days later, with the Braves at Forbes Field, Ralph Kiner hit four home runs in a doubleheader to tie Johnny Mize at 47 for the league lead, helped by the first game going 14 innings, with Higbe all the way for the win.

Kiner and Mize finished the year tied for the home run crown at 51. Ralph became only the fifth player in history to hit 50 in a season and Mize made it number six a few days later. Contrast that with today as the 70 level has been reached by Bonds and McGwire, aided by steroids.

Brooklyn left for St. Louis with that 4½–game lead and took two out of three, the series that Rickey later said won the pennant. They opened with a 4–3 win, with Robinson, Reese, and Lavagetto driving in the runs for Branca, relieved by Behrman.

The Cardinals won the second game 8–7 in another nightmare ending. The top of the ninth was joyous, the Dodgers scoring four runs to take a 7–6 lead. Then Hank Behrman weakened and left with two Cardinals on base.

In came Ralph Branca to face Enos Slaughter. With the count 3 and 2 Country blasted one over Reiser's head for a double, both runs scoring for an 8–7 Cardinal win. Slaughter against Branca in a clutch situation like that was no contest. The wonder of it is they kept giving this guy the ball in situations like that.★

The next game delighted Rickey, not only because the team could come back after such a loss, but because as the deciding game of the series it improved Brooklyn's lead to 5½ as they left town. Branch felt the lead was safe with only 13 Dodgers games left.

"It was a foregone conclusion that we would win once we whipped

---

★Like in October of 1951 with Dressen giving him the ball against Thomson in that game. In previous years Dressen had, on the record, called Branca a choke, the real reason Branca referred to him as "dreck."

St. Louis two out of three in St. Louis," he said later after the Brooks had clinched. Branch must have had some mixed feelings, for those Cardinals were once his boys, almost every one of them out of the farm system he had created.

Hatten now had his groove back and played the iron man role during a double-header in Cincinnati. He went the route in the first game for a 3 to 2 win and then relieved in the second, winning it also after pitching 5 scoreless innings to end it.

It was a great day for Joe, but not for a team going into a World Series to have one of its top pitchers go almost 15 innings in one day. But, as Rud Rennie of the *Herald-Tribune* wrote in his game story, the Dodgers were "ill equipped for pitchers" at the time, a quaint way of saying Taylor was down with a sore arm and Gregg and Behrman were not pitching well. To help, some now familiar names were called up from the minors that day: Banta, Erv Palica, Willard Ramsdell, and Johnny Van Cuyk.

That evening the Dodgers were seven games up with 11 to play while the Cardinals had 13 left. The champagne was being chilled at Ebbets Field, as all of Brooklyn was preparing to celebrate. There would be no repeat of '42 and '46.

The next two days were memorable for all of New York City. The Yankees clinched their 15th pennant when the Red Sox lost to Chicago up in Fenway and the Dodgers upped their lead to 8½ by beating the Pirates at Forbes Field. The Brooklyn lead was now insurmountable, with the magic number four for the pennant.

With the race virtually decided, Mel Ott caused a stir by announcing his retirement, ending a 22-year career that started when he was only 16 years old, another of those few phenomenal ballplayers who never played a day in the minors. He was called Master Melvin in those days, a kid from Gretna, Louisiana, playing big league ball while his friends were still in high school.

Mel was recommended to John McGraw by a friend, and afterward he tried out at the Polo Grounds. Casey Stengel, then managing the Giants' Toledo farm team, said he'd take him to Ohio for seasoning. But McGraw wouldn't trust the 16-year-old with anyone else, not even Casey Stengel.[44] Mel stayed with the Giants, thus starting his Hall of Fame career that included 511 home runs, a .304 lifetime batting average, and six years as manager of the Giants. Mel, at 49, was killed and his wife seriously injured in a head-on auto accident in the New Orleans area in 1958.

After losing to Warren Spahn in trying to close things out, the pennant was decided on the evening of September 23 when the Cardinals were eliminated by the Cubs 6–3 at Sportsman's Park. The club immediately began rounding up convertibles for the victory parade up Fulton Street. Meanwhile, throughout the borough impromptu street celebrations were starting, even though the news from St. Louis wasn't received until after midnight. Yankee fans, jaded by 15 pennants, did not do likewise.

Late as it was, Flatbush Avenue was soon jammed "with a huge mob that milled around going nowhere but having a wonderful time." The focal point was Hugh Casey's Bar and Grill where many of the Dodgers and their wives were awaiting the word. Then about a dozen of the Dodgers players, to the delight of the crowd, danced down Flatbush Avenue in a conga line.[45] Again, there was magic between the fans and that team.

The next day the Dodgers were photographed relaxing and singing in the clubhouse, led in song by Bobby Bragan at a piano wheeled in for the occasion. In an interview query about his piano playing, he said, "I only play chords."[46] Still, how many piano-playing catchers have there been down through the years?

As Brooklyn was preparing for its celebration, Durocher and Day arrived from Los Angeles to discuss with Rickey his return as Brooklyn manager. He was successful, for on December 6 he signed a one-year contract for 1948, an event that made the front page of the December 7 *Times,* above the fold.

The Brooklyn pennant celebration was much like 1941. More than 500,000 milled around Borough Hall, this time under a paper storm as the Dodgers' 17-car motorcade was slowly making its way from Grand Army Plaza to the hall. As usual in the Borough of Churches there was no mayhem, no car fires or serious injuries. In short, as in '41, none of the sickening displays of violence that pass for victory celebrations nowadays.

Baseball was getting set for its first televised World Series. In an agreement reached with TV representatives, two companies, Gillette Safety Razor and Ford, would pay $65,000 for joint sponsorship on video outlets along the Eastern seaboard. Liebmann Breweries of Brooklyn offered $100,000 but was turned down. Chandler told the press he reasoned that it would not look good for baseball to have the Series sponsored by a maker of alcoholic beverages. Of course it wasn't long before sponsorship was wide open to breweries that produced Knickerbocker, Rheingold, Ruppert, and Schaefer, and tobacco companies that sold Old Gold, Camels, and others. The Federal Communications Commission soon drew the line at actual drinking being portrayed during commercials, so broadcasters like Mel Allen would have a glass of beer alongside them during their spiels.

Branca started the first World Series game in Yankee Stadium and went four perfect innings, striking out five of the 12 batters he faced. Then, as Harold Burr of the *Brooklyn Eagle* wrote, the plate started moving around as Ralph came completely apart. DiMaggio beat out a hit to short, George McQuinn walked, and Billy Johnson was hit by a pitch to load the bases.

Johnny Lindell doubled into the left field corner, Branca walked Rizzuto to load the bases again, and after he threw two balls to Bobby Brown he was gone. Hank Behrman walked Brown to force in a run and Henrich hit one through the left side of the infield. The Yankees had five runs, all they needed for their 5 to 3 win. Branca was the loser and Frank (Spec) Shea the winner.

This Branca performance would not go away. Charley Dressen had been circumspect about his thoughts on Branca when he was a coach with the Dodgers, but now as a Yankee coach he obviously confided in James Dawson of the *Times* after the game, since Dawson wrote: "Coach Dressen doubtless anticipated what happened. He knew all about Branca from his coaching in Flatbush ... and he must have sensed what would happen to a pitcher who rattles so easily with a man on base."[47]

It became worse after the Series. Stan Baumgartner, writing in *The Sporting News*, speculated whether Branca's blowup would ruin him for all time. Then he added a crusher: "Did Charley Dressen prove to the baseball world that Branca can't take it; that he has rabbit ears; that when the chips are down he goes up?"[48]

It is no wonder that in future Branca would refer to Dressen as "dreck," Yiddish for garbage or trash. But Charley knew. A future mystery: why did Dressen as manager of the Dodgers give the ball to Branca in 1951 with Bobby Thomson coming up. Sukeforth later said Branca was the decision by default, since Erskine pitched the day before, and there was not enough time to tape Labine's ankles. Sukeforth therefore said Branca was ready, a decision that was to cost him his job, but Charley should have looked back into the past. Branca was never ready in that kind of situation.

All that is mostly forgotten now, as through the years Branca has become a celebrity, appearing at show business and other public functions with Bobby Thomson as part of their occasional baseball act. Celebrity through failure.

Game two was the worst game of Pete's major league career. He was staggering under fly balls as New York ran away in a 10 to 3 score. As the *Times'* John Drebinger wrote: "Pistol Pete, long Brooklyn's idol, had a particularly trying afternoon in center. He was staggered and practically floored by Johnson's towering smash that fell for a triple. Even more horrifying was a single Pete let slip though him for a two-base error."

Others wrote in the same vein, but Red Smith pointed out how sad it was to see "Reiser, one of the genuinely fine craftsmen and competitors of our time, wearing cap and bells. But if he was tragically comical, he had an adequate supporting cast. Hardly anyone in Brooklyn flannels missed an opportunity to contribute a wowser."[49]

No one alluded to Pete's dizzy spells, though all the writers knew about them. Pete had told them a number of times that he sometimes saw two fly balls coming at him. Roger Kahn in his book *The Era* writes that Pete was suffering attacks of vertigo before the game but told no one.[50] It was really worse than that.

Spider Jorgensen recalled that Pete's spells and headaches had struck him again before the Series. "He came back, he played in the World Series but he was punchy then," Jorgensen said. "Sometimes he would take aspirin almost by the handful. He shouldn't even have played, really. I don't know why he did."[51]

Game three was at Ebbets Field where the Brooks pulled one out, 9 to 8, with the day's only effective pitcher being Casey, who gave up just one hit in 2⅔ innings to get the win. Brooklyn's big RBI men were Edwards, Stanky, Furillo, and Jorgensen.

The Series ended for Reiser, except for one important at-bat, in the first inning when he sprained his ankle severely sliding into second base. The X-rays were negative but Dr. Harold Wendler said Pete would "play tomorrow only by some miracle."

Wendler was half right. Pete didn't take the field during the game, the ankle was obviously too painful for that. But he did pinch hit in the ninth inning and, in a daring move on the part of Bucky Harris, was intentionally passed, setting up one of the most glorious moments in Brooklyn Dodgers history.

Before the game Pete spent hours in the whirlpool, hoping to bring the ankle around. As he came into the dugout in the fourth inning Shotton asked him what was going on. "What are you doing here?" Burt asked. "You can't even stand on your feet." But he let him stay.[52]

Bill Bevens went inning after inning until he was deep into a no hitter, a sloppy no hitter since he gave up a run on two walks in the fifth, and going into the ninth had walked an average of one man an inning. Still, the world knew the Dodgers were hitless, as Red Barber announced a number of times as the game went on. He took a lot of criticism on this because he violated baseball's superstition that mentioning a no hitter would jinx the pitcher. Red ignored that silliness, saying that announcers are supposed to tell what's happening and that when there's a no hitter that's what's happening.

Bevens got the first out in the ninth when Edwards flied to Lindell. He then walked Furillo, but got the second out as Jorgensen fouled out to George McQuinn back of first. Shotton looked down the bench and said: "All right Pete." There's some controversy about how Pete got to the plate. Some accounts have him limping but others deny this, saying that Pete faked Bucky Harris into thinking there was nothing wrong with his ankle. Knowing how Pete played the game, it's entirely possible.

Eddie Miksis, watching Pete from the bench, insists that Harris didn't know Pete's ankle was bothering him. "He didn't know it," Eddie said. "They didn't realize he was hurt that bad."

You mean Reiser faked it and walked to the plate normally? he was asked.

"Yeah," Eddie replied. "He walked up there like he wasn't hurt at all. They put him on purposely and I went in to run for him."[53]

The film of the '47 Series doesn't show Pete walking to the plate. There is a shot of him running to first base after the intentional pass. There was a limp, but he didn't look seriously hurt.

Eddie Miksis seems most believable, since he was an eyewitness who was paying close attention, knowing that as the fastest man available, he would be running for Pete. As for the Harris quote, would he admit later that he had been duped?

Some of the following is from memory, with the rest taken from interviews and stories in *The Sporting News* of October 15, 1947, principally the detailed article on page 9 by *TSN*'s Roger Birtwill:

While Pete was going to the bat rack Shotton looked down the bench again and motioned to Al Gionfriddo, telling him to run for Furillo. Al was about 5 foot 6 and the joke around the league was that when Brooklyn traded Higbe to Pittsburgh for $100,000 and Gionfriddo, Al's duty was to "bring the $100,000 to Brooklyn in a satchel and then leave for Montreal." Well, he was small and he wasn't up there very long, but he was involved in two World Series events that have made his name more memorable, in the New York area at least, than some guys who were around 10 or 15 years.

With Gionfriddo on first Pete worked the count to 2 and 1. Then Shotton flashed a sign to third base coach Ray Blades who relayed it to Gionfriddo: *steal.*

"I started for second and slipped on the first step," Gionfriddo recalled. "I thought I was a dead duck. To make up for my slipping I didn't slide feet first. I made a headlong dive for the bag. But I still think any kind of a throw would have had me."

Bevens threw another ball to make the count 3 and 1 with two out. Bucky Harris then made one of the most unusual moves in Series history, the only time it's ever been done: he ordered Bevens to walk Pete, thus putting the winning run on base, a decision that has been second-guessed for decades now.

With Gionfriddo on second, Shotton sent Lavagetto up to pinch hit for Stanky and put Miksis in to run for Pete. Brooklyn now had two good runners on base, Gionfriddo, who could move, and Miksis, one of the fastest men in the game. Lavagetto at first thought he was to run for Pete.

"No, I want you to hit," Shotton said. "I want you to hit for Stanky."

Another seemingly daring move that wasn't. Burt was out of left-side pinch hitters, having used Arky Vaughn earlier. Harry was the best he had left, and even though this was his last year and his average was down to .261, Shotton felt he would at least make contact. Harry had struck out only 244 times out of 3,509 career at-bats.

Bevens got a swinging strike on his first pitch. The next was just where he wanted it, high and away, he said later. Cookie swung and the ball headed out to right field on a line, Tommy Henrich moving back.

Hugh Casey, Pee Wee Reese, Joe Hatten, Eddie Stanky and Dixie Walker (seated) share a brief moment of joy after the Dodgers beat the Yankees 8–6 in the sixth game to tie the 1947 World Series at Yankee Stadium. As usual, the joy didn't last, since the next day Joe Page gave up one hit in five relief innings in winning the seventh and deciding game.

"I ran to about eight feet from the wall," Henrich said. He then played the ball off the wall and it struck his chest, bouncing to the ground on his right side. By the time he got his throw off it was too late. Gionfriddo had scored and Miksis, with his great speed, crossed the plate ahead of the relay, photographed sliding joyously.

Harris defended his decision for the rest of his life, starting with interviews after the game. "I suppose some of you boys will question my judgment ... putting the winning run on," he said. "But I'd do it again tomorrow if I had to. The count is three-and-one and Reiser is a long-ball hitter. I'm not going to give him a chance to whack one over the fence."[54] He also asked the writers who they'd rather pitch to, Reiser or the next hitter, Stanky, adding that Reiser had already hit a home run in a World Series.

The move was debated for some time in the press and one of Bucky's most outspoken defenders was Babe Ruth. The following spring during a visit to the Dodgers' training camp in Florida the subject came up. "I would have done the same thing myself, and would do it every time under the same circumstances," Ruth said. "It is playing percentage to walk a home run hitter if he's the winning run. That's why I say Harris was right. You can't take a chance with dynamite, and Reiser was dynamite."[55]

Game five was all Spec Shea, Yankee righthander, who in his second win of the Series pitched a 2 to 1 four-hitter. The big moment in this pitching duel came in the ninth inning and involved Cookie Lavagetto, again.

The score was 2 to 1 with two outs. The tying run was on second when for the second consecutive day Shotton called on Lavagetto to tie it up. Again Shotton had no lefty to pinch hit, for Arky Vaughn had doubled for Behrman in the seventh. So, batting for Hugh Casey, Cookie worked the count full and then struck out. It was asking a lot but, with Cookie playing the last games of his career, the gods could have been kinder.

The sixth game was 8 to 6 Brooklyn, 27 hits, 38 men used. And it all came down to probably the best catch in Series history. It was the sixth inning and pitchers on both teams were getting cuffed around—Lombardi for the Brooks and, to everyone's surprise, the Yankees' Allie Reynolds and Joe Page were each battered for four runs. Page was hit for his four runs on four hits in one inning.

The Yanks were at bat in the sixth, down 8 to 5. There were two outs and Stirnweiss and Berra on base when DiMaggio stepped in. He hit a screamer to left field where Gionfriddo started tracking it. Al kept going back, back, back until he caught it at the 415 sign and then hit the bullpen gate.

Al saved the game; the Dodgers went on to win it 8 to 6. It was the last game of his brief major league career, the Dodgers having decided to release him at year's end. His problem was that he hit only .175 during that '47 season, far below the norm on that Dodger powerhouse. The wonder is that, after his sensational Series, no other team picked him up, since he was only 25.

DiMaggio, in an uncharacteristic graceless moment, downgraded the catch the next day as he was signing a photograph of the play. "Don't write this in the paper," he told a group of reporters, "but the truth is if he had been playing me right, he would have made it look easy."[56] Joe was obviously bitter about the catch. As he approached second base after the play he kicked the dirt emphatically, one of the few times in his career that he showed emotion on the field.

Game seven was atonement time for Joe Page, one day after being hammered. After starter Shea gave up two runs on four hits in just 1½ innings, Bevens pitched scoreless ball through the fourth. Page then came on and pitched five almost perfect innings—one hit and no runs to take the 5 to 2 win.

At year's end Dixie Walker was traded to Pittsburgh with Gregg and Lombardi for Preacher Roe, Billy Cox, and Gene Mauch. It must have pained Durocher as he took over the team again, for Dixie, along with Higbe, had been one of his stalwarts. But from the overall point of view it was one of the best trades ever, a great pitcher and the best fielding third baseman of his time for three men who didn't have much left.

Dixie's departure was inevitable, given his involvement with the anti–Robinson petition. But there was no bitterness in his leaving. It was understood that players like Walker and Higbe were unable to shed a lifetime of racial stereotyping, of being taught from childhood that people like Robinson were not their equals.

Dixie was even given a choice by Rickey: stay in the Dodgers family as manager of St. Paul, an excellent opportunity, or be traded to Pittsburgh. He said he loved the people of Brooklyn but he was leaving with no regrets.[57] He was 37 years old, had one good year and one mediocre year with Pittsburgh, then went home to Birmingham.

Walker and his fellow Southerners were slow to realize that something fundamental had happened to baseball. Durocher had warned them that Robinson was only the first Negro in the league, that he would be followed by "great athletes, hungry ballplayers" who would "run them out of the park" if they didn't accept the changes.

Some listened and some didn't.

9

1948: Rickey Pads the Walls

As he was reporting to spring training in 1948 Pete was making the mistake of his life, but it wasn't until years later that he admitted it.

Branch Rickey had decided to do everything he could to try to save his prize outfielder's career. His first move was one that seemed the ideal solution, that few ballplayers could have resisted: he asked Pete to take 1948 off at full pay so his injuries, particularly that constantly troublesome ankle, could heal.

Pete rejected all of Rickey's appeals. The Mahatma had all the logic on his side: Reiser was only 29, young enough for his body to heal over a year-long period. But logic wasn't enough to overcome Pete's decision, conscious or not, to play the game until he had nothing left.

Years later Pete ruefully recalled the offer. "That might be the one mistake I made," he told writer W.J. Heinz. "Maybe I should have rested that year."[1]

It turned out to be a mistake for him but it led to two brilliant innovations that, in time, all baseball would follow: in trying to save Pete's career, Rickey padded the walls at Ebbets Field and laid a warning track around the outfield perimeter. The decision was announced on March 13 and the work finished during the first week of April.

By today's standards, where outfielders bounce off walls that are practically cushioned, that first Ebbets Field padding was primitive: foam rubber an inch-and-a-quarter thick covered with waterproof duck canvas. But it was a brilliant concept.

"I think it's still possible for a man to be injured crashing into it," Rickey said in announcing the padding project, "but it undoubtedly offers some protection."[2] Branch lived to see the day when most parks adopted his ideas and to see how they changed the way outfielders play the walls, making catches that would be impossible without the padding and the track. Thus, as daring as they get, today you never see an outfielder carried off the field on a stretcher.

But, as good as the idea was with its promise of reduced injuries, it wasn't immediately adopted, baseball owners being what they are. Some, like Baltimore in 1954, were prompted by injuries. That year Memorial Stadium had bushes and wire fencing around the outfield. They padded the center field wall after Harvey Kuehn cut his face on the wire leaping for a home run ball. Later the rest of the outfield was padded after Curt Blefery injured his hip chasing a Max Alvis fly ball.[3]

During the 1975 World Series Fred Lynn, the Red Sox' prize rookie, lay on the outfield grass of Fenway for some five minutes after he was stunned and twisted an ankle chasing a drive by Ken Griffey. Lynn and the ball struck the concrete at the same time, each bouncing off. Owner Tom Yawkey then ordered that the walls be padded before the start of the 1976 season.[4]

The Cincinnati Reds were probably the last to pad their park, doing so for the 1992 season after coming under heavy criticism when Lenny Dykstra broke his collarbone crashing into the center field wall.[5]

Rickey was determined that that shouldn't happen to Reiser again. Even as the Ebbets Field walls were being padded he made one last try to keep Pete away from them. He sent him to Vero Beach to work out at first base and hired Hall of Famer George Sisler to teach him. The Mahatma also sent Duke Snider along for some hitting instruction, hoping that Sisler, a .340 lifetime lefthander, could teach Snider the strike zone to curb his undisciplined batting habits.

He certainly learned bat control, as shown by his Hall of Fame stats, but self-control was another matter. Duke had the ideal body for a slugger, 6 feet tall, 198 pounds. But inside there was a little boy who sulked too often after a bad at-bat, and never could realize that no one hits .500 and that everyone strikes out on occasion.

Many thought his problem was that everything came to him too early and too easily. Whatever he tried he excelled at—a 63-yard pass to win a high school football game in the closing moments, a no-hitter and 15 strikeouts in his first game as a pitcher, a leading scorer in basketball. Some young athletes never recover from such heady exploits, never gain the equilibrium needed for the inevitable knocks ahead.

Duke was scouted by the Dodgers while in high school in Los Angeles where Pete Rozelle, then a Long Beach sportswriter, was watching and so impressed that he wrote a letter to Branch Rickey urging him to keep an eye on this kid Snider.

Rickey, astute as usual, signed him and sent him to Newport News where he played for Jake Pitler before going into the Navy in 1944. He would be a Brooklyn Dodger for nine full seasons until the team left for

Los Angeles, where he never seemed to fit in and where, if his hitting is any indication, he must have missed Ebbets Field.

Maybe so, but while in Brooklyn for all those fabulous seasons he never seemed to appreciate the borough or its fans, never seemed to accept what all pro athletes must: the fans cheer when you're going good and boo when you're not. If he had looked to his left more often and taken a cue from steady and silent Carl Furillo he would have been a happier ballplayer. Or, to go into science fiction, if Dr. Frankenstein could have put Ben Hogan's head on Snider's shoulders Duke would have hit 900 home runs.

His worst and most childish moment during all those years came on August 26, 1955, when he was in a 27-game slump, his average

Duke Snider at the start of his career. The fans loved his power, his speed, and how he played center field in the smallest park in the majors. Duke never seemed quite happy in Ebbets Field, never was able to cope with booing when things got rough. He missed the little park, however, when he saw the right field distance in that ridiculous LA Coliseum.

dropping from .331 to .299. The fans, of course, were to blame, as he told the press after another hitless night.

"Brooklyn fans don't deserve a pennant," he ranted. "They're the worst fans anywhere." The next day he made it worse. "There are some good Brooklyn fans," he conceded, "but maybe there are more bad ones."[6] All this from a pampered star playing in the best baseball town in the country before fans legendary in their loyalty. That night he got three singles and was cheered.

To give him his due, he was a superb outfielder and a great hitter who could well have had his 500 home runs had it not been for that ridiculous Los Angeles Coliseum. And when he wasn't in one of his moods he was likeable enough, at times a man of good humor who could tell a joke on himself. He recalled later the time five Dodgers were in a car speeding through Prospect Park after a night game, Pee Wee at the wheel. They were pulled over, Pee Wee introduced himself and was let off with a warning.

The next night, Snider was at the wheel and speeding when he was stopped. "Hi officer," he began. "I'm Duke Snider and this is...." The officer cut him off with "I hate baseball."[7]

As Sisler was doing double duty, teaching Snider the strike zone and working with Reiser at first base, Rickey had Reiser and Robinson in mind when on March 6 he traded Stanky to Boston, thus clearing the way to move Jackie to second base, his natural position, and making room for Pete at first base. Stanky had been traded to the Braves for infielder-outfielder Bama Rowell and first baseman Ray Sanders and $40,000.

Eddie was blessed when it came to trades. He was with the Dodger pennant winners in '47, was traded to the Braves, who won in '48, and then went to the Giants and was on the '51 pennant winners. Then he went to the Cards, where he was named manager.

Before all this, as the players were preparing for spring training, two troublesome issues surfaced that had been simmering among the owners. The Mexican situation came up again for discussion by the National League owners, meeting in New York on January 30. They voted unanimously that the five-year ban on all jumpers should hold,[8] giving not even a moment's thought to the Gardella suit filed the previous fall. The structure of their baseball world was safe, for the time being.*

Three weeks later Rickey became a storm center when he stated that 15 of the major league clubs had, in effect, voted against his signing Jackie Robinson to play for the Montreal Royals. In doing so, Rickey said, they unanimously approved a report recommending that all Negroes be barred from playing in organized baseball.

Speaking at Ohio's all-black Wilberforce University, Rickey said copies of the report had been suppressed but "I was at the meeting where it was adopted" and that he would "like to see the color of the man's eyes who would deny it....

"I've had this Robinson story inside me for a couple of years," Rickey said, "and I've decided the time has come for me to tell just how I feel about this whole thing. The denial of equal opportunity to work to anyone is not understandable to me."

The eighteen players affected: Mickey Owen, Luis Olmo and Roland Gladu, Dodgers; Sal Maglie, Danny Gardella, Nap Reyes, Roy Zimmerman, Adrian Zabala, George Hausman, Ace Adams and Harry Feldman, Giants; Rene Monteagudo, Phillies; Max Lanier, Fred Martin and Lou Klein, Cardinals; Alex Carresquel, White Sox; Murray Franklin, Tigers, and Roberto Estalella, Athletics (The Sporting News, 2/11, p. 1).

Rickey, quoted as being shocked at the repercussions caused by his speech, softened his position the next day at a sportswriter's luncheon in New York by handing out a statement stating that the Negro question had been but a small part of a lengthy report and might well have been overlooked by many of the owners.[9]

But it was too late. The talk was drawing heavy fire, as a number of the owners denied Rickey's claim, siding with Larry MacPhail's public assertion that the Brooklyn president was "a liar." The report, MacPhail said, was withdrawn only because it included comments critical of Chandler, the newly appointed baseball commissioner.[10]

Chandler ignored the situation and it gradually went away. "Well," he said in dismissing it, "the Dodgers have Jackie Robinson, don't they?"[11] The logic there was irrefutable: the thing was done, the color line broken, so why go on wrangling about it? Chandler never should have let them call him by that clownish nickname Happy. Looking back, he was a far better man than he seemed at the time.

As the players reported for spring training in Cuba weight became a headline issue, with Robinson the main problem. After his rookie '47 season Jackie was in demand at dinners all over the place, and as a result he came to camp 25 pounds overweight and showed no signs of losing it.

Rickey kept quiet about the situation until May 2 when, after a Joe Hatten win over the Phils, he told the press that Robinson was 18 pounds overweight and Reiser "about 12 pounds too heavy. Without doubt," he said, "this detracts from the speed that is a prime asset of both players."[12] As events proved, Reiser paid attention, Robinson didn't.

Rickey said no more on the subject until he realized Robinson had paid no attention to his announcement. Then on May 26 Gus Steiger ran a copyrighted story in the *New York Mirror* saying that Rickey had put Robinson on waivers, giving the world the impression that he was about to trade him.

Rickey, Steiger wrote, had for some time been displeased with Robinson's condition and as the season went on became more and more emphatic about Jackie's reluctance to get down to his playing weight of about 190. Jackie, he felt, was sluggish and nowhere near the threat he had been on the bases the year before.[13]

Although Rickey was bluffing, it worked. He knew exactly what he was doing. He had 48 hours to remove Robinson from the waiver list, which is what he did. But Jackie obviously took it all very seriously. He got into shape, was assigned second base where he belonged, and finished the year at .296, 108 runs scored, and 22 stolen bases.

For some reason the Reiser experiment at first base didn't work. Leo apparently forgot that Pete came up as a shortstop, and that first base could be a different thing. Many think any clunker can play first, but if you ask a skilled first baseman, he'll say different. Some just never catch on to the footwork.

So Pete went back to center field for the start of his most miserable, and last, season as a Brooklyn Dodger. With Pete in the outfield and Jackie at second there were fill-ins at first base. Guys like Preston Ward played until Gil Hodges, a reserve catcher, was handed the first baseman's glove.

Gil started slowly. In 134 games that year he had 481 at-bats for a .249 average and just 11 home runs. But it was a genius move. In his 18 years Gil had totals that many Hall of Famers do not, plus he was one of the most graceful and skilled first baseman who ever played the position.

Gil was behind the plate with Ward playing first as the Dodgers opened the season at the Polo Grounds with a 7 to 6 win by a patched up lineup: Vaughn in left, Whitman in right, Campanella replacing Hodges for a couple of innings. Roy had been brought up from Montreal on March 30 but was sent to St. Paul without explanation by the club on May 17. That same evening Snider was ordered to Montreal where, it was hoped, he would practice what Sisler taught him about the strike.

Pete's ankle forced him to sit again. On the advice of Dr. Hyland he started X-ray treatments for a calcium chip at the site of the break. He would be out a total of six weeks under Hyland's care in St. Louis, and would not be ready to play again until June 27.

With Reiser out and four other players injured, Durocher was becoming testy with his third-place, patched up lineup. He also wasn't happy about fans chanting "We want Shotton" at Ebbets Field, nor with a newspaper poll that favored the rehiring of Shotton by a wide margin.[14] Idolatry gone, Brooklyn was obviously onto the real Durocher. He exploded as usual, this time taking on the newspaper with the largest circulation in the country when he barred sportswriter Dick Young of the *New York Daily News* from the Dodgers clubhouse for "creating discontent" among his players.[15] Young was brash, opinionated, and a fighter, like Durocher. But he did his fighting with a typewriter, not a blackjack.

He was also one of the great sportswriters of his time, year after year coming up with "inside" stories and great leads. One such lead ranks among the best ever written. Covering the Dodgers in 1956 when they played a number of regular-season games in Jersey City's Roosevelt Stadium, Young began the first game story: "Inching their way westward...."[16] He knew, when most of us didn't, that O'Malley was about to leave his native city because, according to Young, O'Malley told him the Brooklyn area was getting "full of blacks and spics and Jews."[17]

The News defended Young vigorously, calling his work "honest reporting" and adding "he isn't managing the Dodgers, just reporting Dodger doings and observing the discontent, not engineering it."[18] The paper maintained its stand and the clubhouse ban was eventually lifted.

At about this time Rex Barney was starting to look like the great pitcher everyone thought he would be. He was 24 years old, with one of the scariest fastballs of all time—scary because during most of his career he didn't know where it was going. But '48 looked like his coming around year.

On May 17 Spahn beat him 1 to 0, with Rex giving up just three walks and five hits in eight innings. Later in the year, on a misty night in September, he pitched a tight 2 to 0 no hitter against the Giants and finished the season at 15 and 13 with a 3.10 ERA. But the next year the strike zone deserted him forever and no one, psychiatrists included, could figure out why.

Rex had a good life after baseball, though, as a broadcaster for the Baltimore Orioles from 1970 until his death in 1997 at age 72 of a heart attack. What could have served as his baseball epitaph was written many years earlier by Bob Cooke, sportswriter for the *Herald-Tribune*: "Barney pitched as though the plate were high and outside."[19] Often true, and clever, but oh so sad.

That 1 to 0 loss was part of an eight-game losing streak marked by deplorable pitching as starter Harry Taylor and reliever Hugh Casey went down, Harry with an appendectomy and Hugh from an injured back—he slipped walking down the stairs in his home.

With all the other injured, Jorgensen being the latest, the Dodgers were worried about Bruce Edwards' now chronically sore arm. He left for Baltimore's Johns Hopkins Hospital on May 26 for a consultation and possible treatment.[20] Jorgensen's arm was also sore but the Dodgers thought it was just temporary. It wasn't long before it became clear that the arm troubles would shorten the careers of both, two fine ballplayers short on luck.

By late June the team was nine games out and the fans were unhappy. They were a generation not used to losing, with memories that did not go back to the miseries of the '20s and '30s. They were accustomed to being contenders, to '41, '42, '46, and '47, so their calls for Burt Shotton's return continued.

July began with Campanella coming back from St. Paul, and the purchase of George Shuba from Mobile, where they sent Preston Ward the same day. The nucleus of the Dodger powerhouses of the 1950s was now forming as Campanella joined Hodges, Reese, Furillo, Cox, and Robinson, with Snider to come back up for good before season's end.

The Dodgers, though in last place 10 games out, celebrated the 4th of July with a rousing 13 to 12 win over the Giants, rousing because of the way they won. A total of 37 men played and most of them had a great time knocking pitchers around. For the Brooks, Branca, Taylor, Minner, Ramsdell, and Behrman gave up the 12 runs, with the Giants coming up with four in the top of the ninth off Branca before being stopped by Erv Palica. The Dodgers came up down by three, and then down by one when Campanella hit one with Hodges on. Whitman got a pinch single, was doubled to third by Reese, and then Reiser, pinch hitting for Palica, singled both home for the 13 to 12 win. Again, rousing.

It was during this period Los Angeles officials came sniffing east, looking for a team to steal. They concentrated on the St. Louis Browns to the extent that they had owner Richard C. Muckerman warning the fans that if attendance didn't improve he might move west.[21]

Led by Los Angeles County Supervisor Leonard Roach, an apt name for a scavenger, the L.A. people also approached Phil Wrigley, owner of the Chicago Cubs and the Los Angeles minor league club. Roach had with him plans that would make the Los Angeles Coliseum the largest ballpark in the world.*[22] Sadly for Brooklyn, Wrigley turned Roach down.

That same week a baseball legend, Leroy (Satchel) Paige, joined the major leagues, signing with the Cleveland Indians. Taking a cue from Jack Benny, Paige announced his age as 39, but two weeks later his mother told the *Associated Press* that he was 44, that he "changed his age when he left to play in Chattanooga back in 1927, but he's really 44."[23] Whatever, we'll never know how really great this superstar of the Negro leagues would have been in the majors had he come up years earlier.

In mid–July the unbelievable happened: Mel Ott quit as Giants manager and was replaced by Leo Durocher—Leo going over to the hated Giants in a move that made page one of the *Times*. Looking back, it was inevitable. Leo was trouble enough when he was winning, but now the club was under .500 at 37 and 38, so Rickey and O'Malley decided he just wasn't worth the trouble anymore.

The day after he took over the Giants job Durocher revealed that Rickey had asked him to resign July 4 and that he refused, even though he realized he was on his last legs and fading out of the picture in Brooklyn.

"Harold Parrott came to me in the dressing room [in Philadelphia]," Durocher told newsmen, "and he told me the boss wanted me to resign. I said I wouldn't resign. They'd have to fire me. That's the last I heard

---

When they were successful in bribing O'Malley to go west they did indeed make the coliseum the largest ballpark in the country—and the worst. And the fans were no better, so ignorant they thought Wally Moon's disgraceful "Moonshots" 251 feet to left were something to cheer about.

of it until they told me Rickey wanted me in New York. It turned out Stoneham wanted to offer me the job managing the Giants."[24]

Why Stoneham would hire such constant turmoil and trouble is only understandable when you consider that on three or four drinks Horace would do anything, like move his team west at O'Malley's behest, or hire a Leo Durocher. And Stoneham could really drink. As Durocher once wrote: "To say that Horace can drink is like saying Sinatra can sing." And when drunk, Leo added, "he can become unmanageable.[25]

The main reason for the Durocher switch was that Dodger management felt Leo was no longer worth the constant trouble he caused. This was elaborated on by Dan Daniel in a story written for *The Sporting News.*

He said not only was the Dodger management tired of Durocher, but so were the people of Brooklyn.[26] All the scandals had caught up with him—the banishment, the John Christian blackjacking, his disgraceful marriage, and his questionable friends. It got to be too much.

Finally there were the fans. The constant boos proved they had finally wised up to this guy, onto him to the point where attendance was dropping, much to Rickey's alarm. It was time to start planning for 1949 and, since the current season seemed lost, why not bring Shotton back and at least have a contented team, fans looking forward, and the Catholic heirarchy of Brooklyn happy to see, as their Irish priests would say, the back of Leo Durocher.

So Rickey, hearing the shouts of the fans, brought Shotton back to manage the team he had led to the pennant the year before. It was a different team this time, actually a team in transition, with veterans like Walker and Stanky gone and the team of the future forming: Robinson, Cox, Snider, Hodges, Campanella, Roe, and Erskine. The outfield of Walker, Furillo, and Reiser became Hermanski, Furillo, and, temporarily, Marv Rackley.

Burt soon realized that Reiser was no longer the player he had been even the year before. When he took over this second time Pete was being used only as a pinch hitter, mainly because his throwing arm was gone again and didn't seem to be coming around.

From this point on Pete was a part-time outfielder for the rest of the season, or what was left of his career. During the next week he sat out doubleheaders in St. Louis and Chicago and, unlike past years, the writers didn't even take notice, not in print at least. Time was when it was a big deal if he sat out a single inning. The injuries were now old news, his absences taken almost for granted.

Rickey brought up Carl Erskine this same week, replacing Harry Taylor, who was sent down to St. Paul on one day's notice in hopes he could work out his arm troubles. Erskine, small for a fastballer at 5 foot

10 and 165, was one of the gutsiest pitchers ever to pitch for Brooklyn, or any other team.*

He was a Dodger 12 seasons and won 122 games against 78 losses, often in pain because of a sore arm that plagued him his entire career. Imagine pitching all those years, under all that pressure in that small ballpark, with a chronically sore arm.

"I pulled a muscle in my shoulder in my first start, pitching in the rain," he wrote in answer to a series of questions. "It dogged me for the next 12 seasons."[27] This, in what he considered the smallest park in the league. "It had very little foul territory and was a tough park to pitch in."

As to Pete, he knew him for the one year they played together and recalled the dizzy spells and, like Jorgensen, remembered him taking aspirin by what seemed like the handful.

Erskine recalled a sad incident in 1951 when Pete was with Pittsburgh near the end of his career, still plagued by the dizzy spells that finally drove him out of baseball. "He doubled off me one afternoon and slid into second. He got up so dizzy and disoriented he had to be helped off the field."[28]

Carl joined the club in Chicago where, the day before, the mystery of Johnny Schmitz' mastery over Brooklyn continued. In Roscoe McGowen's words, he was "hit hard" in a 10 to 3 win. To McGowen, he was "the Cub southpaw the Dodgers seem unable to beat."

Johnny was 93 and 114 in thirteen seasons, a really fine record considering that his Cubs were usually in last place or near it. Of those 98 wins, 18 were against the Dodgers—almost 20 percent of his wins against a club that ate up lefthanders. Finally, Rickey traded for him in '51 but then passed him on to the Yankees after 10 appearances. During the previous four seasons he had pitched 1,073 innings, apparently too much, for after Chicago he was never the same.

As the Dodgers were settling down under their quiet manager, one of Jackie Robinson's principal tormentors was fired. Bob Carpenter, owner of the Phillies, dismissed manager Ben Chapman as the team dropped to seventh place.[29] The parting, they announced, was amicable and necessary.

On the day Durocher took the Giants job Carpenter announced that a change might help his team. But he fooled no one. The bad publicity from Chapman's treatment of Robinson was still dogging him and the team, and not even the public handshake with Robinson could keep him afloat any longer.

For example, in the '52 World Series, game 5, Carl breezed through the first four innings and was up 4–0 when the Yankees scored five runs in the fifth. He hung on and retired the next 19 batters and was the winner in the 11th innning. Many pitchers would have lost heart after those five Yankee runs, but Erskine was a battler.

The fans of New York, in particular, never forgave him. And not only Brooklyn fans but those at the Stadium as well. They remembered how his bigotry was so offensive that the Yankees finally shipped him to Washington. As Dan Parker wrote in the *New York Mirror,* Chapman "was frequently involved in unpleasant incidents with fans who charged him with shouting anti–Semitic remarks at them from the ballfield."[30] The Stadium, remember, is in the heart of the Bronx, at that time heavily Jewish.

Besides, Ben was doing a lousy job. His seventh-place team had the nucleus of the 1950 Whiz Kids—Robin Roberts, Curt Simmons, Richie Ashburn, Dick Sisler, and Del Ennis, among others. They moved up a notch to sixth place after Eddie Sawyer took over.

Brooklyn, of all teams not sorry to see Chapman go, returned home on July 26 to face Leo Durocher in his first trip to Ebbets Field as manager of the Giants. It was circus time all day along Bedford Avenue, McKeever Place, Montgomery Street, and Sullivan Place. At eight in the morning, almost 13 hours before game time, ticket lines first appeared and eventually were more than three blocks long. Although the crowd was orderly, there were more than 60 policemen on hand just in case.

The umpires were ordered to warn Durocher against any of his usual outbursts but Leo replied: "I'll manage my club the same as always." In the Brooklyn dugout there was nothing to fear from Shotton. It was all anti-climactic, however; the Brooklyn boos were silenced by the sixth inning with the Giants nine runs ahead in a runaway.[31]

That same day, July 27, 1948, saw the release of the worst baseball movie ever made—possibly the worst *movie* ever made. *The Babe Ruth Story* is one of those you had to see to realize how truly awful it was, how Hollywood writers are shameless and careless in their approach to baseball.*

William Bendix was ludicrous as The Babe, playing the role, in the *Times'* film critic Bosley Crowther's words, "as a mawkish, noble-spirited buffoon," who we are to believe was fined $5,000 for missing a game because "he was preoccupied in taking an injured dog to the hospital."[32] One of the two screenwriters was the famous columnist Bob Considine, who thereafter should have had trouble holding up his head among his peers.

On the last day of the month, Lou Brissie, whose life should have been filmed but wasn't, won his 11th game of the year for the Athletics on a leg that was almost blown off by German artillery on the Italian front

---

Example: In Field of Dreams, *Joe Jackson, the second best left-handed hitter who ever lived, bats right-handed. Shoeless Joe hit .356 lifetime, second only to Cobb's .367. Hornsby, at .358, hit right-handed.*

in December of 1944. As inspiring as Monte Stratton's struggle was, as filmed with Jimmy Stewart and June Allyson, Brissie's was more so. Lou was Monte with a happier ending.

Stratton, a star with the White Sox, blew his right leg off in a hunting accident in 1938 and never pitched in the major leagues again. He had come back to pitch Class B ball but, with his mobility limited and fastball gone, he agreed to retire when MGM contracted to film his life story. Unlike the Babe Ruth movie, *The Stratton Story* not only made money, but earned writer Douglas Morrow an Academy Award for the best original screenplay of 1949.[33]

Brissie's shattered leg required 23 operations and finally had to be reconstructed with wire, but he came back to make the Athletics staff in '48 and was 14 and 10 for the fourth-place Athletics. Lou lasted seven years with a final 44–48 record on that injured leg, his career shortened by the osteomylitis that he could keep under control only through doses of antibiotics. Even at this late date, with Brissie now 79, his story in the right hands would make an inspiring movie. The ingredients are there: the war, a Bronze Star and two Purple Hearts, the major leagues, and a man who overcame almost impossible odds to achieve his lifelong goal.[34]

The Dodgers ended July in third place, 6½ games out with a team loaded with outfielders. Furillo, Rackley, and Hermanski were backed up by Snider, Dick Whitman, and George Shuba. George was becoming a fan favorite for no apparent reason. He was featured in Kahn's *Boys of Summer*, where his hitting skills were greatly overstated, calling to question whether he really belonged in that wonderful book. Was he really one of the boys of summer?

He was a part-timer, with the team six years for a total of 355 games, which averages out to 59 a season. He was called "Shotgun," a name from the minor leagues where he was a good hitter. But, possibly because of a bad knee, he didn't bring anywhere near the same bat to Brooklyn. "Shotgun," though nicely alliterative with Shuba, seems an exaggerated nickname for a man who hit only .259 in his six seasons, with but 24 home runs. His fielding was uncertain and his arm questionable, even for a left fielder. But for some reason, and it wasn't his personality, the fans took to him.

Reiser aside, the rest of the team was playing good ball under Shotton, with Hermanski on a hot streak during which he hit three homers in one game against the Cubs. On August 10 they took over second place from the Cardinals on the strength of Barney's complete-game win over Philadelphia, a five-hitter with but one walk. At one point, from the first to the sixth inning, Rex retired 16 consecutive batters. His troubles seemed past, especially during his next outing when he shut out the Phils 1–0, giving up just three walks and, in a "blaze of impressive pitching," struck out the side in the ninth. Again, where did it all go?

On the 16th Babe Ruth died after a prolonged death watch, during which The Babe faded almost by the day, his voice becoming a rasping whisper from the throat cancer that finally killed him. After such a roisterous life, Ruth's death was one you only read about. At his side were his family and the Rev. Thomas Kaufman of Providence College, who blessed him just before he died, and said later: "The Babe died a beautiful death. He said his prayers and lapsed into a sleep. He died in his sleep."[35]

He deserved that peace because he went through an unsuccessful operation and suffered for months, even though on morphine, until a new drug improved his condition before the final relapse. According to the *Times*, Ruth never knew he had cancer; Bill Laurence wrote that it was one of the "best kept secrets of modern times."[36] Hard to believe, but there it is among all the news that's fit to print.

As the month was closing out, the Dodgers were making a run for first place. The club had made a dramatic turnabout. When Durocher left in mid–July their record was 37 and 38, one game below .500. In the six weeks under Shotton they were 31 and 15, proving that sometimes bombast and turmoil work and sometimes they don't.

On September 2 Brooklyn went into first place by a half game, beating Johnny Schmitz for a change, routing him with five hits and five runs in the first three innings. But that was it for the year, as a combination of slumps and bad pitching did them in.

Four straight losses, to the Giants and Braves, started the slide. Besides the pitching, a major factor was a horrendous slump by Reese— two hits in 47 times at bat. At the time the team couldn't survive this. Pee Wee hit .274 that season and had become the best leadoff man in baseball. Even with that kind of slump he still scored 96 runs. Without him the attack came to a virtual standstill.

During the "Great Reese Drought," as it was known in Brooklyn, the team lost eight out of 10 games, and the slump spread.[37] The Braves took the lead for good on September 6 when the Dodgers scored just one run in 21 innings against Warren Spahn and Johnny Sain, later famous as the "Spahn and Sain and pray for rain" duo.*

The double loss to the Giants on the 11th killed any chance the Brooks might still have had, a heartbreaking doubleheader for a team that had made a terrific run at the Braves for more than two months. This was a team that was in last place on July 2, halfway through the season. But the chase was over. Hatten lost the first 2–1 after pitching into the

---

Fan refrain for the Braves from the 1948 World Series when the Braves lacked pitching depth as they went up against a Cleveland staff among the best in history. It didn't rain. Cleveland won 4 games to 2.

13th inning and giving up just one run. He weakened then, loaded the bases, and walked in the winning run.

The second game was even worse. The Dodgers were leading 4–3 in the sixth inning when infielder Bobby Rhawn, just up from Minneapolis, hit a three-run homer at 7:15 P.M. as it was getting dark. Because of the Sunday blue laws then in effect, umpires Scotty Robb and Babe Pinelli were unable to order the lights on so that the game could be completed. Thus Brooklyn lost 6–4 in six innings.

There was just one bright spot amidst all this: Rex Barney's 2–0 no hitter at the Polo Grounds. It was played in mist and then rain, at which point Red Barber started predicting that the game would be called if the Giants got a hit. The no hitter, however, didn't help. Brooklyn left the park 3½ games behind the Cardinals and never made it up.

Four days later Pete started at third base as Shotton was looking for a spot for him where the walls wouldn't pose a danger. He knew that Pete had been an infielder when he came up, and at the time Billy wasn't yet recognized as the great Cox, and Spider's arm was hurting.

It didn't work. Pete became dizzy whenever he looked up for a ball in the air[38] so Shotton turned to Tommy Brown the next day, continuing the constant third base shuffling. The *Eagle,* in an analysis story on Brooklyn's prospects for the next year, pointed out that they hadn't had a permanent third baseman all during 1948, that after Spider Jorgensen's arm went dead eight other men played the position at one time or another, including Billy Cox.[39] Shotton hadn't yet realized that Billy was a better third baseman than he was a shortstop, that he had at hand one of the best third baseman of all time.

The Brooks wound up in third place, one-half game behind the Cardinals when on the last day of the season they lost to the Phillies 4 to 2. Pete's last at-bat as a Dodger was as a pinch hitter and he was struck out by bonus baby Curt Simmons.[40]

When the season and the World Series were over, with the Cleveland pitching staff too much even for Spahn and Sain, Rickey had to decide what to do with Pete, whether to risk trading him or keep hoping he'd recover physically. The Mahatma was afraid of the second guess: if he traded Pete and he recovered his health, Rickey knew the fans would call for his head.[41] As it was, they were unhappy with the team, as shown by the year's attendance figures: just under 1,300,000, down 400,000 from 1947.

Pete himself helped solve Rickey's dilemma. Toward the end of the season, embittered because of his diminished role on the team, Pete inexplicably "seemed to form a strong dislike for his employers," John Drebinger reported in the *Times,* and went so far as to vow "he would never play in a Dodger uniform again."[42]

One can sympathize with Rickey here. Trading Pete was really his only alternative and he, in turn, had a right to be bitter. He had done everything he could to save Pete's career, and paid him star money while hoping he would recover.

You can hear the Mahatma saying: Pete's ailments are of his own making, but even so we did all we could—the best salary of his career when he was a part-timer, padded the walls and laid down the warning track, and even offered him a year off at full pay so that he could recover from his injuries.

Given all that, the inevitable happened on December 15 when Pete was traded to the Boston Braves for outfielder Mike McCormick and a player to be named later.[43]

Thus Pistol Pete Reiser left the borough where he had really been three Pete Reisers: the 22-year-old budding superstar of 1941, the Reiser of the mid–1940s who squandered his gifts against the walls of Sportsman's Park and Ebbets Field, and the hurt, struggling, and finally bitter man who left for Boston.

Bitter? That, too, is understandable if he was remembering that as a young man of 23 the organization, from MacPhail on down to Durocher, failed to protect him. He could have been thinking that they should have brought him in from center field to third base, away from the walls.

But as a grown man of 29 he should have realized that he himself was responsible for most of his troubles, that he, for example, at age 28 should have accepted Rickey's offer to sit out 1948 at full pay, that at that age he should never have played while injured. He admitted again after the trade that he cost Brooklyn the '42 and '46 pennants because he would not sit down.[44] He played hurt at 27 and 28 because he wanted to, not because Durocher was some kind of Svenghali. Why else would he refuse to sit out 1948 at full pay?

After he was traded he told Ray Gillespie of *The Sporting News* that part of his troubles with management were because "he was permitted to play" when he should have been resting in a dispensary, that he "hurt the ballclub" by playing while injured.

"And all this," he said, "led to a very unhappy state of affairs between me and the Brooklyn front office."[45] But again, it's one thing to play hurt at 23, when after hitting the wall in St. Louis he saw "two balls" coming at him while batting. It's quite another to do so at 28 and 29. There's a question of maturity involved here.

The thought that he should have gotten psychiatric counseling at some point seems beyond questioning. Once he hit that first wall in mid–1942 some one should have realized that in his intensity, his fearlessness, he could not control himself out there. "The walls were never there for Pete," was Eddie Miksis' explanation. And that was the real problem. Not the manager, not the front office, but Pete himself.

10

1949: Jackie Robinson, Batting Champion

As the 1949 spring training season was starting, Branch Rickey decided to take the wraps off Jackie Robinson by freeing him from his vows of silence and pacifism. Jackie immediately served notice that he would no longer turn the other cheek as he had been doing through two tough and wearing seasons.

On the first day in Florida he told a sportswriter: "They better be rough on me this year because I'm going to be rough on them." The quote got him called before Commissioner Chandler for an explanation.

"I told him exactly how I felt, that while I had no intention of creating problems, I was no longer going to turn my cheek to insults," Jackie said in his autobiography. "Chandler completely understood my position, and that was the end of the interview."[1] But he also said he couldn't help wondering if Chandler would have called up Ty Cobb, Frankie Frisch, or Pepper Martin—all white and given to sounding off—for the same thing.

Rickey had been pondering the move for some time, knowing that many in baseball didn't understand Jackie's lack of reaction to all that was done to him. "They could be made to respect only the fighting back," he said, "the thing that is the sign of courage to men who know courage only in its physical sense. So I told Robinson that he was on his own. Then I sat back happily knowing that, with the restraints removed, Robinson was going to show the National League a thing or two."[2]

It didn't take long for the real Robinson to surface. He recalled years later that he got into a hassle with a young Brooklyn farmhand that almost came to blows.[3] *The Sporting News* elaborates on this, revealing the rookie to be 6 foot 6 Chris Van Cuyk, a 22-year-old out of Wisconsin.

What began as banter in an intra-squad game turned nasty after Robinson felt he was being ridden too hard. It appeared Van Cuyk threw at Robinson's head twice, causing a confrontation after the game during which Jackie described "in lurid detail" what he would have done if either pitch had hit him.

"He'd been trying to make a fool of me, so I just reared back and fired one at him," the pitcher said afterward. "Only one though. The second one came close, but it slipped." After quoting the pitcher, writer Bill Roeder observed that "this is no longer the meek, inoffensive, uncomplaining Robinson" of 1947.[4] Obviously, though, the confrontation wasn't held against the Van Cuyk. He was brought up in '50 and in three years pitched 160 innings for a 7–11 won-lost record.

Rickey kept his word as Jackie was asserting himself. He sat back and watched, happy with the racial makeup of the team. As the year began he had Robinson and Campanella and was about to bring up Newcombe, his 17 and 8 pitcher at Montreal. But, being Rickey, he wanted more.

He wanted Monte Irvin so that the Brooklyn outfield would be one of the best in modern times: Furillo in right, Snider in center, and Irvin in left. And he almost got him.

Monte at the time was 30 years old and under contract to the Newark Eagles. He had been a star athlete since his days at Orange (New Jersey) High School where he earned 16 letters in baseball, basketball, and football. While enrolled at Lincoln University in Pennsylvania he starred in football, basketball and track. Since the school had no baseball team he was allowed to sign with the Eagles, at that time in the Negro National League.

In 1940 when he was 20 years old he hit .422 for the Eagles, followed by .393 the next year. After three years in the Army he returned to further stardom in Newark.[5] By this time interest in signing black stars was rising, and Rickey was watching.

In January, as he was thinking of an unfettered Robinson, Rickey boldly signed Irvin for St. Paul, a Brooklyn farm team in the American Association, without contacting anyone associated with the Newark Eagles. He would have gotten away with it if it hadn't been for one determined lady, Effa Manley, owner of the Eagles. Irvin was under contract to her and she was going to fight. She took her case to Commissioner Chandler, arguing that Irvin's contract "was the same as that covering all of major and minor league baseball."[6]

Rickey at first paid no attention to this because he didn't take Negro League contracts seriously, claiming they were not valid because of teams barnstorming, uneven scheduling, and the fact that for many of the players there was no such thing as a contract. Arthur Mann, a former Chandler troubleshooter and now Rickey's personal assistant, went further, saying the Mahatma maintained that Negro ballplayers were therefore free agents at the end of each season, meaning that he did not have to compensate Negro League teams for any players he intended to sign.[7]

Rickey's main argument was specious but there was some logic to his stand. The Negro leagues were showing signs of breaking up, a major reason for Manley's announcement that she was moving her Newark Eagles franchise to Houston. She had already lost Larry Doby, Don Newcombe, and Roy Campanella to the big leagues and had been looking at dwindling crowds for two years as many black Newarkers headed for Ebbets Field to see Robinson, Campanella and Newcombe. Thousands of others stayed at home, watching on television.

People like Rickey and Manley could clearly see what was happening as leading Negro ballplayers were jumping their teams for the big time. To many the death knell had sounded the year before when Satchel Paige, Negro star of stars, signed with the Cleveland Indians. Less than a decade after that signing the Negro leagues were down to a handful of struggling teams, and these were eventually gone.

An entire way of life was thus swept away in a few short years. The Homestead Grays, the Kansas City Monarchs, the Baltimore Elite Giants and the rest gradually dwindled away as more and more Negro stars were grabbed up by big league teams.

Against this background Rickey might have gotten away with signing Irvin, but he bowed to Manley's wishes and released the Negro star, who was then signed by the Giants for their Jersey City farm club. "Rather than get into any kind of hassle," Irvin recalled years later, "Mr. Rickey called Mr. Stoneham and recommended that he sign me."[8]

With all these signings, stars as well as second-liners like Sam Jethroe and Dan Bankhead, there were those in the South who still would not come to terms with blacks being in the big leagues. Three days after Irvin signed with Jersey City they were at it again. Ku Klux Klan Grand Dragon Dr. Samuel Green said he would investigate to see if the Georgia segregation law would be violated if Robinson and Campanella played in a scheduled spring exhibition game in Atlanta against the Crackers.

"In my opinion it's illegal," he said, backed by Governor Herman Talmadge, who said the matter would probably come before him and that "I'll look into it then."[9]

Rickey reacted heatedly, saying: "No one can tell me anywhere what players I can or cannot play. If the Negroes are barred from playing I will request a cancellation."[10] Surprisingly, according to an Associated Press poll, there were a number of Atlantans who agreed with him.

Of 50 people polled, 40 said they approved of whites and Negroes playing baseball together. "If the Klan's against it I'm for it," one male respondent said. "I haven't seen a ball game since I was a kid. I'll see one of these."[11]

He and his kind prevailed, for during the exhibition season, as the Dodgers were playing their way up from Florida, Robinson took the field against the Macon Peaches before a racially mixed crowd. It was the first time a Negro ever played baseball with whites in the state of Georgia, and although Jackie was both cheered and booed in his first at-bat, his drawing power was such that 6,532 fans filled a park that seated only 4,000. Jackie had three straight singles and two RBIs.[12]

The game also included the major league debut of Kevin (Chuck) Connors, later famous as a Hollywood actor and as TV's *The Rifleman.* Although he was an All-American out of Seton Hall and a Brooklyn native, Connors had no chance with the Dodgers. Like all other first base candidates he couldn't get by Gil Hodges. He lasted just one regular season game with Brooklyn and then joined that long list of first basemen, led by the likes of Dee Fondy and Wayne Belardi, unlucky enough to be of Hodges' generation.

The Dodgers began the season against the Giants at Ebbets Field with a 10–3 win. Jackie, batting cleanup now, led the team with 3 for 5 including a homer. Shotton opened with Joe Hatten, who would be one of his four starters all year, along with Newcombe, Roe, and Branca.

It was a fitting beginning for Robinson, a sign of things to come, for 1949 would be the season of Jackie's life: batting champion, Most Valuable Player, leader of the team that would win the pennant. And it was something Dodger fans were not expecting.

For although Robinson was by then the complete ballplayer, he gave no sign of becoming one of the top players in the game. He was viewed by the Flatbush Faithful as a steady, solid second baseman and, with years of .297 and .296 behind him, a good hitter who knew the strike zone and could not be intimidated by brushbacks.

Robinson's becoming cleanup hitter was a surprise to many, since the previous season Jackie had hit just 12 home runs along with a .296 batting average, decent but not nearly impressive enough to merit fourth spot in the order. Those surprised forgot about or didn't know about Alan Roth, Rickey's statistical wizard.

Roth had been hired by Rickey at the start of the 1947 season as the first team statistician in baseball history. At the time Roth was a statistician for the National Hockey League. According to *The New York Times,* he approached Rickey with a proposal that would change the way the game was played: Wouldn't it help a manager, Roth asked, if he knew a certain batter hit .220 against right-handed pitchers and .300 against left-handers? An intrigued Rickey hired him.[13]

He started immediately to analyze hitters and pitchers in ways never before even approached. He was the first, for example, to compile a hitter's average with men on base. In his book *The Numbers Game,* Alan Schwarz writes that when Roth told Rickey that Jackie, despite his .296 average, hit for .350 with men on base, Jackie then took over the cleanup spot.

Schwarz also claims that Dixie Walker, despite a .306 average in 1947, was traded by Rickey to Pittsburgh the following year not only because of the Robinson situation, but because Roth's analysis of his hitting showed Walker wasn't pulling the ball, a sure sign of aging.[14] Maybe so, but there are those of us who feel Rickey didn't need statistics to tell him when a ballplayer was aging and slowing down.

Without question that type analysis has made the game more interesting and, unlike football, subject to fan discussion almost year round. The old "Hot Stove League" still exists, perhaps hotter now than ever since there is so much more to analyze and argue over than in the pre–Alan Roth days.

It can be daunting to those of us who had trouble with algebra in high school. Bill James' "Pythagorean Theory" for analyzing won-lost records has the following formula: team wins over team losses equals runs scored over runs allowed. Or his runs created: hits plus walks times total bases divided by plate appearances.[15] Interesting but sometimes a bit much.

Schwarz cites one example of Bill James showing that record performances are not always what they seem. In his Leadoff Efficiency category, he analyzes Rickey Henderson's all-time high 130 stolen bases in 1983, pointing out that Henderson got caught stealing 42 times.

"That's 42 outs he took away from some Oakland batter," James says. "The actual increase in runs scored resulting from Henderson's baserunning: 4½ runs. Four-and-a-half goddam runs and they want to give him an MVP award for that."[16] If he hasn't already, James should look into Reggie Jackson's career totals. Yes, 563 home runs, but also 2,597 strikeouts, the most in baseball history. Is there a stat for runners stranded? (In contrast, in 1941, the year of Joe DiMaggio's 56-game hitting streak, he struck out but 13 times—13 times in an entire season.)

Schwarz' book makes it clear that it takes some dedication to be a regular-game statistician, at least one of the caliber of Alan Roth. During the course of a regular Brooklyn Dodger season Roth would chart every one of some 40,000 Dodger pitches and in doing so would avoid liquids so that he wouldn't miss any of the action by having to use the men's room.[17] That's dedication.

Long before Roth's analysis made Robinson a cleanup hitter, everyone knew he was one of the best base runners in memory, one of the best ever. In his first two seasons he had stolen 51 bases and had become adept at the hardest steal of all, third to home. Vic Raschi years later recalled the 1949 Series game he lost to Roe 1–0 when Hodges singled Jackie home for the lone run.

It was not Hodges who beat him, he said, it was Robinson on third bluffing a break for home. "I had never seen anything like him before, a human being who could go from a standing start to full speed in just one step. He did something to me that almost never happened: he broke my concentration and I paid more attention to him than to Hodges."[18]

The season had barely started when Robinson showed that his skills on the bases had not been affected as they were by his weight problems of 1948, when Rickey put him on waivers as a disciplinary measure. In this off-season he refused many of the dinner invitations that caused his problems after his

Tragedy struck Roy Campanella in his late 30s but before that he was one of the best catchers in baseball history, a Hall of Famer with his .276 lifetime average, 242 home runs and three Most Valuable Player awards. On January 28, 1958, Roy's car skidded on an icy road, hit a pole and flipped over. Campy spent the rest of his life in a wheelchair.

first historic year. He was now playing at his usual 190 to 195 pounds, not the 220 he weighed starting the '48 season.

This was evident on April 23 as the Brooks opened their second series of the year against the Phillies at Shibe Park. Robin Roberts had been routed and former Giant Ken Trinkle was pitching when Snider opened the sixth with a line single. Robinson, trying to sacrifice, forced Snider at second. Then the incredible: Jackie stole second on the first pitch, stole third on the next, and scored when Stan Lopata's hurried throw to Puddin' Head Jones went into left field. When he trotted to the dugout after scoring, the Brooklyn team was on its feet applauding him. The run was insurance in an 8–6 Brooklyn win.

The next day Campanella became Brooklyn's first-string catcher in the second game of a doubleheader against the Phils. Bruce Edwards had caught the opener but his chronically sore arm forced him to the bench. Campy's Hall of Fame career as a number one catcher started in high fashion: 3 for 4 and a run scored in a 6–5 win over Curt Simmons.

Roy had shown tremendous talent early. At just 16 he was the first-string catcher for the Baltimore Elite Giants, a team with a tradition going back to 1918 when it was founded in Nashville. Campy joined the team in 1938, the year it settled in Baltimore for the next decade. In those days if you weren't a Satchel Paige or a Josh Gibson, life in the Negro leagues was tough. They played often and often in pain, as Campanella recalled years later.

"You didn't get hurt in the Negro Leagues," he said. "You played no matter what happened to you because if you didn't, you didn't get paid." As an example he cited a day he caught four Elite Giants games on one Sunday, working a doubleheader in Cincinnati in the afternoon and another in Youngstown that evening.[19]

The Dodgers had scouted Campy for some time when Charley Dressen was told to approach him during an exhibition game in October of 1946 at Newark's Ruppert Stadium. Roy was catching for a Negro All-Star team that was playing a collection of major leaguers when Dressen came up to him between innings to say, "Campy, can I talk to you after the game?"

They met outside the clubhouse, where Roy agreed to report to the Dodgers offices in Brooklyn at 10 o'clock the following morning. "It was the first time anyone spoke to me about coming to the Dodgers," Campy said years later.[20]

As he sat across from Rickey it was evident from their conversation that the Mahatma was raising some doubts in Roy's mind, most certainly to make him more amenable to signing, for that was Rickey's intention after all the scouting and reports from Dressen and Clyde Sukeforth.

"What do you weigh, Campy?" he asked.

"Two fifteen to two twenty."

"Judas Priest," Rickey shouted. "You can't weigh that much and play ball."

"All I know," Roy answered, "is that I've been doing it every day for years and it's worked out fine."

Rickey then took another tack. "The one thing that puzzles me is your age," he said. "I have your age noted in this book. You sure this is your right age?"

"Sure it's my right age," Roy replied. "I'm 23. I was born November 19th, 1921. I'll be 24 next month."

"You look older," Rickey said to a somewhat annoyed Campanella.

"Mr. Rickey," he said, "I've been playing ball a long time."[21]

All those years finally paid off after Campanella signed. The

Mahatma convinced Roy to report to Nashua, New Hampshire, and then brought him up to Brooklyn after stops in Montreal and St. Paul.

Roy was 28, old for a first-time starter, as he took over from Edwards behind the plate in Philadelphia that afternoon. But he was nevertheless a known quantity. He had played 83 games the year before, backing up Edwards and sometimes Hodges, and hitting .258. As we know, he made the most of his scant 10 major league years.

After Roy became a star and could speak out, his relationship with Robinson became strained because of their different outlooks on the role of the Negro in society and baseball. In Robinson's words Campanella felt that blacks in America would be better off if they were "to stop pressing to get too far too fast." Jackie further quotes Roy as saying "I am no crusader" during a discussion of hotel accommodations for black players.[22]

The nationally known black sportswriter A.S. Young used the word "feud" in summing up the situation: "Background for this feud is found in the differences in personalities between these two stars. Campy is a Dale Carnegie disciple who believes in 'getting along' at all costs, in being grateful for any favor or any deed interpreted as a favor. Jackie is an aggressive individualist who is willing to pay the price and, once having paid it in full, does not believe that effusive thank you's are a necessary tip."[23]

Young, however, didn't take into account their vastly different backgrounds: Campy's boyhood in 1920s Philadelphia, his life in the Negro leagues catching doubleheaders at 16 instead of being in school, all those years on the road in old buses, sleeping in rundown hotels, and playing for minimum money.

In contrast, Jackie was a Californian, raised in Pasadena, a star in four sports at UCLA, an Army officer during World War II, a star, again, with the Kansas City Monarchs, and a nationally famous figure as the man who broke baseball's color line. It is no wonder that they looked at the world from different points of view.

In Duke Snider's opinion Campanella was fortunate that Jackie was the first to break the color line, for Roy with his easygoing personality could never have done it, could never have put up with racial slurs and personal attacks that Jackie put up with so stoically.

"Many people feel Campy could have been the man to break baseball's color barrier, but Rickey knew his personnel," Duke says in his autobiography. "The reason people give for saying Campy could have been the first—his easygoing, happy-go-lucky disposition—is the very reason he couldn't have done it."

Jackie, Snider said, was militant and knew that history had placed him in a special role and he never ducked it and never removed himself from that role—things that "Campy could never have done" because of his personality. "However, Campy could well have become the first black manager, something I don't think Jackie could have handled," he added. "Jackie could have been a good general manager, but Campy had a thorough knowledge of the game, an outstanding attitude, and he got along with the press."[24]

Duke should have said that Campanella got along with everyone, as anyone who followed the Dodgers during those years would attest. Young should have used a milder word than feud. Campy and Robinson had their differences but to call those differences a feud is an exaggeration. Campy never feuded with anybody, not even with any of the 1950s Yankees at their most imperious.

And they could be imperious bordering on the obnoxious. Roger Kahn wrote of covering a Yankees spring training game in 1952, when he was new on the Dodger beat. As he was interviewing Stengel, Raschi and Reynolds were ringing the front of his shoes with tobacco juice, as if to punctuate Casey's remarks.

"Years later I asked Reynolds about his behavior," Kahn wrote. Reynolds replied: 'We knew who you were, and it was nothing personal. We were just making sure that you knew who *we* were. The New York Yankees."[25] Now *there* were teams Campy could have feuded with during all those World Series games if he was the type. But he got along even with them, though it must be said that no one ever intimidated Roy Campanella.

Two days after Campy took over the catching job, Shotton replaced Cal Abrams with Hermanski, who had lost his starting job during spring training. The results, in the words of the *Times'* McGowen, "probably astonished even the self-contained Dodger pilot."

Gene not only homered in the first inning, but started a triple play—baseball's rarest happening—with an extraordinary catch that got Preacher Roe out of a tough inning in a 5–2 win over the Braves.

Sain and Stanky had both singled, putting men on first and second. Alvin Dark hit a twisting fly to short center. Both runners advanced, thinking no one could make the catch, but Gene made a last-second desperate reach, just barely stayed on his feet, and threw to Robinson. Jackie doubled Sain off second and fired to Hodges to get Stanky.

On the 28th the Brooks came down from Boston for another Giants series and opened up with a 15–2 win as just about everyone got at least one hit. It was bad news, however, for the pitching staff as Erskine, Ramsdell, and Ed Chandler were optioned out, with Carl and Willard on 24-hour recall. Chandler was never heard of again.

The following week Shotton, realizing that Jorgensen's arm would never really come around, named Billy Cox his first-string third baseman. The man who would become the best of his era—the "acrobat" as Casey Stengel was to call him—would kill baseline doubles for the next seven years.

Billy was born in Newport, a small town in central Pennsylvania where he played high school ball. He started his pro career with the Harrisburg Senators in 1940 when he was 21 years old and good enough to be called up by the Pittsburgh Pirates the next year. After only 10 games in 1941 he was drafted and spent the next four years in the Army, including 18 months on Guadalcanal. That time in the Pacific affected the rest of his life.

The story around Ebbets Field was that Billy caught malaria there and never really got over it. Bill McNeil in his *Dodgers Encyclopedia* confirms this, writing that Cox came home from the war a skeletal 130 pounds and never fully recovered his health.[26]

Billy Cox was the best-fielding third baseman of his generation. Casey Stengel called him "an acrobat" after watching him play against his Yankees. A scrawny 150 pounds, Billy might have become the hitter he was as a young man but for the persistent malaria he caught while in combat in the South Pacific. As it was, he hit .266 over 11 seasons.

That would account for his baseball physique—150 pounds on a 5 foot 10 frame, and the fact that Billy was never a 154-game third baseman. His highest total was 142 in 1951, but years of 100, 116, and 119 games were more common.

Those games he did play, however, were magic. It was a common sight in Ebbets Field to see him capture a double on the baseline, straighten up and then *look the ball over* before throwing to Hodges for the out. Such was his arm, a Furillo at third base.

And the glove he wore was unbelievable, probably the smallest used by any third baseman of modern times.

Later in the month, on May 15, Don Newcombe, the first great black pitcher in the major leagues, joined Brooklyn in Chicago after a year at Montreal where his 17 and 6 led the pitching staff. Newcombe had come out of Madison, New Jersey, where, large for his age, he began pitching semi-pro ball when he was only 13 years old.[27] By the time he signed with the Newark Eagles five years later, he was 6 foot 4, 220 pounds.

When he arrived at Ebbets Field he brought with him a world of stuff, a buzzing fastball, control worthy of Carl Hubbell, and a batting eye that eventually made him one of the best hitting pitchers in the game. And, contrary to critics of the day, he also had a lot of heart, something made obvious by the box scores of the big games he supposedly "blew."

Over the years he has been accused of choking down the stretch drive for the 1951 pennant. The box scores tell the real story, as usual: On September 26 he went nine innings to beat the Braves. On the 30th he shut out the Phillies, 5–0, going all nine. The next day he relieved and gave up only one hit in 5⅔ innings as the Dodgers beat the Phils in 14 innings. After pitching 14⅔ innings in two days, he went 8⅓ innings against the Giants before Bobby Thomson hit his historic homer off Branca. This is choking?

Don Newcombe was the first of the great black pitchers signed after the color barrier was broken. Because of the bottle he lasted only 10 years but still compiled a 149–90 record. When Don finally conquered his drinking problem he became a counselor for the Los Angeles Dodgers, helping young players to avoid or get over drug and alcohol problems.

His Dodger debut, however, was a disaster. A week after he arrived he relieved Barney in the sixth inning against the Cardinals. The result: four hits in one-third of an inning, the last a three-run double into the farthest corner of Sportsman's Park by Enos Slaughter.

He took the mound just two days after that pounding and shut out the Reds 5 to 0 at Crosley Field, the first step on his way to one of baseball's great rookie years: 17 and 8 with a 3.17 ERA. He was, naturally, named Rookie of the Year that fall.

Newk ended up at 149–90, a very respectable record, except that he should have been much better—200 wins at least from a man with his skills. But in mid-career alcohol got to him and by 1960 he was through. The only pitcher to ever win Rookie of the Year, Cy Young, and

Most Valuable Player awards was finished at 31 after just 10 years in the majors.

In later years he conquered the bottle and went back to the Dodgers organization as a counselor, telling young players about his battles against alcohol. "I had friends who died young because nobody cared about them drinking," he would say. "The Dodgers care, I care. You can come to me."[28]

By this time the team that would dominate the National League for most of the '50s had jelled, with the racial and other animosities now mostly in the past. Robinson says in his autobiography that the team "had improved tremendously in closeness," with racial tensions "almost completely dissipated." All the team cared about through that season was "acquiring talented players."[29]

Cox was now at third, Robinson had already been moved over to his natural position at second base, Campanella took over as the starting catcher, and Hodges, after an uncertain 1948, was soon to be recognized as one of the great first basemen of the game.

Gil, the son of an Indiana coal miner, was now 25 years old and was afraid of nothing, as he proved in the Marine Corps, where he became a legend in the Pacific Theater. He served at Pearl Harbor, Okinawa, and Tinian before he was discharged as a sergeant in 1946.

Don Hoak, who joined the Dodgers in 1954 as a third baseman, also served in the Pacific and remembered that "we kept hearing stories about this big guy from Indiana who killed Japs with his bare hands."[30] That's not hard to believe, for Hodges' strength was legendary throughout the National League. Reese recalled a fight he had with Dee Fondy of the Cubs and how it ended. Hodges grabbed the front of Fondy's shirt, lifted him easily off the ground and said: "I don't know where you're going, Dee, but you're not going near Pee Wee." Fondy was 6 foot 3 and 200 pounds.[31]

The sentiment to get him into the Hall of Fame has been strong, but time is passing and it may never happen now, unless the newly reconstituted Veterans Committee votes him in. It almost happened in 1992 when he lost out by one vote, undoubtedly because his friend and teammate Roy Campanella, who died the following year, was too ill to attend the meeting.

If he ever does get in, the hall's standards would not be lowered as they have in some past elections. Gil was the finest fielding first baseman of his time during an 18-year career, hit 370 homers, drove in 1,274 runs, and scored 1,105. And if character counts, as it certainly should—dope peddler Orlando Cepeda notwithstanding*—Gil was one

*On December 16, 1976, Cepeda was sentenced to five years in prison and fined $10,000 in federal court in San Juan on his conviction for smuggling 165 pounds of marijuana into Puerto Rico (New York Times, 12/17/76, p. B13). He was paroled 10 months later. A convicted dope trafficker in the Hall of Fame is bad enough, but his hall credentials are not all that impressive: a .297 batting average with 379 home runs.

The Dodgers are on their way to victory in the fourth game of the 1955 World Series as Gil Hodges scores on a fourth-inning home run that helped in the 8–5 win over the Yankees. Greeting Gil are batboy Charlie DiGiovanni, Carl Furillo and Jackie Robinson.

of the best, a family man who was never involved in a scandal of any kind.

With the infield now set, by early May Robinson was becoming one of the great hitters in baseball. From May 9th until the 31st he hit .493— 38 hits in 77 times at bat. He closed out the month with three home runs against Pittsburgh, one a game winner, and a bases loaded single that beat Warren Spahn 3–2 on May 29 at Ebbets Field.

On June 5 Commissioner Chandler, no doubt because of threats to the reserve clause, commuted the sentences of all those still out of baseball because they jumped to Mexico. He even allowed the clubs to go over the player limit "for a reasonable time" to accommodate the returnees.[32]

This left Branch Rickey with a problem: what to do with the returning Mickey Owen. Olmo was coming back too, but Luis was a decent-hitting outfielder, only 30 years old, and in shape from playing in the Caribbean. Mickey was 33 and had been one of the best catchers in baseball but he hadn't played in the majors for four years. Brooklyn had Campanella, whom nobody was going to push onto the bench by this time, Edwards when his arm was right, and Hodges for emergencies.

The problem was solved when Mickey signed with the Cubs after Rickey sold him to Chicago on waivers. He shared the catcher's job with Rube Walker until Rube was traded to the Dodgers on June 15, 1951. Mick had a good first year at .273, but faded to .243 and in his last National League season, .184 in 1951.

As the second week in June opened Jackie was the star of the National League, its best hitter at .345 as well as leading in RBIs with 45 and hits with 66. At this time the top of the standings was so crowded that in just one game on June 5 Ralph Kiner's game-winning homer against Brooklyn knocked them from first to third place.

Jackie brought them back into first place several days later with a one-man show against the Cubs. With Barney going the distance, he hit a triple that took a weird hop past Andy Pafko, a single, and sacrifice fly to drive in all three runs for a 3 to 1 win over Bob Muncrief.

The next day Jackie, aware of his drawing power, announced that in 1950 he would demand that his contract contain a bonus clause based on Dodger attendance. As the *Brooklyn Eagle* noted, no one could deny that Robinson had become the "greatest gate attraction the club has had in years."[33]

Two days later one of the most sensational stories ever to hit baseball came out of Chicago when 19-year-old Ruth Steinhagen shot Phillies first baseman Eddie Waitkus after luring him to her room in the Edgewater Beach Hotel.

Eddie was 29, single, and a lifetime .300 hitter at the time. Miss Steinhagen, a six-foot brunette, got him to her room just before midnight and soon after he entered she shot him in the chest with a .22-caliber rifle. She then called the desk to report that she had just shot a man.

When they got Waitkus to the hospital they put him on oxygen and gave him two blood transfusions before pronouncing him in fair condition with the bullet lodged near his heart. Miss Steinhagen was booked on a charge of assault with intent to murder. She told police that, although she had never met Waitkus, she had a twisted fascination for him, and a desire to be in the limelight. Police later found she had been obsessed with Eddie for two years and kept a file of newspaper pictures and stories about him.

"He reminded me of my father and I wanted the thrill of murdering him," was the only explanation she gave to the police for the shooting. She added that she had intended suicide but lacked the nerve.

Under questioning she said she brought the gun and a knife into the hotel, had three drinks and called Waitkus. "He entered the room and sat down in a chair and I said I have a surprise for you," she said. "I got the gun out of the closet and I told him to get up and move toward the window and he said, 'what in the world goes here.'"

"Before he had a chance to say anything else I shot him. He slumped to the floor and said 'oh baby, what did you do that for,' or something to that effect."[34]

It was almost a month later, on July 11, that Eddie was able to get up and take walks in his hospital room. He was released the following week but, because of the seriousness of the wound and the four operations it took to heal it, his doctors ordered that he not play until the next spring training. Miss Steinhagen was sent to a mental hospital for an indeterminate term and was released sometime in 1955. Eddie, after months of recuperation, rebounded well from the shooting. For the next three years, before he became a part-timer, he played in 445 games, averaging .277 over the three seasons.

Eddie retired after the 1955 season but by that time he was on his way to becoming famous as the real-life Roy Hobbs, the hero of Bernard Malamud's best-selling novel *The Natural*. Hobbs, a ballplayer like Waitkus, is lured to a Chicago hotel room and then shot by a girl he'd never met.

In 1972 Eddie died of cancer and 12 years later, in 1984, memories of the shooting were revived when Robert Redford made the movie *The Natural* based on the book. Eddie was only 53 when he died and is remembered today more for the shooting and Roy Hobbs than for the fine ballplayer he was.

On the 18th Brooklyn beat the Cubs, 2–1, with Newcombe going all the way, Hodges singling in the ninth to drive Snider in with the game-winner, Campy homering, and Jackie getting two hits and a steal.

With games like that it was becoming more and more obvious to the Flatbush Faithful that a new era was beginning with these youthful Dodgers. The days of Reiser, Walker, Stanky, and Casey were remembered fondly but without regret. With Shotton as manager, also gone were the chaotic days of Durocher and his umpire baiting.

It was also becoming obvious that this new team and the New York Giants were major factors in the demise of minor league baseball in nearby New Jersey where the Newark Bears, Jersey City Giants, and Newark Eagles had drawn respectable crowds for decades.

The drawing power of Jackie Robinson since 1947 had started the decline. Now he was joined by Campanella and Newcombe, with Monte Irvin and Hank Thompson over on the Giants. Blacks, by 1949 a significant fan base in the Metropolitan area, could now see black ballplayers not only at Ebbets Field and the Polo Grounds, but on television, which by this time was broadcasting a Dodgers or Giants game almost every day of the season.

The New Jersey teams had already lost most of their white fans to television and therefore could not survive black abandonment as well, as Manley saw when she planned to take her Newark Eagles to Texas.

By the beginning of 1949 the Eagles were gone and just one year later so were the Newark Bears and Jersey City Giants. The Bears, for example, were abandoned by their parent Yankees with General Manager George Weiss stating that declining attendance was the major factor in the sale of the team to the Chicago Cubs.

By 1949, with the flow of talent from the Yankees non-existent, the plight of the Bears was so desperate that one of the Newark newspapers announced a move unprecedented in the relationship between a local sports team and the media covering it.

The *Star-Ledger* announced on June 25 that it would no longer include the Bears in the International League standings section of its sports pages "because they obviously do not belong in Triple A competition." The paper said the team was "18½ games out of first" and would not be restored to the International League listings "until they are again a Triple A ball club."[35] It never happened. On January 12, 1950, the Chicago Cubs bought the team, announcing it would be transferred to Springfield, Massachusetts.

As June was ending Joe DiMaggio once again had the country watching as he came off the bench after 65 games on the disabled list with a heel spur. It was probably the most dramatic return within memory, for he was to face the Red Sox, the team the Yanks battled all year for the pennant. How would Joe fare after being out so long, the New York press asked in print.

His playing at all was totally unexpected because the heel had been giving him pain for weeks and had shown no signs of improving. But one morning he stepped out of bed and discovered the pain was gone. A few days later, on the afternoon before an exhibition game, he walked into Casey Stengel's office and said: "I think I'll give it a whirl tonight, Case."

"Great," Stengel replied. "You can play as long as you want. Just let me know when you're ready to quit." He didn't, but instead played the entire exhibition game and was ready for the Red Sox at Fenway the next night.[36]

In the first of the three-game series he hit a two-run homer and a single in a 5–4 Yankee win in which he had a hand in all the scoring. In game two he hit two homers, the second the winning run in a 9–7 New York victory. In the third game his fourth homer of the series, this one with two on, drove in the winning runs as the Yanks won again 6–3. Joe had five hits in eleven times at bat and drove in nine runs during the three games. This after being out 10 weeks and playing in the Sox home park. "I really surprised myself," Joe said years later. "We shocked 'em. They didn't say a word. Not even my brother [Dom]."[37]

It has been called by some the game's greatest comeback, and they could well be right. The claim is enhanced when it is pointed out that Joe hit two of the four homers off Mel Parnell and Ellis Kinder, among the best pitchers in the game that year.

By the time the series was over it had become such a national sensation that *Life* magazine paid Joe the then-very-large-sum of $6,000 for his personal account of it.[38]

And, as it turned out, the series was crucial even though it was still fairly early in the pennant race. Boston was eight games out when the series ended on June 30 but, rather than being disheartened, the Sox kept pressing the Yankees so hard that they were tied for the pennant going into the final game of the season.

The Yanks won behind Vic Raschi, 5–3 at the Stadium, the key hit being Jerry Coleman's bloop double over first with the bases loaded, scoring all three with the winning runs. So all three of those DiMaggio games were important, for if just one had gone the other way the Sox might well have won the pennant.

As Joe's story was appearing in *Life*, Horace Stoneham decided to bring Irvin and Thompson up from Jersey City. Irvin at the time was leading the National League at .385 and 41 RBIs. The *Times'* account of his promotion pointed out that "He had one of the best throwing arms in baseball."

Thompson was 23, out of Los Angeles, and played for the Kansas City Monarchs before reporting to Jersey City. He had been up for a brief trial with the St. Louis Browns in 1947 and joined the Monarchs after he was cut. At Jersey City he was hitting .303 with power: 12 home runs, two triples, and nine doubles.

Thompson, Hammering Hank as he was known, had a good nine-year career, hitting .267 with 129 homers and 462 RBIs, mostly as a third baseman. Hank didn't fare well after baseball. He drove a cab in New

York City for a while and then, after a divorce, went to Texas in 1963 where he was convicted of armed robbery and sentenced to 10 years in prison. He was paroled after four years and died two years later of a heart attack at age 43.[39]

Though his life was short and ended badly Thompson has his moment in history, ignored though it has been. Not even a footnote has been devoted to the July 8 game at Ebbets Field during which Hank, filling in for the injured Bill Rigney, faced Don Newcombe, the first time a black batter faced a black pitcher. He went 0 for 5.

On July 6 the league office announced that seven Dodgers had been named to the All-Star game: Robinson and Reese as starters, Roe, Newcombe, and Branca to the pitching staff, and Hodges and Campanella as reserves. The American League won 11–7 with Newcombe taking the loss and Joe DiMaggio leading his squad with a single, double, and three RBIs.

American League manager Lou Boudreau was criticized for naming DiMag, since Joe, out for most of the year with the heel spur, had not been part of the fans' balloting. When pressed as to why he skirted the rule to name Joe, Boudreau replied: "Joe DiMaggio is Joe DiMaggio."[40]

In mid–July the House Un-American Activities Committee, recognizing Robinson's now national stature, asked him to testify before it to counter statements by Paul Robeson that Negroes would not fight against Russia if the need arose. This, at the height of the Cold War.

"Rachel and I had long talks about it," Jackie recalled. "I knew that Robeson was striking out against racial inequality in the way that seemed best to him. The newspaper accounts seemed to picture the great singer as speaking for the whole race of black people. With all the respect I had for him I didn't believe anyone had the right to do that."[41]

He testified on July 18, calling the Robeson statement "silly and untrue." He told the committee that he was not an expert on communism, but that he was "an expert on being a colored American, with 30 years experience at it."

"Negroes were stirred up long before there was a Communist party," he said, "and they'll stay stirred up long after the party has disappeared. We can win our fight without the Communists, and we don't need their help."

Robeson, he told the committee, "has a right to his personal views, and if he wants to sound silly when he expresses them in public that's his business not mine. He's still a famous ex-athlete and a great singer and actor."[42]

That night Jackie was back in Ebbets Field and was, as was becoming usual, the offensive star. In a 3–0 win over the Cubs he stole home and drove in another run with a triple. The steal of home was becoming typical Robinson: he walked, stole second and when Mickey Owen's throw was wild, went to third. He then stole home as the Cubs' Bob Rush was pitching to Furillo.

The Brooks closed out July 1½ games behind the first-place Cardinals and with Robinson at the top of the league leaders, hitting .366. They started August with a three-game sweep at Pittsburgh and a win at Cincinnati. Then the improbable cost them a game.

In the eighth inning at Crosley Field, Billy Cox, that most sure-handed of third basemen, committed three errors to tie a National League record, snapping a six-game winning streak and depriving Branca of his 12th win. The dubious record was first set by Bill Grier of Boston in 1904 and tied by Lou Riggs of the Dodgers in 1942. Billy tied it by throwing high to first on a grounder, then fumbling a bunt down the line, and finally dropping a throw as Harry Walker slid into third base.

The next day the pennant race took one of its usual twists as the Dodgers took a double-header from the Reds, putting them back into a tie for first with St. Louis. Joe Hatten played Iron Man again, with a shutout in the first game and saving Barney's win in the second.

Why Shotton would risk a starter of Hatten's quality in this fashion was not asked by the *Times'* McGowen. Burt had Jack Banta, Paul Minner, and Irv Palica, among others, that he could call on. Even if they weren't going good, anything would have been better than to risk the left arm of one of his starting four.

As the month wore on Brooklyn and St. Louis fought for first place and were tied on the 11th as Robinson's two-run homer beat the Phillies in the ninth inning 7–5. Then, to Shotton's dismay, they lost two straight to the Phils, were swept in four by the Braves and came home to Ebbets Field for the three-game series with the first-place Cardinals.

They lost the afternoon opener 5–3 as Joe Hatten was knocked out early, proving possibly that the Iron Man business doesn't usually work, especially as late as August in a tough campaign. The loss was the seventh in eight games, leaving the Brooks three full games behind the Cardinals.

Shotton, as usual, didn't scream and shout at his players as Durocher would have, but he couldn't keep it in entirely, since the team seemed to be playing itself out of the race. He spoke to the beat writers, probably with as much frustration as was in the man, telling them: "They just don't do anything right. They don't even think right. They are not taking advantage of openings and are leaving too many men on third base. You'd think they never saw a curve ball before."

As if in answer, the team turned it around that night when Roe, pitching one of the most important games of his career, beat Howie Pollett, who with 16 wins was the ace of the Cardinal staff. The game opened on a bad but familiar note for Roe as Musial, the scourge of Ebbets Field, hit one out with a man on in the first inning.

Roe, knowing a loss would put the team four games back, held Musial off the rest of the way, giving up eight hits and pitching out of trouble several times. The somewhat forgotten Mike McCormick, who came to Brooklyn in the Reiser trade, drove in the first run in the fourth and then made two great fielding plays that probably kept Roe in the game.

Mike drove in the tying run in the fourth when, with Robinson on third, he hit a roller down the line to Tommy Glaviano. As Jackie broke for home Glaviano, rushing because of Robinson's speed, threw the ball wildly into the Brooklyn dugout. The winner came in the eighth on consecutive doubles by Campanella and Snider. The game ended 4–3 on a play that brought the fans to their feet—a spectacular stab by Cox of a hot grounder by Lou Klein followed by Billy's usual bullet throw to Hodges for the out.

The Brooks were now back to being two games out, with any cause for panic dissipated by Roe's gutsy nine innings. Things improved even more the following day as Newcombe pitched what the *Times'* Louis Effrat called a "masterpiece," a six-hit shutout that brought the team to within one of first place.

Big Don was ahead 3–0 on home runs by Furillo, Campanella, and Hodges going into the eighth inning. In the Dodger half, Newk, a .271 career hitter, put the game out of reach with a base-clearing three-run double. The shutout was his second in a row, both under intense pressure.

The Cardinals kept up that pressure during the following week, opening up a 2½ game lead again until the Dodgers closed out August with the best kind of win—coming from behind in the ninth inning.

Rex Barney had gone the route but was behind 3–2 to the Pirates when, with one out in Brooklyn's last at-bat, Campanella singled, Miksis ran for him, and then Hodges hit a towering home run into the left field seats, no doubt the most satisfying of his 23 that year. As he crossed the plate the team was waiting, led by Campanella, Robinson, Hermanski, Newcombe, and Reese.

It was a good way for the Dodgers to start September, the final month of one of the closest and most grueling pennant races of the decade, one that was decided on the final day of the year by the margin of a single game. The race for the batting title was also heating up as Robinson dropped to .348, six points ahead of Slaughter.

By September 8 the Dodgers had won 12 out of 16 games and were 30 above .500 but still trailed the Cardinals by a game and a half. The next day Eddie Stanky's aggressiveness, plus the tension building up with every game, caused an explosion from the most mild-mannered man on the ballfield.

In the fifth inning against the Braves at Ebbets Field Spider Jorgensen punched his way out of the game. Johnny, during one of those periods when his arm was right, was covering third when Stanky, instead of merely sliding, "jumped him" as the *Brooklyn Eagle* described it, with his spikes cutting Spider's right leg. Johnny came up swinging as both benches erupted and the park police rushed onto the field.

When things quieted down Jorgensen and Stanky were ordered out of the game. Later, as Johnny was being treated for five superficial spike wounds, Stanky entered the Brooklyn clubhouse

John "Spider" Jorgensen, Brooklyn's smooth-fielding third baseman, hit .274 in his rookie year to help the Dodgers win the 1947 pennant. Spider's luck didn't hold, however. After that first year his arm went bad, one reason for the Billy Cox trade. He was a part-timer for the next four seasons and retired after one year with the '51 Giants.

to apologize. Jorgensen, after all, had been his teammate for a year and was popular with everyone.

"I'm sorry Spider, I'm sorry it happened," Eddie said, holding out his hand.

Jorgensen, pointedly ignoring the hand, simply said "I'm sorry too." Eddie persisted as he said again, hesitantly, "I'm sorry about it Spider." This time Johnny took the outstretched hand. "I never got into a fight on the ballfield before," he said with his usual good-natured grin.[43]

The fight turned out well for the Dodgers, for Spider's replacement was Eddie Miksis. With the Brooks down 5 to 4 in the eighth inning

Eddie came up against Nelson Potter with a man on and hit one into the left field stands for the winning runs. It kept the team one behind the Cardinals.

Another win in late innings came about the next day against the Giants when Erv Palica in relief of Newcombe topped a roller toward first in the ninth inning. First baseman Joe Lafata missed his grab for it as Bruce Edwards crossed the plate with the winning run. But such was this pennant race that out in Cincinnati, Musial, with two on and two out and the Cards trailing by one in the ninth, hit a game-winning home run, keeping his team one up.

At the mid-month mark the Cards increased their lead to 2½ games, but on the 19th Barney shut out the Cubs 4–0 as the Cardinals were losing to Phil's rookie Jocko Thompson 4–3. Rex had a no-hitter until the eighth when Cavaretta singled. The lead was again 1½ games and the teams were poised for a stretch drive almost the equal of 1946.

On the 22nd Brooklyn exploded with 19 hits against six Cardinal pitchers for a 19–6 win behind a relaxed Joe Hatton. The teams had split a doubleheader the day before, thus Brooklyn took the series and cut the lead to one-half game.

During the next week each team lost a tough one. Brooklyn blew one to Philadelphia when Branca, moving into the eighth inning leading 3–1, was replaced by Jack Banta on Shotton's decision that Ralph couldn't continue because of a blister that had seemed to break. Banta came on for one of his few bad outings, four hits and three runs in just one-third of an inning.

The blister was a matter of controversy, with Branca saying it had been no problem and that he'd been taken out before he ever showed it to Shotton. "It wasn't bothering me," the pitcher insisted. Campanella had aggravated matters by telling the manager that Branca "didn't have a thing," that he couldn't throw his curve, relying on fast balls alone for the previous two innings.

As Branca kept saying that he shouldn't have come out, thereby second-guessing his manager, the matter became a debate in the clubhouse, with Shotton so upset that the *Brooklyn Eagle* printed rumors that Branca would be traded the following spring. The *Eagle,* having it both ways, also printed rumors that the whole rhubarb was set up to get rid of Shotton.

The matter, however, was settled within a day. Shotton was not so crazy as to throw away a 23-year-old pitcher who, disappointing as he had been at times, was seen to have great potential.

As the Dodgers were rained out on the 27th the Cardinals lost to the Pirates 6–4 on a grand slam by Tom Saffell, a 27-year-old rookie just up from Indianapolis. The Cardinal pitching was uncertain and the defense jittery, with reliables like Schoendienst making key errors. Eddie Dyer threw in five pitchers, including his 20-game-winner Pollett, in trying to keep his team's lead intact. But by nightfall and with just four games remaining the Cardinal lead was down to just one-half game again.

The Cardinal slide continued the next day as the Dodgers, responding magnificently to the occasion, took a doubleheader from the Braves while St. Louis was losing to the sixth-place Pirates.

It was an unusual day for both teams. The Dodgers overwhelmed Boston at Braves Field, 9–2 and 8–0, and in doing so knocked out two of the game's best pitchers, Warren Spahn and Johnny Sain. Roe and Newcombe each went all the way in a drizzling rain. The Dodger offense drove Spahn off the mound in four innings and scored five runs in the first inning of the second game to get rid of Sain in just two-thirds of an inning.

The Cardinals went up against their old ace, Murray Dickson, who went all nine while the Cardinal pitching again faltered and the defense continued committing key errors, another by Schoendienst and one by Slaughter. "It wasn't breaks that beat us," Dyer said after the game, "it was just bad baseball."

These games were something totally unexpected from the team of Musial, Slaughter, Marion, and Schoendienst. St. Louis had lost in '41 and '47, but always with their gloves up and bats ready. Their play in that Pirates series was such that Pittsburgh manager Billy Meyer said: "That [Cardinal] club out there just can't win the pennant."

The Cardinal collapse continued the next day in Chicago as the Cubs beat them 6–5 in a game they fought to the last out. With Musual and Slaughter coming up in the ninth there was still a chance, but Stan fouled two long ones off the right field wall and then hit a grounder the first baseman bobbled. The win was still possible with Slaughter up there fighting Robinson for the batting title, but Enos rolled one down to first for the final out.

On Sunday, October 2, both the Dodgers and Cardinals lost, leaving the pennant to be decided on the last day of the season. Brooklyn, with Branca pitching, had gone into the sixth inning leading 3–1. But then, typical of Branca in a clutch game, Dick Sisler tripled and Del Ennis homered. Shotton, aware of Branca's sudden blowups, quickly brought on Erskine, who took the 6–4 loss. The Dodgers still had an edge, however, in that if they won the next day they'd be champions, regardless of how the Cardinals fared.

Looking back now, that final day had to be the most exciting finale in baseball history, for over in the American League the Red Sox and Yankees were also tied on their very last day.

The Red Sox had come into the Stadium the day before needing to win one out of two for the pennant. But the Yankees, once behind by four runs to Ellis Kinder, eventually tied it and then won it in the eighth inning when Johnny Lindell, a .242 hitter, homered for the winning run.

The Dodgers won their pennant at Shibe Park, beating the Phillies in a 10-inning thriller, 9–7. A string of pitchers followed starters Russ Meyer and Newcombe, both of whom were gone early. Kenny Heintzelman, 17 and 10 and always tough on the Brooks, was pitching into the tenth inning when Snider singled up the middle, driving in Reese with the pennant-winning run.

The pitcher of the day was Jack Banta, who pitched shutout ball for 4⅓ innings and the win. It was a great 10 and 6 year for Jack but it was his only one. He was 4 and 4 the next year with arm trouble and then was gone at the age of 25. Next to Snider probably the happiest hitter of the day was Robinson, whose 1 for 3 assured him of the batting title at .342 over Slaughter's .339

Vic Raschi and the Yanks took care of the Red Sox 5–3 that same afternoon as Kinder lost his sixth against 23 wins. As Rizzuto, Henrich and Coleman were delivering clutch hits, Raschi held the top of the Boston order—DiMaggio, Pesky, and Williams—hitless, which hurt the Boston attack. The Sox scored three in the ninth, but Raschi then toughened up to get Birdie Tebbtts on a foul pop with Billy Goodman on first to finish it off.

It was Coleman's hit that killed the Red Sox that day, the bloop bases-loaded double that drove in the decisive runs. Forty years later Ted Williams still could not get over it, as he was being interviewed by the writer David Halberstam. "Oh God, that cheap hit," Williams remembered, "that cheap goddamn hit. Coleman is up. Tex [Hughson] makes a good pitch. A damn good pitch. Then Bobby [Doerr] is going back and Zeke [Zarilla] is coming in. Oh Jesus, I can still see it with my eyes closed. Zeke is diving for it, and then I see it squirting to the foul line."[44] Forty years later one of the best hitters of all time still sees it in his mind. And no wonder.

As the Dodgers got on the train in Philadelphia, Furillo was visiting his ill father in Reading. He had been one of the better hitters down the stretch but no one had seemed to notice. That was one of the things about Carl; he was a silent man who never pushed himself forward and was therefore often overlooked.

Clem Labine once said that Carl's eighth grade education probably hampered him socially, that "he may have felt some of the other players were aloof because they had a better education. He wouldn't socialize," Clem added, "he just wouldn't do it."[45]

But he was one of baseball's best hitters and on the train they started talking about him. The writers asked Reese to name the player who did the most down the stretch (had it been Snider or Robinson the question would not have been necessary). "Furillo," Reese answered, "Furillo and about 24 other guys, but put Furillo first."

It was spelled out by Bill Roeder of *The Sporting News:* In Carl's final 46 games he was almost unstoppable, hitting .426 on 79 hits in 186 at-bats, driving in almost a run per game.[46]

Not even the Dodger killer of the '40s and early '50s, Max Lanier, could get by Furillo consistently. Like Detroit's Frank Lary against the Yankees, Lanier was one of the few pitchers in the National League who dominated the Dodgers year after year.

In an interview conducted by mail because of Lanier's hearing problems, Max recalled loving to pitch against Brooklyn. "I can't explain it completely but I

The Reading Rifle: Carl Furillo may one day make the Hall of Fame if the Veterans Committee takes a look at his figures. His .299 career average, his batting championship and the arm that made him one of the best right fielders of his time are worth considering. Carl was blackballed after winning an injury-based suit against the Los Angeles Dodgers.

had great luck against Brooklyn. I remember pitching them—Reiser in particular—high fast balls mixed in with curve balls low and away. Of that whole team Carl Furillo hit me better than anyone."[47]

Max had more than luck. *The New Yorks Times* pointed out that when he jumped to Mexico in 1946 he was 21 and 7 against Brooklyn, surely making the Dodgers happy that he was gone.[48]

Furillo hit well not only against Lanier but most of the league's pitchers, as his .299 lifetime average shows. Carl was truly one of the Boys of Summer, a solid-hitting and silent right fielder whose fearsome arm prevented even the fleetest from taking the extra base. During his career he threw out seven men by throwing to first behind them as they took the wide turn. Even more remarkable, he once got a putout from right field on what would have been a single.

"I caught seven rounding the bag," he told Roger Kahn. "There's only one guy I really threw out. Mel Queen. A pitcher. He hit a liner at me, I grabbed it on a hop and my throw beat him."[49]

During his 15 years with the Dodgers he was fearless, at one time charging at the entire Giants team to get at Durocher. It was on September 6, 1953, and Furillo was leading the league at .344 on his way to the batting championship that year. There was, of course, bad blood between the Dodgers and Giants and on this day at Ebbets Field. Durocher was riding Carl for several innings until, with Carl at bat, Leo was heard to shout "stick it in his ear" to pitcher Ruben Gomez.

Gomez then hit Furillo on the right wrist and Carl, knowing the order came from Leo, went for the Giants manager, reaching him in front of the Giants dugout. There were punches thrown before the two grappled and went down, with Furillo's hands around Durocher's throat, choking him. Carl said later that while he was down someone stepped on his left hand, breaking a bone and ending his regular season.

It was one of the truly frightening brawls on a ballfield. As the *Times*' Louis Effrat pointed out, "It had been a long time brewing." The bad feeling between Furillo and Durocher started in 1949, Effrat wrote, after Carl was struck by a Sheldon Jones pitch and had to be hospitalized. He blamed Durocher for it at the time and his simmering resentment finally turned into rage as he charged the Giants team.

Even as his hand was being treated in the clubhouse he was still boiling, vowing further revenge, not satisfied that he had wrestled Durocher to the ground and was throttling him before they were separated. "I will get him," he said. "The first time I see him, the first time we come face to face I will get him. He has crossed me once too often."[50] The feud gradually died away, however, as Durocher apparently decided against further provocations. Leo Durocher was no fool.

Carl Furillo was raised near Reading, Pennsylvania, where he started playing ball for $80 a month in the Eastern Shore League. While working his way up through the Dodgers farm system he was nicknamed "The Reading Rifle" for his great throwing arm. To many Carl has Hall of Fame credentials: a batting championship, the .299 lifetime average, power enough for 194 home runs, 1,058 RBIs, and having been a team leader in seven World Series.

He was unyielding in standing up for his rights, a proud, stubborn man when crossed. Because of this his career ended badly when he was released after suffering a torn calf muscle. He sued and won $21,000 back pay on the grounds that releasing an injured player was illegal.

It cost him dearly, however. In later years he often said he was blackballed from baseball. He died January 21, 1989, never having been offered a coaching or even scouting job.[51] Given his skills and experience he was no doubt right. He was dealing, after all, with Walter O'Malley.

After visiting his father, Carl rejoined the club in plenty of time for the Series opener two days later and was in right field to see Tommy Henrich's line drive go over his head into the Stadium's "short porch," the lower stand, for a 1–0 last-inning win over Don Newcombe. Newk and Allie Reynolds had fought through a scoreless eight innings when Henrich, first up in the ninth, hit it out.

Roe got the Brooks even the next day in a six-hit, 1–0 masterpiece. The run came early when Robinson doubled off Vic Raschi and scored on a Hodges single. In the fourth inning the Preacher stopped a liner by Johnny Lindell that broke the index finger of his right hand. A lefty, he pitched right on, going all the way.

Roe was a study in sublety

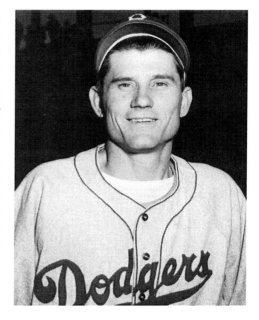

Elwin "Preacher" Roe came to Brooklyn from Pittsburgh along with Billy Cox in December 1947. Preacher was one of the smartest pitchers of all time. Lacking a major-league fastball, he pitched to spots and batter weaknesses, compiling a 93–37 record in seven years as a Dodger. After he retired he revealed that he threw a spitter on occasion.

and cunning both on and off the mound. He would play the role of hick from the Ozarks, often getting the advantage over those foolish enough to believe him. In truth, his father was a medical doctor, his brother a schools superintendent and Roe himself a part-time high school mathematics teacher.[52]

On the mound he was a mystery that Dodgers fans could never figure out. He had good control but he wasn't a power pitcher. He had a decent curve ball but not the hard fast ball to go with it. How, then, could this skinny guy, 6 foot 2 and just 170 pounds, be such a great pitcher?

Well, as Casey Stengel once said, he was one of the smartest pitchers around and he knew how to pitch to spots and to weaknesses. But there was something else: after he retired he admitted in a magazine article that he often threw the spitter during his Brooklyn glory days.[53]

The team knew about his spitter. Furillo, for one, could spot it from right field. "When Preach went to his cap with two pitching fingers together, that was our signal," he said. "That meant it was coming. If he went to his cap with fingers spread, then he was faking."[54] Preacher was clever enough, however, that he was never caught, even though a suspicious umpire would occasionally ask for the ball. During his shutout there was none of this, nor did any Yankee complain to the press about "a wet one."

The Series moved to Ebbets Field the next day where the Yanks won again, despite a fine eight-inning performance by Branca. But Ralph weakened in the ninth, gave up two runs and left with a man on who scored off Jack Banta, pinning the loss on Branca. Yankee reliever Joe Page won in relief of Tommy Byrne.

Bobby Brown, the medical student and future heart specialist, was the hitting star of the fifth game. He hit a bases-loaded triple in the fifth inning that routed Newcombe as the winning runs scored in a 6–4 struggle that gave the Yankees a commanding two-game lead. Allie Reynolds, of all pitchers, won in relief.

The last game of 1949 was a 10–6 Yankee win. Shotton used five pitchers in relief of Barney, who turned up wild again and was gone by the third inning. Hodges hit one with two on in the seventh but it was too late. Raschi won again with Page in relief.

The Dodgers' problem was that they never got into a sustained hitting attack, never had one of those big innings they often enjoyed during the season. As a team they hit .210 over the five games. During the season the starting Dodger eight had a team batting average of .295. Nobody beats the New York Yankees batting .210.

But the Yankees again had terrific pitching: Vic Raschi, Allie Reynolds, Eddie Lopat and, possibly the best reliever ever when he wasn't drinking, Joe Page.

In later years Birdie Tebbetts was often asked by people: who had the better team in the 1940s, the Yankees or the Red Sox?" The Red Sox," he would reply. The comeback was always: Why didn't you win?

"I'll give you the answer in two words," Birdie would say: "Joe Page."[55]

If any of the Brooklyn Dodgers had been asked the same question during those years the reply would, or should, have been the same.

So closed the 1940s, with another World Series loss for Brooklyn. Looking back over more then 50 years it's still hard to believe the team would be gone within a decade and the ballpark torn down soon after. Dick Young wrote in his "Obit on the Dodgers" the team went west because of "an acute case of greed, followed by severe political complications."[56]

Just one year before they left the Dodgers cleared $500,000, more than any other big league club, with O'Malley announcing that they were out of debt and owned real estate assets of about $5 million.[57] The announcement came as a surprise, since Walter was usually devious about the team's finances. In November of 1951 for instance, he released figures purportedly showing that because of its farm system the Dodgers organization lost almost $130,000 the year before.

Rep. Emanuel Cellar, chairman of the House Judiciary subcommittee, came up with the true figures the next day, pointing out that O'Malley wrote off a $167,000 loss incurred in promoting the Brooklyn Dodgers football team, a separate operation from the baseball club.

Cellar's committee was investigating organized baseball to look into accusations of anti-trust laws violations. He revealed that between the years 1945 through 1949 the Brooklyn Baseball Club netted $2,364,500, not including certain salaries and bonuses paid to club officials.[58]

Even after years of such earnings O'Malley was not happy. As Red Smith so aptly put it at the time: "No other Irishman excels O'Malley at musical keening, at crying with a loaf of bread under each arm."[59] While he was selling Ebbets Field for $4 million he was supposedly interested in property at the intersection of Atlantic and Flatbush avenues, the site of an obsolete Long Island Railroad terminal.

Some historians today feel that Robert Moses forced the Dodgers out of New York. Moses was certainly a powerful, arrogant and sometimes cruel man to deal with, but O'Malley moved the Dodgers, not Moses. In the final analysis, New York would not, or maybe could not, meet the bribes Los Angeles ultimately threw at him. How about starting with 300 acres of prime land in downtown Los Angeles? O'Malley gratefully accepted.

The crux of the matter in New York was that O'Malley insisted on the Atlantic-Flatbush Avenue property while Moses was equally insistent that Title I money under the Federal Housing Act was for slum clearance in that area, not a ballpark.[60]

As an alternative Moses offered Flushing Meadows but O'Malley was adamant, even after the Queens Chamber of Commerce, backing the Moses offer, recommended construction of a municipal stadium on the site of the 1939 World's Fair grounds.[61]

Those who write of this today are too young to have ever seen O'Malley in action, the lawyerly O'Malley who never tipped his hand and whom nobody could fathom. It took Red Barber and Branch Rickey years to read the man. Carl Furillo couldn't, George McLaughlin, even when not in his cups, couldn't, nor could his old friend, Harry Hickey, the man O'Malley refused to take to Japan lest he'd have to pay to ship his body back.

And these were people who dealt with Walter all the time. Was he honest with Mayor Robert Wagner and other officials or was he double-dealing and negotiating with Los Angeles all along, as many people think? We'll never know. His son, Peter, refuses to make his father's correspondence public.[62]

But Dick Young, for one, knew what he was talking about. An excellent reporter, he heard conversations in the flesh and didn't have to depend on documents 50 years later to know where the blame lay. O'Malley's remark to him about "niggers and spics and Jews" in Brooklyn resonates down through the years.

Ebbets Field was part of the excuse for moving, and there is no doubt the park had to go, since it only seated around 32,000. O'Malley worried over the parking situation and the demographic changes in the area, the changes Dick Young heard discussed.

Given those O'Malley concerns, what could have been wrong with Flushing Meadows? The New York Mets have been there for years and have prospered, despite some of the worst front-office management teams in the game's history.

A deceptive view of Ebbets Field: The old ballpark appears to be in its heyday as the Yankees and Dodgers battle through another World Series in the 1950s. At the time none in the packed stands would ever believe that the wrecker's ball was just a few short years away. But even as Robinson scores and the Duke approaches the plate, Walter O'Malley knew.

If at the time O'Malley wanted territory where there were not many blacks or Hispanics, there it was in Queens, with the proffered municipal stadium, plenty of parking and in an area accessible to millions of people. But it lacked the millions of dollars O'Malley knew could be made quickly in Los Angeles. The businessman in Walter, the greed and meanness that were always part of his nature, said go, and he went, leaving the Brooklyn Dodgers, in Dick Young's words, "the healthiest corpse in sports history."[63]

The *Times'* Dave Anderson, who was a sportswriter on the *New York Journal-American* when O'Malley moved out, is on Dick Young's side. His feelings: "They annoy me, these people who blame Moses for the Dodgers moving. Listen, they could have built a mile-high wall around Los Angeles and O'Malley would have broken through it to get his team there. The Mets are in Flushing now at the very place Moses offered O'Malley. Walter kept saying, 'Oh, I can't move the Dodgers to Queens.' No, so he moved them to Los Angeles."[64]

The team packed up and left at the end of the 1957 season, leaving a deserted ballpark that was gone within three years, replaced eventually by an apartment complex, the aptly named Ebbets Field Apartments. But the legacies of Ebbets Field live on in virtually every ballpark in America.

That first telecast in 1939 has taken over baseball, just as Larry MacPhail thought it would. As we know, TV rules the game, to the extent that we have World Series games at night in the November cold. (MacPhail never envisioned such abuse when he brought night ball to the majors in 1935.)

The batting helmet MacPhail had designed in 1941 now covers not only the head but includes a protective cheek guard. Today it would be unthinkable for a batter to face a 90-mile-an-hour fastball wearing just a cloth cap.

Jackie Robinson walked onto the infield at Ebbets Field in April of 1947, the only acknowledged black man in the history of major league baseball. There have been many times since when blacks have outnumbered whites on many teams and nobody gives it a second thought.

In fact, as pointed out by the writer Marty Appel in a piece he wrote on baseball milestones, the ultimate happened at Forbes Field on September 1, 1971, when the entire Pittsburgh starting lineup was black in a game against Philadelphia. There they are in the *New York Times* boxscore: Al Oliver, Rennie Stennett, Jackie Hernandez and Dave Cash in the infield, Willie Stargell, Gene Clines and Roberto Clemente in the outfield, Manny Sanguillen catching, and Dock Ellis the starting pitcher. The *Times* in its National League roundup wrote up the game without mentioning the team's racial makeup.[65]

Those first thin pads on the walls of Ebbets Field in the spring of 1948 have become cushions that outfielders literally bounce off of, knowing they are free to be more daring—and more effective—than in the days of uncovered concrete.

Of course there is always resistance to new ideas, no matter how good and sensible they may be. Remember, it was almost twelve years after MacPhail introduced the batting helmet that Don Zimmer, wearing his cloth cap at the plate, was almost fatally beaned and spent 13 days in a coma. And he wasn't alone in resisting the helmet.

It was the same with the padding. Club owners were hesitant to spend the money at first but came around slowly, some only after star players were injured. For Cincinnati, for example, to wait until 1992 when Dykstra broke his collar bone cannot be justified by any argument.

Now all those Ebbets Field developments—television, batting helmets, blacks in baseball, padded walls, warning tracks, team statisticians—are integral parts of baseball throughout the country. The contributions of MacPhail and Rickey live on, their ballpark gone these many years.

But is it? Listen to Red Barber when asked about the destruction of Ebbets Field:

"Ebbets Field meant so much to me that I never went back to look at the place after it became a ghost park. I never have gone back because I can still see Ebbets Field [in my mind]. As far as I'm concerned, it is still standing."[66]

That from the best baseball broadcaster who ever lived.

Notes

Chapter 1

1. Streak results: *New York Herald-Tribune*: 3/23–3/28, 1939 (Sports sections).
2. We didn't want anyone else to see him: *Ibid.*
3. Becomes a weekend pitcher: *Ibid*, p. 286.
4. Description of St. Louis: *Missouri, a WPA Project*, p. 295.
5. Brother dies: Honig, *Baseball When the Grass Was Real*, p. 287.
6. They'd sign him at 15: *Ibid*, p. 288.
7. Father a warehouse foreman: *American Magazine*, July 1947, p. 126.
8. St. Louis Cardinals "working agreements": *New York Times*, 3/24/38, p. 28.
9. Lomax on Rickey as commissioner: Frommer, *Rickey & Robinson*, p. 77.
10. Veeck on sale of Phillies: Veeck, *Veeck as in Wreck*, p. 172.
11. Veeck buying Phillies not true: SABR, *The National Pastime*, 1998, No. 17, pp. 3–13.
12. Rickey on Winsett: Parrott, *The Lords of Baseball*, pp. 89–90.
13. Hornsby-Rickey fight: *New York Times*, 11/13/23, p. 17.
14. Hornsby's lateness and absences: Polner, *Branch Rickey*, p. 89.
15. Shotton breaks up fight: Fitzgerald, *The Story of the Brooklyn Dodgers*, p. 175.
16. $275,000 offer for Hornsby: *New York Times*, 12/12/23, p. 26.
17. Cards trade Hornsby: *New York Times*, 12/21/26, p. 1.
18. Giants trade Hornsby: *Ibid*, 1/11/28, p. 1.
19. Stoneham reacts to insults: Hynd, *The Giants of the Polo Grounds*, p. 271.
20. Winding ball tighter: Light, *Cultural Encyclopedia of Baseball*, p. 54.
21. Reiser signs for $100: *The Sporting News*, 2/6/41, p. 4.
22. Pete's reaction to the $100: *Ibid.*
23. Learns to hit left-handed: Honig, *Baseball When the Grass Was Real*, p. 290.
24. MacPhail furious with Durocher: *Ibid*, p. 123.
25. Battle of the Biltmore: Warfield, *The Roaring Redhead*, p. 220.
26. MacPhail and first night game: *Ibid*, p. 59.
27. Brooklyn's inferiority complex: Barber, *Rhubarb in the Catbird Seat*, p. 17.
28. Smith on Brooklyn-Philadelphia: Parrott, *The Lords of Baseball*, p. 97.
29. Smith: Dodger fans as cockroaches: *New York Herald-Tribune*, 10/21/47, p. 29.
30. Smith: Brooklyn a provincial outpost: Kahn, *The Era*, p. 112.
31. MacPhail brings radio to N.Y. baseball: Warfield, *The Roaring Redhead*, pp. 81–82.
32. I broadcast the ball: Barber, *Rhubard in the Catbird Seat*, p. 274.
33. The smallest crowd in Stadium history: Barber, *The Broadcasters*, p. 218.
34. The firing of Red Barber: *Ibid*, p. 220.
35. MacPhail brings TV to N.Y. baseball: Warfield, *The Roaring Redhead*, p. 91.
36. Red pays for the memento: Barber, *The Broadcasters*, p. 155.
37. Durocher fired "60" times: Durocher, *Nice Guys Finish Last*, p. 129.

38. Leo strands Larry at 125th Street: Creamer, *Baseball in 1941*, pp. 292–293.

39. Objections to Elmira order: Honig, *Baseball When the Grass Was Real*, p. 293.

40. Yankees offer $100,000-plus: Red Smith, *New York Times*, 11/2/81, p. C 10.

41. Gehrig streak ends amid great emotion: *Ibid*, 5/4/39, p. 29.

42. Bill Killefer, Alexander's batterymate: Reichler, *Baseball Encyclopedia*, p. 1135.

43. The injury jinx starts: *Elmira Star-Gazette*, 4/19/40, p. 22.

44. Learns to throw left-handed as elbow heals: Heinz, "The Rocky Road of Pistol Pete" in *The Baseball Reader*, Edited by Charles Einstein, pp. 164–116.

45. MacPhail gives up Elmira, Interview of Al Mallette, retired sports editor of the *Elmira Star-Gazette*, in Elmira on 3/27/01.

Chapter 2

1. Is Brooklyn still in the league: *The Sporting News*, 2/1/34.

2. MacPhail upgrades Ebbets Field: Warfield, *The Roaring Redhead*, pp. 73–74.

3. You mean $50,000 for the whole team: Golenbock, *Bums*, p. 33.

4. Purchase price $35,000 and four players: *The Sporting News*, 12/9/56, p. 9.

5. Cronin says Reese will never make it: Durocher, *Nice Guys Finish Last*, p. 133.

6. Reese nicknamed Pee Wee after winning marble tournament: *New York Times*, 8/6/99, p. B7 (Obit).

7. No one at the bank even blinked at MacPhail deals: *Brooklyn Eagle*, 6/13, p. 1.

8. Dissension on Cards involved Medwick: Warfield, *The Roaring Redhead*, p. 96.

9. Reese through for year after breaking heel sliding: *Brooklyn Eagle*, 8/16, p. 13.

10. Reese lost ball against white-shirt background: Golenbock, *Bums*, p. 63.

11. Medwick beaned by Bowman: *New York Herald-Tribune*, 6/19, p. 29.

12. O'Dwyer investigates "bad blood" behind beaning: *Ibid*, p. 6/20, p. 27.

13. Leo decides to play despite injuries: *Ibid*.

14. Medwick plate-shy: *Brooklyn Eagle*, 8/19/46, p. 19.

15. Casey hits Passeau; starts bench-clearing, injury-free melee: *Ibid*, 7/20, p. 10.

16. MacPhail loses bet against Reiser

speed: Honig, *Baseball When the Grass Was Real*, p. 291.

17. Reiser possibly fastest man on earth: Kahn, *The Era*, p. 108.

18. Two pitches three outs: *New York Times*, 7/24, p. 25.

19. Coscarart-Frey brawl: *Ibid*.

20. Yankees call up Henrich: Mayer, *The 1937 Newark Bears*, pp. 111–112.

21. Hershberger commits suicide: *New York Times*, 8/4, p. 5.

22. Arnovich, McKechnie comments: Hershberger upset at being Lombardi backup; McKechnie to team that day: *The National Pastime* (SABR), 2000, No. 20, p. 72.

23. Suicide ran in Hershberger family: *Ibid*.

24. Team votes Hershberger's mother full Series share of $5,803, *Ibid*.

25. Abe Stark never gave up suit: Parrott, *The Lords of Baseball*, p. 87.

26. Umpire Magerkurth attacked by fan: *New York Times*, 9/17, p. 29.

27. Higbe to Dodgers causes Philly fans to talk boycott: *Brooklyn Eagle*, 11/28, p. 15.

Chapter 3

1. Anybody can play center field: Honig, *Baseball When the Grass Was Real*, p. 298.

2. Pete so fast he tried for everything: Howie Schultz interview.

3. The walls were never there for Pete: Eddie Miksis interview.

4. Stadium center field toughest: *Where Have You Gone Joe DiMaggio?*, p. 40.

5. Ballpark dimensions: Lowry, *Green Cathedrals*, pp. 61, 196, 117, 118.

6. Bat left-handed only: Honig, *Baseball When the Grass Was Real*, p. 298.

7. Pete saved by MacPhail inserts: *New York Times*, 5/1, p. 28.

8. Medwick rushed back too soon: Creamer, *Baseball in 1941*, p. 111.

9. MacPhail has doctors design helmet; saves Reese: *New York Times*, 3/9, p. S1.

10. Between 1910 and 1920 four minor leaguers killed by fastballs: Light, *The Cultural Encyclopedia of Baseball*, p. 87.

11. Ray Chapman, 29, only major league fatality: *New York Times*, 8/18/20, p. 15.

12. Carl Mays' unpopularity because of dusters: *Ibid*, 8/19/20, p. 10.

13. Mickey Cochrane's career-ending injury: *Ibid,* 5/26/37, p. 1.

14. Don Zimmer beaned: *St. Paul Pioneer Press,* 7/8/53, p. 15.

15. Don hospitalized 28 days; operated on twice: *St. Paul Dispatch,* 8/3/53, p. 15.

16. He wasn't wearing a helmet: Joe Hennessy column, *St. Paul Pioneer Press,* 7/9/53, p. 23.

17. Actually four holes in my head, Zimmer says: *Zim,* p. 9.

18. Don't hurt Zim. He's got a plate in his head: *Ibid,* p. 116.

19. Clemens denies deliberately hitting Piazza: *CBS Sixty Minutes,* 4/22/01.

20. Bobby Valentine says different: *New York Times,* 7/8/00, p. S1.

21. Headhunters Maglie, Drysdale, Wynn: Bobby Bragan interview.

22. Thank God for Mr. Rickey's helmet: Eddie Miksis interview.

23. Hank Greenberg into Army: *New York Times,* 5/5, p. 27.

24. Club announced injury not serious but Pete out eight days: *Ibid,* 5/18, p. 56.

25. Leo not interested in tomorrow: *The Sporting News,* 9/11, p. 9.

26. Joe DiMaggio 56-game streak starts: *New York Herald-Tribune,* 7/18, p. 16.

27. Joe starts another streak: *New York Times,* 8/4, p. 17.

28. Pete hits grand slam off Pearson, who beaned him month before: *Ibid,* 5/26, p. 25.

29. Poll on who plays Gehrig in Goldwyn movie: *The Sporting News,* 10/9, p. 16.

30. Back from the war, Mulcahy weakened by tropical disease: Light, *The Cultural Encyclopedia of Baseball,* p. 80.

31. Draftee's appeal must go to the president: *New York Times,* 6/12, p. 30.

32. Average major league salary $7,000 in 1941: Light, *The Cultural Encyclopedia of Baseball,* p. 642.

33. Various prices in 1941: *New York Times,* 6/15.

34. Deferments tougher after Pearl Harbor: Creamer, *Baseball in 1941,* p. 331.

35. Dick Wakefield first bonus baby: *New York Times,* 6/28, p. 18.

36. Dodgers need suit of armor: *Brooklyn Eagle,* 7/1, p. 15.

37. We should get combat pay: Honig, *Baseball When the Grass Was Real,* p. 305.

38. Coscarart on Durocher: it was either love or hate: Pete Coscarart interview.

39. Durocher shoves Ruth into locker: Creamer, *Baseball in 1941,* p. 51.

40. Ruth hit three homers last day of his career: Pete Coscarart interview.

41. What's wrong with loosening up a hitter?: *The Sporting News,* 9/4/46, p. 2.

42. Wyatt warns DiMaggio against digging in: Honig, *Baseball When the Grass Was Real,* p. 307.

43. After second knockdown of DiMaggio, both benches emptied: *New York Times,* 10/7, p. 28.

44. Joe says the strain is over: *The Sporting News,* 7/24, p. 16.

45. Slaughter out for season: *St. Louis Post-Dispatch,* 8/11, p. S1.

46. Slaughter's competitive fire: Connor, *Voices From Cooperstown,* p. 315.

47. Enos' face went white: *St. Louis Post-Dispatch,* 8/11, p. S1.

48. Jubilant fans escort Pete around the bases: *New York Times,* 8/19, p. 25.

49. Moore wore no protective cap: *Ibid,* 8/21, p. S1.

50. Cecil Travis' frozen feet from Battle of the Bulge: *The Sporting News,* 7/9, p. 11.

51. Crowd forms victory line after 10th-inning win: *Ibid,* 9/8, p. 13.

52. Sportsman's Park: worst in majors: Turner, *When the Boys Came Back,* p. 172.

53. Roy Sievers agrees Sportsman's Park the worst: Roy Sievers interview.

54. Ford Frick takes command: *St. Louis Post-Dispatch,* 9/13, p. S1.

55. Who is Alf Anderson: Creamer, *Baseball in 1941,* p. 285.

56. Umpires hate being showed up: *New York Herald-Tribune,* 9/20, p. 15.

57. No one dared challenge Magerkurth: SABR's *National Pastime,* (1993) No. 13, p. 14.

58. Magerkurth blocked from Series: *Ibid.*

59. Durocher sucker punches AP writer: *New York Herald-Tribune,* 9/20, p. 15.

60. Leo rides Maj on radio shows: Parrott, *The Lords of Baseball,* p. 153.

61. Dixie the "People's Choice," not Cherce: *Ibid* p. 111.

62. A peaceful celebration, 1941 style: *New York Herald-Tribune,* 9/30, p. 21.

63. Leo claims Casey pitch not a spitter: *Nice Guys Finish Last,* p. 161.

64. Henrich says Casey's pitch exploded: Creamer, *Baseball in 1941,* p. 310.

65. "I really think it was a spitter." Pete Coscarart interview.

66. "It was a little wet slider," Reese said: Golenbock, *Bums,* p. 74.

67. It was a "spitball," Casey tells Tommy Holmes: Holmes, *The Dodgers*, p. 89.

68. Reiser gets one vote in Athlete of the Year poll: *New York Times*, 12/8/41, p. 42.

Chapter 4

1. The Green Light letter from FDR to Landis: *New York Times*, 1/17/42.

2. MacPhail says 1941 team can't repeat: *Ibid*, 11/28/41, p. 29.

3. Says he drew up lists of undesirables for trades: *Ibid*.

4. Reiser gets Rookie of the Year Award from Chicago writers: *The Sporting News*, 1/15, p. 10.

5. Brooklyn was the big leagues: Pete Coscarart interview.

6. Reiser and Reese married on same day, 3/29: Florida State Office of Vital Statistics.

7. Pete fined $200 for missing day; fine sticks: *Ibid*, 4/6, p. 20.

8. Pete: They never asked me if I could; they always asked me if I would: Honig, *Baseball America*, p. 278.

9. Navy refuses French leave to go for win 200: Pietrusza, Silverman and Gershman, *Baseball: The Biographical Encyclopedia*, p. 382.

10. After injury, Ed Head switches to right arm: *The Sporting News*, 4/30, p. 5.

11. Beazley injures arm in service: *Ibid*, 4/30/90, p. 45 (Obit).

12. Ballplayers must stay on field during air raids: *Ibid*, 4/11, p. 17.

13. Glow from ballparks helped U-boats: *Ibid*, 5/19, p. 25.

14. Capt. Eddie Grant only big leaguer killed in action in WW I: *Ibid*, 4/15, p. 28.

15. Lost Battalion down to 650 survivors: Stallings, *Doughboys, the Story of the AEF*, pp. 267–2791.

16. Pete known for his vicious swing: *The Sporting News*, 5/28, p. 3.

17. Pete never cheated out of a swing: Eddie Miksis interview.

18. Pete a bad ball hitter: Fitzgerald, *The Story of the Brooklyn Dodgers*, pp. 117–118.

19. Grimm, Cubs manager, delighted to get Dean: *Ibid*, p. S7.

20. Dean on reported $150,000: I don't think they got enough: *Ibid*, 4/18/38, p. 18.

21. Cards stunned and sad about Dean leaving: *Ibid*, 4/17/38, p. S1.

22. Pitcher Jim Tobin's three consecutive homers in one game: *New York Herald-Tribune*, 5/13, p. 24.

23. Leo throws towel in umpire's face: *Ibid*, 6/29, p. 9.

24. Leo says umpires picking on Dodgers: *New York Times*, 6/30, p. 25.

25. Bob Feller claims to have invented the slider: *Ibid*, 7/3, p. 21.

26. Years later Feller credited George Blaeholder of the St. Louis Browns: Einstein, *The Baseball Reader*, p. 114.

27. Foxx says Blaeholder toughest pitcher in the AL: Pietrusza, Silverman and Gershman: *Baseball: The Biographical Encyclopedia*, p. 92.

28. Bithorn throws at Leo in dugout: *New York Times*, 7/16, p. 25.

29. Pete at .350 when he hit wall, not .380: *New York Times*, 7/19, 7/20.

30. *Brooklyn Eagle* on Pete hitting the wall: 7/20, p. 11.

31. Leo again oblivious to seriousness of Pete's injury: *Ibid*, 7/21, p. 11.

32. MacPhail charges doctor keeping Pete from playing against St. Louis: Honig, *Baseball When the Grass Was Real*, p. 303.

33. Pete plays too soon after injury: *Brooklyn Eagle*, 7/26, p. 1C.

34. Pete was oblivious of the walls: Gene Hermanski interview.

35. Rickey on MacPhail handling of Reiser: Parrott, *The Lords of Baseball*, p. 139.

36. Don't ever speak to me again: Frommer, *Rickey & Robinson*, p. 150.

37. The headaches and dizzy spells start: *New York Times*, 8/5, p. 23.

38. A powerful umpire bloc content with status quo: *Brooklyn Eagle*, 8/10, p. 13.

39. These are real men from Missouri: *Ibid*, 9/17, p. 1.

40. Case settled amicably: *Ibid*, 10/6, p. 26.

41. Reiser: I cost the Dodgers the pennant in '42: *The Sporting News*, 1/5/49, p. 3.

42. MacPhail to beautify Ebbets Field: Parrott, *The Lords of Baseball*, p. 99–100.

43. Larry left club in good financial shape: Warfield, *The Roaring Redhead*, p. 144.

44. O'Malley buys 25 percent of the Dodgers: Helyer, *Lords of the Realm*, p. 43.

45. McLaughlin a political power: *New York Times*, 12/8/67, p. 42 (Obit).

46. O'Malley McLaughlin's driver: Helyer, *Lords of the Realm*, p. 40.

47. O'Malley won't risk cost of shipping body back from Japan: Parrott, *The Lords of Baseball*, p. 24–25.
48. MacPhail: I've talked enough. Let's have a drink: Warfield, *The Roaring Redhead*, p. 145.
49. Breadon resented money Rickey was making from selling players: *American National Biography*, pp. 480–481.
50. Rickey and Durocher, the odd couple: Polner, *Branch Rickey*, p. 38–39.
51. Rickey dubbed The Mahatma: *Ibid*, p. 122.
52. Durocher never kept money won from players: *New York Times*, 11/20, p. 28.
53. Frank Graham compares Rickey and MacPhail: *The Sporting News*, 11/5, p. 9

Chapter 5

1. American Legion offers to buy Dodgers: *New York Times*, 2/9/45, p. 19.
2. Legion schedules meeting to discuss offer but no Dodger exec attends: *Ibid*.
3. Rickey denies any knowledge of offer: *Ibid*.
4. Legion wants all Dodger stock or nothing: *Ibid*, 2/10/45, p. 15.
5. The Mulveys insist their stock is not for sale: *Ibid*.
6. The following week no comment from either side; deal dead: *Ibid*, 2/18/45, p. S2.
7. Boxing promoter Mike Jacobs formed syndicate to buy club before the war: *New York Herald-Tribune*, 8/18/40, p. 20.
8. *Herald-Tribune* account says Jacobs group wants all stock or nothing: *Ibid*.
9. Jacobs denies syndicate; says he's alone: *Brooklyn Eagle*, 8/9/40, p. 13.
10. Things too good for Mrs. Mulvey to sell: *New York Herald-Tribune*, 8/8/40, p. 20.
11. McLaughlin does about face, saying no deal: *New York Times*, 8/9/40, p. 8.
12. George M. Cohan and George Jessel attempt ignored: *Ibid*, 11/20/40, p. 31.
13. Jessel unacceptable, married 16-year-old. *New York Times*, 5/26/84, Sec. 4, p. 12 (Obit).
14. Years before, Col. Huston, once a Yankee owner, made offer that was refused by Dodger president Stephen McKeever: *Ibid*, 2/10/34, p. 10.
15. O'Malley gets total control: Light, *The Cultural Encyclopedia of Baseball*, p. 421.

Chapter 6

1. Browns wartime outfield: Goldstein, *The Spartan Seasons*, p. xiii.
2. Red Barber on wartime baseball: *Ibid*.
3. Chapman to Ruth about salary: *New York Times*, 7/8/93, p. D19 (Obit).
4. Chapman banned for one year: *Ibid*.
5. I'm a changed man: *The Sporting News*, 6/8/44, p. 6.
6. Chapman to Dodgers: *Ibid*, 8/10/44, p. 7.
7. Fired as Phillies manager: *New York Times*, 7/17/48, p. 10.
8. Chapman chastised by Chandler: *Ibid*, 7/8/93, p. D19 (Obit).
9. Shepard to Walter Reed Hospital: SABR *The National Pastime*, 1999 No. 19, p. 75.
10. Works out as POW: Peitrusza, Silverman and Gershman, *Baseball: The Biographical Encyclopedia*, p. 1030.
11. Shepard: I'll do okay with special leg: Goldstein, *Spartan Seasons*, p. 211.
12. Shepard pitching coach: Turner, *When the Boys Came Back*, p. 84.
13. Not the "push-off" leg: SABR *The National Pastime*, 1999 No. 19, p. 76.
14. Gets DFC and Air Medal: Goldstein, *Spartan Seasons*, p. 212.
15. Gray taught himself to catch and throw: *New York Times*, 8/1/02, p. A19 (Obit).
16. Gray MVP of Southern Association: *Ibid*.
17. Cost us eight to ten games: Pietrusza, Silverman and Gershman, *Baseball: The Biographical Encyclopedia*, p. 430.
18. Gray a gate attraction: *New York Times*, 8/1/02, p. A19 (Obit).
19. He could do things others could not: *Ibid*.
20. An inspiration to those at Walter Reed Hospital: *Ibid*.
21. Gray retired because of tougher competition: *Ibid*, 4/23/46, p. 28.
22. With two arms, who knows?: *Ibid*, 8/1/02, p. A19 (Obit).
23. I don't care what they write: Holmes, *Brooklyn's Babe*, p. 220.
24. Babe a rich poultry farmer: *Baseball Magazine*, 9/45, p. 331.
25. Babe wouldn't have to run too much: Holmes, *Brooklyn's Babe*, p. 220.
26. The many tales about Babe Herman: *Ibid*, p. 221.

27. To the press, same old Babe: Holmes, *Ibid*, p. 222.

28. A battery that totaled 32 years in age: Goldstein, *Spartan Seasons*, p. 163.

29. Nuxhall signed by Cincinnati at 15: *The Sporting News*, 2/24/44, p. 4.

30. McLeod a first-class receiver: *Newark Evening News*, 4/11/45, p. 23.

31. The Don Newcombe fastball: *Ibid*.

32. Just 32 remained from wartime ball: Goldstein, *Spartan Seasons*, p. xiii.

Chapter 7

1. Pete offered $100,000 to jump to the Mexican League: *Brooklyn Eagle*, 5/5, p. 9.

2. Luis Olmo and Danny Gardella jump: *New York Times*, 2/19, p. 29.

3. Chandler announces five-year suspensions: *The Sporting News*, 3/14, p. 2.

4. Court enjoins Mexicans from luring other Dodgers: *New York Times*, 5/7, p. 27.

5. Lavagetto's "not interested" mood of other Dodgers: *Brooklyn Eagle*, 3/28, p. 15.

6. Reiser and Rojek stay after meeting with Rickey: *Ibid*, 5/5, p. S3.

7. Triplett not allowed to play in Mexico: *The Sporting News*, 9/4, p. 8.

8. Fan with broken jaw says Durocher attacked him: *New York Times*, 6/11/45, p. 1.

9. Leo denies charges: *Brooklyn Eagle*, 4/24, p. 1.

10. Judge congratulates jury on acquitting Durocher: *Ibid*.

11. Brawl continues next day: *Ibid*, 5/24, p. 15.

12. Ruth says MacPhail refused him Newark job: *Ibid*, 6/2, p. S1.

13. Ruth praises the Pasquels: *Ibid*, 5/16, p. 25.

14. Ruth agrees baseball a monopoly: Ibid, 5/22, p. 27.

15. A union movement in Pittsburgh: *Ibid*, 6/6, p. 26.

16. Coscarart shipped to Pacific Coast League: Pete Coscarart interview.

17. Pirates vote against union: *Ibid*, 8/20, p. 30.

18. Veeck sends midget up to bat: *New York Herald-Tribune*: 8/20/51, p. 1.

19. Move stayed with Veeck after death: *Ibid*, 1/3/86, Sec. II, p. 4 (Obit).

20. Baseball's "darkest hour" bus crash: *Spokane Review*, 6/20/71, p. 36.

21. Fund for crash victims' families: *Ibid*.

22. Dean: Don't fail to miss tomorrow's game: *New York Times*, 7/21, p. S4.

23. A guy's got to do that sort of thing in this business: *Ibid*, p. 1.

24. Owen: Pasquels the real power in Mexico: *The Sporting News*, 8/14, p. 1.

25. Owen appeals, says others await decision on him: *New York Times*, 8/9, p. 23.

26. Phillies approve resolution condemning jumpers: *Ibid*.

27. Vern Stephens urges continued ban: *The Sporting News*, 8/14, p. 4.

28. Gardella's suit charges restraint of trade: *New York Times*, 10/3/47, p. 34.

29. Dismissal based on 1922 Oliver Wendell Holmes ruling: *Ibid*, 10/10/22, p. 17.

30. Court reinstates Gardella suit: *Ibid*, 2/10/49, p. 39.

31. Gardella bribed to withdraw suit: *Ibid*, 6/16/50, p. 32.

32. Chandler lifts ban on jumpers: *Brooklyn Eagle*, 6/6/49, p. 13.

33. An 86-day work stoppage in 1972 is settled: *Ibid*, 4/14/72, p. 1.

34. Seitz rules reserve clause binds for just one year: *Ibid*, 12/24/75, p. 1.

35. Mexican owners promise no further raids: *Ibid*, 10/29/47, p. 38.

36. Giants split doubleheader: *New York Times*, 8/5/12, p. 11.

37. Philadelphia splits doubleheader: *Ibid*, 5/31/12, p. 10.

38. Owners agree to players' demands: *Ibid*, 8/29, p. 1.

39. Higbe and Casey on the town: McNeil, *The Dodgers Encyclopedia*, p. 59.

40. Pete's seventh steal of home: *Brooklyn Eagle*, 9/8, p. 13.

41. Each Dodger gets new Studebaker: *Ibid*.

42. O'Malley starts anti–Rickey campaign: Parrott, *The Lords of Baseball*, p. 20.

43. Walter would ridicule not playing Sunday: Frommer, *Rickey & Robinson*, p. 38.

44. O'Malley gripes about Studebaker gifts: Golenbock, *Bums*, 105–106.

45. When Rickey gave his word, that was it: Frommer, *Rickey & Robinson*, p. 31.

46. "Merkle" game a replay, not a playoff: *Brooklyn Eagle*, 9/24, p. 17.

47. Merkle not touching second common then: Anderson, *More Than Merkle*, p. 17.

48. Rickey pledges playoff proceeds to employees: *Brooklyn Eagle*, 10/3, p. 16.

49. Films show Pesky didn't freeze: Stout and Johnson, *Red Sox Century,* p. 257.
50. Slaughter "knew" he could score: Halberstam: *Teammates,* p. 153.
51. Doerr deplores condition of Sportsman's Park: *Ibid,* p. 157.
52. Scorer "took the romance" out of a great play: *Ibid,* p. 156.

Chapter 8

1. Pete offered full salary for year off: Heinz, *The Rocky Road of Pistol Pete,* p. 237.
2. Ebbets Field refurbished; stands enlarged: *The Sporting News,* 2/5, p. 16.
3. CYO demands Durocher be replaced: *New York Herald-Tribune,* 3/1, p. 15.
4. Calls Durocher trial fixed: Marshall, *Baseball's Pivotal Era,* p. 114.
5. Gamblers had run of Dodger clubhouse: Polner, *Branch Rickey,* p. 123.
6. Leo ordered to cut ties to underworld: Marshall, *Baseball's Pivotal Era,* p. 105.
7. "Stop nodding," Durocher told: Arthur Daley, *New York Times,* 4/10, p. 32.
8. Chandler to George Raft: Marshall, *Baseball's Pivotal Era,* p. 106.
9. Minor leaguers accused of throwing game: *New York Times,* 1/27, p. 18.
10. Anti-gambling rules: *Ibid,* 1/31, p. 19.
11. Laraine Day's husband names Leo: *The Sporting News,* 12/11/46, p. 10.
12. Durocher arguing in Day's bedroom: Marshall, *Baseball's Pivotal Era,* p. 10.
13. Who can shed a tear for Durocher?: Marshall, *Ibid,* p. 115.
14. Stadium crowd on Chandler's side: *New York Times,* 4/28, p. 1.
15. Robinson in antagonistic camp: *The Sporting News,* 3/12, p. 17.
16. Robinson names those responsible: Robinson, *I Never Had It Made,* p. 57.
17. Reiser, Hodges, Barney and Snider the first to befriend Robinson: Marshall, *Baseball's Pivotal Era,* p. 142.
18. They'll run you right out of the ballpark: Durocher, *Nice Guys Finish Last,* p. 205.
19. I was brought up a Southerner: Higbe, *The High Hard One,* p. 107.
20. Schoendienst says no strike planned: Frommer, *Rickey & Robinson,* p. 138.
21. Robinson strike plot, UCLA and

barbarism and discrimination in Philadelphia: Robinson, *I Never Had It Made,* pp. 59–64.
22. Shaking hands with Chapman: *Ibid,* p. 63.
23. Hermanski suggests everyone wear #42: Snider, *The Duke of Flatbush,* p. 24.
24. Everyone relaxed a bit: Gene Hermanski interview.
25. Pee Wee's hand on Jackie's shoulder: *New York Times,* 8/16/99, p. B7 (Obit).
26. A gesture of support: Robinson, *I Never Had It Made,* p. 65.
27. Rickey's search for the right man: Frommer, *Rickey & Robinson,* p. 96.
28. Rickey finds Robinson, *Ibid,* p. 106.
29. Robinson goes to 215 Montague Street: Robinson, *I Never Had It Made,* p. 30.
30. Childhood, UCLA and Joe Louis: Robinson, *Ibid,* pp. 4–12.
31. Troubles in the Army, *Ibid,* pp. 15–23.
32. Rickey wants someone with guts *not* to fight back: *Ibid,* pp. 33–34.
33. A certain amount of jealousy: Frommer, *Rickey & Robinson,* pp. 113–114.
34. Abrams was slow: Eddie Miksis interview.
35. One of the most dramatic putouts in game's history: *New York Times,* 6/5, p. 33.
36. Hermanski explains the catch: Gene Hermanski interview.
37. Calls for rubber walls and gravel warning track: *Brooklyn Eagle,* 6/5, p. 20.
38. The lights made a difference: Pete Coscarart interview.
39. Stanky breaks up Blackwell no-hitter: *New York Times,* 6/23, p. 21.
40. Veeck gets letters protesting Doby signing: Veeck, *Veeck as in Wreck,* p. 170.
41. Doby would point to his hand: *Ibid,* p. 179.
42. Cub trade destroyed team camaderie: Eddie Miksis interview.
43. Spider ran out of gas: Spider Jorgensen interview.
44. McGraw trusts Ott with no one: Hynd, *The Giants of the Polo Grounds,* p. 266.
45. Dodger fans do conga line: *Brooklyn Eagle,* 9/23, p. 1.
46. Bobby Bragan at the piano: Bobby Bragan interview.
47. A pitcher who rattles so easily: *New York Times,* 10/1, p. 37.

48. That when the chips are down, he goes up: *The Sporting News,* 11/26, p. 9.
49. Pete wearing cap and bells: Red Smith, *New York Herald-Tribune,* 10/2, p. 29.
50. Pete was having dizzy spells but told no one: Kahn, *The Era,* p. 108.
51. He was punchy by then: Spider Jorgensen interview.
52. Shotton: What are you doing here?: *The Sporting News,* 10/15, p. 9.
53. He walks up there like he wasn't hurt at all: Eddie Miksis interview.
54. Harris: Reiser is a long-ball hitter: *New York Times,* 10/4, p. 12.
55. Ruth: You can't take a chance with dynamite: *The Sporting News,* 3/24/48, p. 7.
56. DiMaggio: He could have made it look easy: Halberstam, *Summer of '49,* p. 49.
57. Dixie leaves with love and few regrets: *New York Times,* 12/8 p. 41.

Chapter 9

1. Maybe I should have rested: Heinz, *The Rocky Road of Pistol Pete,* p. 237.
2. Rickey announces padding of Ebbets Field walls: *Brooklyn Eagle,* 3/14, p. 3.
3. Baltimore pads walls after Kuehn and Blefery injuries: *Internet to Google to Padded Walls to Memorial Stadium.*
4. Fenway walls padded: Light, *The Cultural Encyclopedia of Baseball,* p. 256.
5. Reds pad walls in '92 after Dykstra injury: *Ibid.*
6. Brooklyn fans don't deserve a pennant: *New York Times,* 8/27/55, p. 10.
7. Cop: I hate baseball: Snider, *The Duke of Flatbush,* p. 100.
8. Owners nix amnesty for jumpers to Mexico: *The Sporting News,* 2/11, p. 1.
9. Backs down the next day: *Ibid,* 2/19, p. 31.
10. MacPhail calls Rickey a liar: *Ibid,* 2/21, p. 16.
11. Chandler: The Dodgers have Jackie Robinson, don't they?: *The Sporting News,* 2/25, p. 1.
12. Rickey critical of overweight Robinson: *New York Times,* 5/2/48, p. S2.
13. Rickey puts Robinson on waivers: *New York Daily Mirror,* 5/26, pp. 42–43.
14. "We want Shotton" cries heard at Ebbets Field: *The Sporting News,* 5/12, p. 2.

15. Durocher bans Dick Young from Dodgers clubhouse: *Ibid.*
16. Inching their way westward: *New York Times,* 9/1/87, p. B 7 (Dick Young Obit).
17. O'Malley: too many blacks and spics and Jews: Kahn, *The Era,* p. 327.
18. *The Daily News* vigorously defends Dick Young: *The Sporting News,* 5/12, p. 2.
19. Barney pitched as though the plate were high and outside: Kahn, *The Era,* p. 123.
20. Edwards joins Jorgensen on arm trouble list: *Brooklyn Eagle,* 5/27, p. 24.
21. LA officials try for the St. Louis Browns: *The Sporting News,* 7/7, p. 2.
22. Plans to make the LA Coliseum world's largest ballpark: *Ibid.*
23. Paige's mother: He changed his age back in 1927: *New York Times,* 7/18, p. 26.
24. Durocher's version of Giants job offer: *Ibid,* 7/18, p. S 2.
25. To say Stoneham can drink is like saying Sinatra can sing: Durocher, *Nice Guys Finish Last,* p. 288.
26. Dan Daniel: Both the Dodgers and Brooklyn tired of Durocher: *The Sporting News* 7/28, p. 3.
27. Erskine's 12-year pulled muscle: Erskine mailed reply to questions, 11/26/99.
28. He was so dizzy he had to be helped off the field: *Ibid.*
29. Robinson tormentor Ben Chapman fired as Phillies manager: *New York Times,* 7/17, p. 10.
30. Ben Chapman's anti–Semitic shouting: Frommer, *Rickey & Robinson,* p. 137.
31. Durocher's return to Ebbets Field an anti-climax: *New York Times,* 7/27, p. 20.
32. The Babe taking an injured dog to the hospital: *Ibid,* p. 18.
33. Movie about Monte Stratton wins Oscar: John Eames, *The MGM Story,* p. 224.
34. The incredible comeback of Lou Brissie: Westcott, *Splendor on the Diamond,* Chapter on Lou Brissie.
35. The Babe died in his sleep: *New York Times,* 8/17, p. 1.
36. One of the best kept secrets of modern times: *Ibid,* 8/17, p. 5.
37. The Great Reese Drought: *Brooklyn Eagle,* 9/8, p. 24.
38. Things went black when Pete looked up: *The Sporting News,* 9/22, p. 6.
39. After Spider's arm went dead eight men tried at third: *Brooklyn Eagle,* 9/29, p. 15.

40. Pete's last at-bat as a Dodger: *Ibid,* 10/4, p. 13.
41. Rickey afraid of the second guess: *Ibid,* 12/16, p. 21.
42. Pete: I'll never again wear a Dodger uniform: *New York Times,* 12/16, p. 43.
43. Reiser traded to Boston: *Brooklyn Eagle,* 12/16, p. 21.
44. Pete admits again he cost Brooklyn two pennants by playing hurt: *The Sporting News,* 1/5/49, p. 3.
45. A very unhappy state of affairs: *Ibid.*

Chapter 10

1. No longer to turn the other cheek: Robinson, *I Never Had It Made,* pp. 80–81.
2. Jackie will show the league a thing or two: *Ibid,* p. 79.
3. Robinson and farmhand almost came to blows: *Ibid,* p. 81.
4. No longer the meek, inoffensive Robinson: *The Sporting News,* p. 2.
5. Monte Irvin of the Newark Eagles: *Ibid,* 6/25, p. 25.
6. Mrs. Manley fights Rickey's move: *New York Times,* 1/12, p. 38.
7. Rickey felt he didn't have to buy Negro stars: Alvarez, *The Perfect Game,* p. 211.
8. Irvin: Rickey didn't want the hassle: Frommer, *Rickey & Robinson,* p. 155.
9. Grand Dragon says it's illegal: *New York Herald-Tribune,* 1/15, p. 36.
10. Rickey: if Negroes barred I'll cancel: *Ibid.*
11. If the Klan's against it I'm for it: *Ibid,* 1/18, p. 25.
12. Fans turn out to see Robinson: *New York Times,* 4/8, p. 33.
13. Rickey hires Alan Roth: *Ibid,* 3/5/92, p. B15 (Obit).
14. Dixie wasn't pulling the ball: Schwarz, *The Numbers Game,* p. 55.
15. Bill James' formulas: *Ibid,* p. 125.
16. Henderson caught stealing 42 times: *Ibid,* p. 124.
17. Roth wouldn't take time out for the men's room: *Ibid,* p. 54.
18. Raschi: I lost my concentration: Halberstam, *Summer of '49,* p. 258.
19. You don't get hurt in the Negro Leagues: *Ibid,* 6/28/93, p. B 8 (Obit).
20. Roy approached by Dressen: Golenbock, *Bums,* p. 200.

21. I've been playing a long time: Frommer, *Rickey & Robinson,* pp. 109–110.
22. Campanella: I'm no crusader: Robinson, *I Never Had It Made,* pp. 96–97.
23. Jackie an aggressive individualist: *Ibid,* p. 98.
24. Snider: Campy couldn't have been the first: Snider, *The Duke of Flatbush,* p. 77.
25. Those imperious Yankees: Kahn, *Memories of Summer,* p. 65.
26. Billy caught malaria on Guadalcanal: McNeil, *The Dodgers Encyclopedia,* p. 39.
27. Newcombe started pitching at 13: Pietrusza, Silverman and Gershman, *Baseball: The Biographical Encyclopedia,* p. 828.
28. Newcombe: You can come to me: Pietrusza, *Ibid,* pp. 828–829.
29. Racial tensions dissipated: Robinson, *I Never Had It Made,* p. 86.
30. Hodges killed Japs with his bare hands: *New York Times,* 4/3/72, p. 1 (Obit).
31. Hodges protects Pee Wee: *Ibid.*
32. Chandler commutes jumper's sentences: *Brooklyn Eagle,* 6/6, p. 13.
33. Jackie demands attendance bonus clause: *Ibid,* 6/14, p. 13.
34. The shooting of Eddie Waitkus: *New York Herald-Tribune,* 6/16, p. 1.
35. The *Star-Ledger* drops the Newark Bears: *Ibid,* 6/26, p. S1.
36. DiMaggio ready to play: Durso, *DiMaggio,* p. 47.
37. DiMaggio: They didn't say a word: Anderson, *Pennant Races,* p. 109.
38. Joe got $6,000 from *Life* for his story: Halberstam, *Summer of '49,* p. 145.
39. Thompson convicted of armed robbery: *Ibid,* 10/2/60, p. 47 (Obit).
40. Joe DiMaggio is Joe DiMaggio: *Sporting News.com: '49 All Star Game.*
41. Jackie decides to answer Paul Robeson: Robinson, *I Never Had It Made,* p. 84.
42. If he wants to sound silly that's his business: *New York Times,* 7/19, p. 1.
43. Jorgensen accepts Stanky's handshake: *Brooklyn Eagle,* 9/9, p. 11.
44. Oh that cheap goddamn hit: Halberstam, *Summer of '49,* p. 286.
45. Labine: Furillo would not socialize: Pietrusza, Silverman and Gershman, *Baseball: The Biographical Encyclopedia,* p. 387.
46. Furillo led team down the stretch: *The Sporting News,* 10/12, p. 23.
47. Hit Lanier consistently: Max Lanier interview.

48. Max 21 and 7 against Dodgers when he jumped: *New York Times:* 5/15, p. 27.

49. Carl throws out Mel Queen from right field: Kahn, *The Boys of Summer*, p. 339.

50. He has crossed me once too often: *New York Times*, 9/7/53, p. 1.

51. Carl says he was blackballed: *Ibid*, 1/22/89, p. 26 (Obit).

52. Roe not hillbilly he pretended to be: Kahn, *Boys of Summer*, pp. 294, 295, 303.

53. Preacher often threw the spitter: *Sports Illustrated*, 7/4/55.

54. He signaled the team when it was coming: Kahn, *Boys of Summer*, p. 306.

55. Birdie Tebbetts on Joe Page: Halberstam, *Summer of '49*, p. 287.

56. An acute case of greed: Dick Young, *Obit on the Dodgers*, in Halberstam's *Best American Sports Stories of the 20th Century*, p. 174.

57. O'Malley: Dodgers sitting pretty financially: *Ibid*.

58. Rep. Emmanuel Cellar refutes loss: *New York Times*, 11/8/51, p. 39.

59. O'Malley's loaf of bread under each arm: Smith, *The Red Smith Reader*, p. 147.

60. Moses: Title I money only for slum clearance: *Ibid*.

61. Queens Chamber of Commerce proposes Flushing Meadows site: *Ibid*.

62. Peter O'Malley refuses access to father's correspondence: Shapiro, *The Last Good Season*, p. 323.

63. Dodgers healthiest corpse in sports history: Young, *Obit on the Dodgers*, p. 176.

64. Anderson on O'Malley: Dave Anderson interview.

65. Pittsburgh's all-black lineup: Marty Appel: Noting the Milestone in *The Armchair Book of Baseball*, p. 26; *New York Times*, 9/2/71, p. 44.

66. Ebbets Field is still there: Barber, *Rhubarb in the Catbird Seat*, p. 291

Bibliography

Books

Allen, Lee. *The Giants and the Dodgers.* New York: G.P. Putnam's Sons, 1964.

Allen, Maury: *Where Have You Gone Joe DiMaggio?* E.P. Dutton, New York, 1975.

Alvarez, Mark: *The Perfect Game.* Barnes & Noble, New York, 1993.

Anderson, Dave: *Pennant Races.* Doubleday, New York, 1994.

Anderson, David W.: *More Than Merkle.* University of Nebraska Press, 2000.

Angell, Roger: *Game Time.* Harcourt, Inc., 2003.

Barber, Walter (Red): *The Broadcasters.* Dial Press, New York, 1970.

_____. *Rhubarb in the Catbird Seat.* University of Nebraska Press, 1968.

Cohen, Stanley: *Dodgers.* Birch Lane Press, Carol Publishing, New York, 1990.

Colbert, David: *Baseball.* Time Life Books, New York, 2000.

Connor, Anthony: *Voices From Cooperstown.* Promontory Press, New York, 1998.

Creamer, Robert: *Baseball in '41.* Viking Press, New York, 1991.

Durocher, Leo: *Nice Guys Finish Last.* Simon and Schuster, New York, 1975.

Durso, Joseph: *DiMaggio.* Little, Brown, Boston and New York, 1995.

Eames, John: *The MGM Story.* Crown Publishers (Sundial), New York, 1975.

Einstein, Charles: *The Baseball Reader.* Bonanza Books, New York, 1989.

Fitzgerald, Ed: *The Story of the Brooklyn Dodgers.* Bantam Books, New York, 1949.

Frommer, Harvey: *Rickey & Robinson.* MacMillan, New York, 1982.

Geitschier, Steven: *American National Biography.* Oxford University Press, New York, 1999.

Goldstein, Richard: *Spartan Seasons.* Macmillan, New York, 1980.

Golenbock, Peter: *Bums.* G.P. Putnam's Sons, New York, 1984.

Halberstam, David: *The Best American Sports Writing of the 20th Century.* Houghton Mifflin, Boston and New York, 1999.

_____. *Summer of '49.* William Morrow, New York, 1989.

_____. *Teammates.* Hyperion, New York, 2003.

Helyer, John: *Lords of the Realm.* Villard, New York, 1994.

Higbe, Kirby: *The High Hard One.* University of Nebraska Press, 1998.

Heinz, W.J.: *Once They Heard the Cheers.* Doubleday & Company, New York, 1979.

_____. *The Rocky Road of Pistol Pete.* Fawcett Publications, Greenwich, Conn., 1958.

Holmes, Tommy: *The Dodgers.* Rutledge Books, Macmillan, New York, 1975.

Holmes, Tot: *Brooklyn's Babe*. Holmes Publishing, Gothenburg, Neb., 1990.

Honig, Donald: *Baseball America*. Macmillan, New York, 1985.

_____. *Baseball When the Grass Was Real.* Coward, McCann & Geoghegan, New York, 1975.

Hynd, Noel: *The Giants of the Polo Grounds*. Doubleday, New York, 1988.

Kahn, Roger: *The Boys of Summer*. Harper & Row, New York, 1971.

_____. *The Era*. Ticknor & Fields, New York, 1993.

_____.*Memories of Summer*. Hyperion, New York, 1997.

Leventhal, Josh: *Take Me Out to the Ballpark*. Black Dog & Leventhal, New York, 2000.

Light, J.F.: *The Cultural Encyclopedia of Baseball*. McFarland, Jefferson, N.C. 1997.

Lowry, Philip: *Green Cathedrals*. Addison-Wesley, Reading, Mass., 1992.

Marshall, William: *Baseball's Pivotal Era, 1945–1951*. Univ. Press of Kentucky, 1999.

Mayer, Ronald: *The Newark Bears*. Rutgers University Press, New Brunswick, N.J., 1994.

McNeil, William: *The Dodger Encyclopedia*. Sports Publishing, Champaign, Ill., 1997.

Mead, William B.: *Even the Browns*. NTC/Contemporary Publishing, Chicago, 1978.

Parrott, Harold: *The Lords of Baseball*. Praeger, New York, 1976.

Pietrusza, Silverman, Gershman: *Baseball: The Biographical Encyclopedia*. Sports Illustrated, Kingston, N.Y., 2000.

Polner, Murray: *Branch Rickey*. Atheneum, New York, 1982.

Reichler, Joseph: *The Encyclopedia of Baseball*. Macmillan, New York, 1988.

Robinson, Jackie: *I Never Had It Made*. Ecco Press, Hopewell, N.J., 1995.

Robinson, Ray: *The Iron Horse*. W.W. Norton, New York, 1990.

Schwarz, Alan: *The Numbers Game*. Thomas Dunne Books, New York, 2004.

Shapiro, Michael: *The Last Good Season*. Doubleday, New York, 2003.

Smith, Walter (Red): *The Red Smith Reader*, edited by Dave Anderson, Random House, New York, 1982.

Snider, Edwin (Duke): *The Duke of Flatbush*. Kensington Publishing, New York, 1998.

Stallings, Laurence: *Doughboys: The Story of the AEF.* Harper & Row, New York, 1963.

Stout, Glenn and Johnson, Richard: *Red Sox Century*. Houghton Mifflin Company, .Boston, New York, 2000.

Thomson, Bobby: *The Giants Win the Pennant*. Kensington, New York, 1991.

Thorn, John: *The Armchair Book of Baseball*. Charles Scribner's Sons, New York, 1987.

Turner, Frederick: *When the Boys Came Back*. Henry Holt, New York, 1996.

Veeck, William: *Veeck as in Wreck*. G.P. Putnam's Sons, New York, 1962.

Warfield, Don: *The Roaring Redhead*. Diamond Communications, South Bend, Ind., 1987.

Westcott, Rich: *Splendor on the Diamond*. University of Florida Press, Gainsville, 2000.

W.P.A. Writer's Program in Missouri: *Missouri*. Duell, Sloan & Pierce, New York, 1941.

Zimmer, Don: *Zim*. Sports Illustrated, Kingston, N.Y., 1980.

Interviews

Dave Anderson
Bobby Bragan
Pete Coscarart
Carl Erskine
Herman Franks
Gene Hermanski
John (Spider) Jorgensen
Clem Labine
Max Lanier
Eddie Miksis
Howie Schultz
Roy Sievers

Newspapers

Baltimore Sun
Brooklyn Eagle
Elmira Star-Gazette

New York Daily Mirror
New York Herald-Tribune
New York Times
Newark Evening News
Newark Star-Ledger
Philadelphia Inquirer
Pittsburgh Post-Gazette
St. Louis Globe-Democrat
St. Louis Post-Dispatch
St. Paul Dispatch
St. Paul Pioneer-Press
Spokane Review
The Sporting News

Other

American Magazine, July 1947
Baseball Magazine, September 1945

CBS 60 Minutes, 4/22/01
CBS Sportsline
David Jordan, Larry Gerlach, John Russell, *A Baseball Myth Exploded,* 1998, #17, p. 3
Joe Naiman, *Bert Shepard,* 1999, #19, p. 75
The National Pastime: a publication of the American Society for Baseball Research: Tom Knight, *George Magerkurth,* 1993, #13, p. 13
The 1947 World Series (video)
Sports Illustrated, May 7, 1984
Brian Wigley, Dr. Frank Ashley, Dr. Arnold LeUnes, *Willard Hershberger & the Legacy of Suicide,* 2000, #13, p. 72

Index